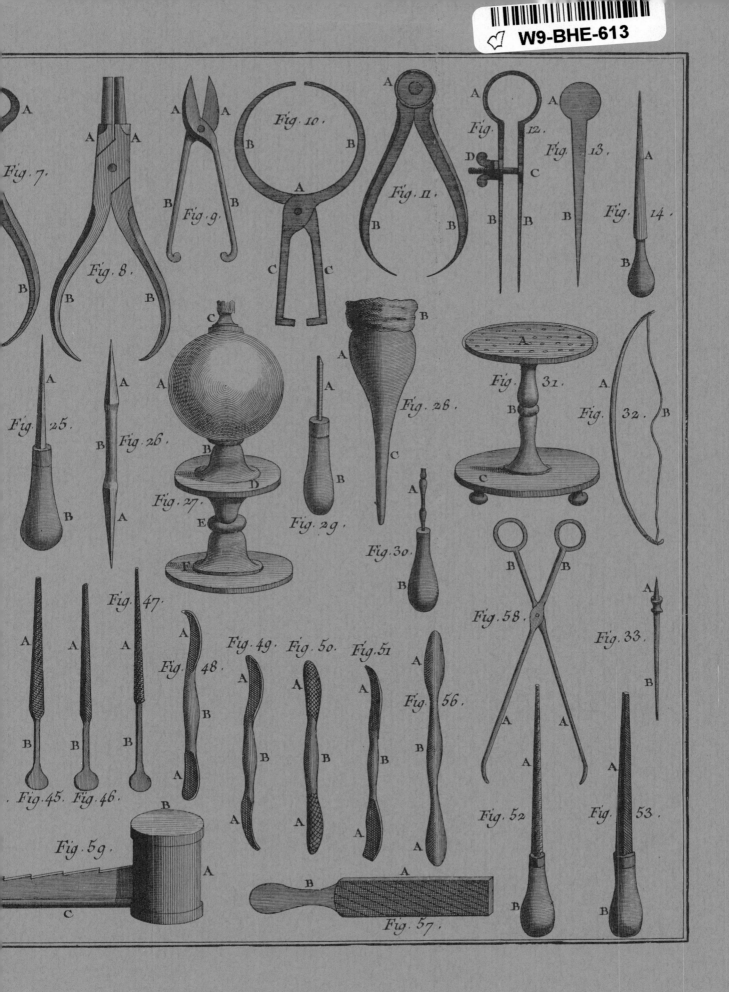

The Diamond

PADDINGTON PRESS LTD
NEW YORK & LONDON

The Diamond

BY GEORGE G. BLAKEY

Library of Congress Cataloging in Publication Data

Blakey, George G.   1934–
   The diamond.

   Bibliography: p.
   Includes index.
      1.   Diamonds.   I.   Title.
TS753.B47   553'.82   77-5003
ISBN 0-448-22062-8

Printed in England by
BAS Printers Limited, Over Wallop, Hampshire
Bound in England by Kitcat Ltd., London
Color separations by Rowley Studios Ltd., Hull, England
Color sections printed by Shenval Press, Harlow, England

The quotations from Ian Fleming's *Diamonds Are Forever*, which
appear on p. 12 and on the back of the jacket, are reprinted with
the kind permission of Glidrose Productions Ltd. (London),
International Creative Management (New York, N.Y.) and the
book's publishers, Jonathan Cape Ltd. (London).

Jacket photograph courtesy of the Diamond Information Center,
New York, N.Y.

Designed by Colin Lewis

In the United States	PADDINGTON PRESS LTD. Distributed by GROSSET & DUNLAP
In the United Kingdom	PADDINGTON PRESS LTD.
In Canada	Distributed by RANDOM HOUSE OF CANADA LTD.
In Australia	Distributed by ANGUS & ROBERTSON PTY. LTD.
In Southern Africa	Distributed by ERNEST STANTON (PUBLISHERS) (PTY.) LTD.

Acknowledgments

No book about diamonds could possibly be written without the active assistance of De Beers, and I wish to extend my sincere thanks to the many officers of the company who aided my research. I should like to mention in particular Lionel Burke, James Courage and John Roux of the Public Relations Department in London and Howard Vaughan in Johannesburg; Craig Matthew of the Photographic Department in Kimberley and Frank Beresford of the Kimberley Mine Museum; Susan Farmer of the Jewelry Section in London and Rosemary May of the Photographic Library; and Paul Daniel and Alan Bullock of the Industrial Diamond Division in Ascot. For technical help, I am deeply indebted to Roy Huddlestone of the Diamond Grading Laboratories in London; Alfred Montezinos of Montezinos, Inc., in New York City; Ben Bonas of Bonas & Co., London; and Basil Watermeyer of Jooste's in Johannesburg. Finally, for his invaluable assistance in gathering together many of the photographs for the chapter on jewelry, I should like to thank Albert Middlemiss of Christie's in London.

PLEASE NOTE: Unless otherwise indicated, all photographs are courtesy of De Beers Consolidated Mines, Ltd.

TABLE OF CONTENTS

INTRODUCTION

A tiny diamond in an engagement ring bought by a young man for his fiancée has as much magic as a great stone bought by a prince for a princess. Both are unique and yet share a common origin. They were both formed a hundred or more million years ago by unimaginable pressures deep beneath the surface of the earth. They are both so hard that they can scratch the hardest steel. And yet both can be fashioned into a gem with a fire and brilliance unmatched by any other.

Beauty rarely exists in any but the most fragile forms, and the fact that a diamond not only possesses exceptional beauty but is virtually indestructible makes it one of the wonders of nature. These awe-inspiring qualities of the diamond also mean that its popular romantic image remains unsullied by affectation. Nothing so perfect could ever be regarded as sentimental.

Certainly there was nothing sentimental about the lengths to which the Indian princes were prepared to go to lay their hands on a great diamond. As a symbol of power and prestige in ancient India, the diamond was unparalleled, and it was soon to be regarded in the same way by the sovereigns of medieval Europe. Thousands of slaves toiled for centuries in India and Brazil to wrest these crystals from the earth, and today in South West Africa the mightiest fleet of earth-moving equipment in the world is employed in the same task. In the frozen wastes of Siberia at temperatures of 70° below zero, jet engines have been adapted to thaw the rock-hard ground before the excavators move in. Mighty business empires have been created to mine and market diamonds and yet, contrary to popular opinion, the end product is not simply a beautiful but ultimately

useless gem dedicated to "the vanity of
woman and the greed of man." More than
four-fifths of the world's natural diamond production and all synthetic production are destined to
be used by industry.

It is no exaggeration to say that if the supply of diamonds were
abruptly cut off, many of our high-technology industries would grind
to a halt and many other industries would be severely dislocated.
Diamonds are the only material capable of achieving the high-precision, mass-
production work necessary for a modern engineering industry. Without diamond
dies, wire drawing for the electronics industry would be infinitely more laborious and
much less accurate. The machining of vital parts for space vehicle guidance and control devices would fall far short of the precision required and now being achieved
thanks to diamonds.

It is no coincidence that while Soviet Russia exports nearly all its production of gem diamonds, not a single carat of industrial diamonds is
allowed to leave the country. Diamonds are used to machine the
lenses we wear in our spectacles, to cut the glasses we drink
from, to shape the billiard balls and dice we play with, and to
make possible the ultimate in sound reproduction by forming the points of the styli on the record players we
listen to.

In the light of the diamond's close involvement
with almost every aspect of our daily life, it
is remarkable that the many and varied
roles it plays are so little known. This
book is written in an effort to
make the reader more aware
not only of this involve-
ment but also of the
deeply fascinating
history behind it.   **George G. Blakey**

THE ROMANCE OF DIAMONDS

After his defeat in battle in 1833, the Afghan prince Shah Shuja was blinded and tortured for days before he would give up the Koh-i-Noor diamond to Runjeet Singh, the victorious Lion of the Punjab. His captor, curious at his stubbornness, asked him why he had resisted for so long.

"Because," answered the sightless shah, "it brings good luck and has ever been the bosom companion of him who has triumphed over his enemies."

This story illustrates only too well the fascination and power that a small "colorless" stone has exercised over the minds of men for centuries. "To win them, temples have been profaned, palaces looted, thrones torn to fragments, princes tortured, women strangled, guests poisoned by their hosts, and slaves disemboweled. Some have fallen on battlefields, to be picked up by ignorant freebooters, and sold for a few silver coins. Others have been cast into ditches by thieves or swallowed by guards, or sunk in shipwrecks, or broken to powder in moments of frenzy. No strain of fancy in an Arabian tale has outstripped the marvels of fact in the diamond's history."

So wrote Gardner Williams, the American mining engineer who became general manager of De Beers in the 1890s. But sixty years

OPPOSITE The Bridal Pair. *This South German portrait of about 1470 shows both the bride and the groom wearing rings. The custom of giving betrothal rings had been well-established for centuries before this picture was painted.*

later Ian Fleming in *Diamonds Are Forever* described the fatal allure of the diamond even more dramatically. James Bond has just examined a piece of quartz handed to him by "M," and mistaken it for a diamond. "M" now gives him a top-quality diamond to look at, a blue-white stone of 20 carats:

> What he now held had a heart of blue white flame, and the infinite colours reflected and refracted from its depths, lanced into his eyes like needles. With his left hand he picked up the quartz dummy and held it beside the diamond in front of his glass. It was a lifeless chunk of matter, almost opaque beside the dazzling translucence of the diamond, and the rainbow colours he had seen a few moments before were now coarse and muddy.
>
> Bond put down the piece of quartz and gazed again into the heart of the diamond. Now he could understand the passion that diamonds had inspired through the centuries, the almost sexual love they aroused among those who handled them and cut them and traded in them. It was a domination by a beauty so pure that it held a kind of truth, a divine authority before which all other things turned, like the bit of quartz, to clay. In those few minutes Bond understood the myth of diamonds, and he knew he would never forget what he had suddenly seen inside the heart of this stone.

But the diamond is more than just a beautiful stone. It has properties that set it apart from every other gem. It is the hardest natural substance yet discovered—the name itself is derived from the Greek *adamas*, meaning unconquerable—and it is also the purest. Yet, almost paradoxically, the diamond is composed of one of the commonest elements in nature, carbon, in crystalline form. The diamond thus combines the ordinary with the extraordinary, in a sense mirroring the human condition.

It is therefore not surprising that diamonds have always been associated with religion and the concept of eternity. To quote Gardner Williams once more, "the diamond that gleamed with such strange fire in an idol's eye before the rising of the Star of Bethlehem may be sparkling today with more dazzling radiance in the crown of an emperor. Koh-i-nûr and Darya-i-nûr and Taj-e-mah and Regent and Orloff and Sancy and Shah will shine no less resplendent when the sovereigns that now treasure them shall be dust." The diamond is as indestructible as the human spirit—if a little more tangible—and while the Hindus divided diamonds according to their qualities into the same castes as men—that is, into Brahmins, Kshatriyas, Vaisyas and Sudras—other religions and beliefs were prepared to ascribe to diamonds even greater powers.

In the first century A.D., the Roman author Pliny the Elder wrote of diamonds: "They resist blows to such an extent that the hammer rebounds and the very anvil splits asunder, but this invincible element which defies Nature's two most violent forces, iron and fire, can be broken by ram's blood. But it must be steeped in blood that is fresh and warm and, even so, many blows are needed."

Pliny was right, but only up to a point. A diamond will penetrate the jaws of a steel vice—a phenomenon often demonstrated by the eminent nineteenth-century physicist Sir William Crookes—but like other objects of great hardness, it is relatively brittle and can be shattered by a well-placed blow. The Swiss mercenaries who defeated that early diamond fancier Charles the Bold, duke of Burgundy, in 1476, found many diamonds in his baggage

and, believing the old story, tested them to destruction with their war hammers. Centuries later in India and in South Africa, merchants who knew the true facts were reputed to have encouraged miners to use this drastic testing procedure . . . and then to have picked up the broken pieces of diamond after the disappointed miners had left. The use of ram's blood in Pliny's alchemical instructions then becomes purely incidental— and later perhaps a deliberate deception perpetuated by diamond merchants eager to hide the profitable secrets of their trade.

Recognition of the diamond's unique qualities meant that very early in its history the diamond seemed to be invested with magical properties. It was worn in battle as a symbol of courage and virtue, and in the sickbed as an aid to healing. It was also reckoned to be of use in winning the heart of a reluctant maiden and there is a story that the arrows of Cupid were tipped with diamonds. This is probably the only legendary attribute of diamonds that has as much credence today as it had over a thousand years ago.

There was more room for doubt about the medicinal properties of diamond especially when, instead of being worn or held next to the body, it was actually administered in powdered form. Ancient authorities are remarkably divided as to whether powdered diamond would kill or cure.

The Hindus pronounced that only the powder of a flawless diamond would cure and impart energy, strength, beauty, happiness and long life, while that of a flawed diamond was poisonous. This qualification could well have been a case of being wise after the event. By the mid-sixteenth century Ivan the Terrible had no doubts. While exhibiting the contents of his treasury to the English ambassador to Moscow, Sir Jerome Horsey, the latter reports that the czar pointed to a diamond and observed, "The least parcel of it in powder will poysen a horse geaven to drink, much more a man."

But elsewhere in Europe, powdered diamond still seems to have been used fairly indiscriminately, in one century as a poison and in another as a medicine. The death of the Emperor Frederick II in 1250 was widely blamed on an administration of powdered diamond, as was that of the Turkish sultan Bejazet in 1512 along with the victims of Catherine de Medici and her infamous *poudre de succession* in the mid-sixteenth century. Yet in 1532 the unfortunate Pope Clement VII was liberally dosed with powdered diamond. He is reported to have expired after the fourteenth spoonful, but the prospect of a bill of 40,000 ducats must take at least a part of the blame for his death!

By this time, not surprisingly, the consensus had come down on the side of the diamond being poisonous, and it is probably not unduly cynical to believe that this view was officially encouraged in order to stop workers smuggling stones out of the mines by swallowing them.

The stories of the finding of the first diamonds are also cloaked in mystery and imagination. The legend of the Valley of Diamonds begins in or around 350 B.C. with its discovery by Alexander the Great during his campaign in India. It was guarded by great and terrible snakes whose gaze could allegedly kill a man. Alexander instructed his soldiers to polish their shields to a mirror-like finish before advancing on the snakes. With their gaze turned back on themselves, it was the snakes and not the soldiers who were struck down. Carcasses of freshly slain sheep were then thrown into the valley. The diamonds stuck to the greasy carcasses and eagles, attracted by the meat, swooped down into the valley to carry them off. But Alexander's bowmen, who were positioned around the edges of the valley, shot the birds as they emerged and recovered the diamonds.

This story bears a remarkable similarity to that of Sinbad the Sailor who, during one of his adventures, was stranded in a diamond valley which, apart from being full of diamonds, was also swarming with snakes and vipers "each as big as a palm tree." The resourceful Sinbad, noticing that great chunks of fresh meat were lying on the ground and recalling the legend of the valley from which diamond-studded meat was "plucked by eagles," wrapped himself in one of the carcasses after filling his pockets and his turban with the choicest diamonds. Before long Sinbad, concealed in his carcass, was swept up by an eagle and carried out of the valley to safety.

One thing both these tales demonstrate is an early familiarity with two special characteristics of the diamond. These are its inability to be wetted by water and its affinity to grease. In fact, a grease belt over which the diamond concentrate passes plays an important part in the recovery process today, serving exactly the same purpose as the fatty sheep carcasses of two thousand years ago.

There is no lack of evidence documenting the fact that diamonds were known to the ancients, but pinpointing the first undoubted reference to them before Pliny is quite another task. Much has been made by some writers of the references in the Bible to the "diamond" in the breastplate of the high priest in Exodus, the "stones of fire" of Ezekiel, and the "diamond" penpoint of Jeremiah. Unfortunately, in this premineralogical era, the word *adamas* might have been applied to any stone or object of exceptional hardness; and, given the comparative rarity of diamonds and their limited source, there must be considerable doubt as to the authenticity of these Old Testament references. Nevertheless, it is interesting to record that Edwin Streeter, one of the most celebrated writers on precious stones in the nineteenth century, not only regards the finding of stone implements in Kimberley as evidence of prehistoric diamond

The popular idea that one of the twelve stones in the breastplate of the High Priest is a diamond has its origins in the translation of the Hebrew word jahalom *in Exodus 28:18 as* diamond *in the Authorized version of the Bible. Since the word derives from* halom, *meaning "to beat or to overcome,"* jahalom *could be interpreted as "unconquerable," thus setting up a clear link with the Greek word* adamas. *Most historians believe that the stone was probably corundum, the family of the ruby and sapphire, which is next in hardness to the diamond.*
FROM *DIAMONDS AND PRECIOUS STONES* BY HARRY EMANUEL

mining, but suggests that the area was the origin of the "diamond" in the breastplate of the high priest as well as of those presented to King Solomon by the Queen of Sheba.

With Pliny, however, the historian is on much safer ground. Not only does he stress the rarity of diamonds—"the most valuable thing on earth," he wrote, "is the diamond, known only to kings and to very few of those"—and as we have seen, describes its characteristic hardness, but he also adds the first clear description. The true Indian diamond, he says, is "colorless, transparent, with polished facets and six angles ending either in a pyramid with a sharp point or with two points like whipping tops joined at the base." These are perfect descriptions of an octahedron crystal and a dodecahedron, the most common of the classic rough diamond shapes.

It is India which from then on continues to supply allusions to diamonds both as ornaments and as tools. The Hindus are said to have repelled the early Aryan invaders with dazzling swords of remarkable cutting power; and they are known to have been early users of diamond-tipped tools and diamond-edged knives. Because of their unique value as cutting tools, these instruments became greatly sought after and soon formed the basis of a very valuable export trade. They were in great demand in China particularly, where they were employed in jade cutting.

The earliest references to diamonds in Western Europe are found in a lapidary dating from the first half of the eleventh century. The description of the diamond along with that of other precious stones is brief but to the point: "There is a certain stone called Diamond; neither iron nor steel nor anything hard will cut it, but each is the worse for touching it." These lapidaries, or accounts of the mystical and medicinal properties of the many varieties of precious stones, are very much a feature of medieval literature and serve to illustrate the great importance ascribed to such stones. Perhaps the most comprehensive of these early descriptions of the attributes of the diamond is that contained in the Anglo-Norman document of 1243 known as the *Sloane Lapidary*:

Diamonde comes from Inde and some from Arabie; that wich cometh from Inde is clipped males, ye other female. The male is broun appon light shininge, ye female is whit & bewtifull of coulor like Cristall. Thes diamonds is very pretious to thee and of great hardnesse, for they will graue in Iron or steele, taking no

harme. If a man weare it, it strengthen him & kepith him from dreming in his sleepe, from faintnes and from poyson, from wroth & chiding. It sendeth & helpeth men to great worth. It defendeth a man from his enemies, & kepeth a man in good estate wher he findeth him; it comforte a man witt, & support him of ritches. And though a man do fall downe from a cart or a wale he shall not break any of his bones if the stone be on him. . . . It destroyth Lechery; and he shall not lightly be acombred so yt he feare god. And it will keepe the seede of a mans body within a womans body, so yt the children's limmes shall not be wrong ne crooked. And it must be sett in the mettle of steel & bore of a mans left halfe.

But for all the familiarity the world was beginning to have with diamonds, there was little knowledge of their origin. It was as if the extraordinary qualities of the diamond were quite enough to make people content to accept extraordinary and romantic ideas of where they came from. Some believed that such marvelous stones were indeed splinters of the stars, and others that they were formed when lightning bolts struck the earth. Plato thought they might be the purest and noblest

part of the finest quality gold, which had fused into a brilliant and transparent mass. Some Hindu miners believed that diamonds grew like onions and that size and quality denoted age. Another school supposed that rock crystals were simply immature diamonds.

The belief that diamonds are living, growing things is still held in some parts of India, where the miners actually expect the diamond beds to yield a new harvest of stones every twenty years. Another theory was that diamonds were created by the supernormal hardening of dewdrops, something which occurred only very rarely at a special conjunction of the stars. But perhaps the most attractive story of where diamonds come from is this one related by the Griqua servant of an early South African digger:

After the passing of many moons, and when there was great sorrow in the land, a spirit, pitying the wants and difficulties of mankind, descended from Heaven with a huge basket full of diamonds. The spirit flew over the Vaal River, starting beyond Delport's Hope, dropping diamonds as it sped on. Past Barkly West and Klipdam it flew toward the place now called Kimberley, ever throwing out handful after handful of gems from its huge basket. On reaching Kimberley, where at that time large trees were growing, one of the spirit's big toes caught in a branch of a camelthorn tree, and tripping, he upset the basket, emptying out all the diamonds, and thus forming the Kimberley Mines.

A camelthorn tree and a lone African are the sole features in this Kimberley landscape of 1870. Within a year this peaceful scene was to be totally transformed following the discovery of diamonds at Colesberg Kopje in July 1871.

Today the Indian beds are largely exhausted, but it was to those Indian diamonds and the growing trade with the Orient from the fifteenth century onward that Europe owed its early familiarity with gemstones. The growth of Greece as a trading nation from about 500 B.C. had marked the beginning of the flow of precious stones from East to West, a flow which quickened with the conquests of Alexander the Great and became a flood as the Roman Empire spread eastward. After Pompey's victory over Mithridates in 66 B.C., precious stones and pearls poured into Rome and desire for them rose to such a passion that Pliny could write: "We drink out of a mass of gems crusting our wine bowls, and our drinking cups are emeralds." Later writers record that Lollia Paulina, wife of Caligula, wore a dress completely covered with pearls and emeralds; that Nero showered his mistresses with pearls; and that by A.D. 330, Constantine could challenge the splendor of the Oriental monarchs by riding into Rome in a gold chariot studded with precious stones.

But despite the apparently limitless wealth and desire for display manifested by ancient Rome, allusions to diamonds are few and far between. And apart from their rarity—none have been discovered during the excavations of Herculaneum and Pompeii or even of the

A selection of famous diamonds: 1 The Koh-i-Noor after recutting; 2 The Stewart, a 123-carat South African stone; 3 The Orloff; 4 A Brazilian stone known as Mr. Dresden's; 5 The Great Mogul; 6 The Shah; 7 The Koh-i-Noor in its original Indian cut.

most celebrated temple sites and royal tombs—the reason is almost certainly the limitations the unique hardness of the diamond placed on the skill of the early jewelers. Diamonds had obviously acquired something of a cult following among the princes of the East who valued them chiefly for their size. Brilliance was very much a secondary factor. Tavernier, for example, records that the Moguls were quite content to have a stone simply rounded off and the pits polished. The idea of creating a more brilliant and valuable jewel by cutting away the greater part of it, as commonly happens today, would have been regarded with horror even had it been possible. As a result, a fine white diamond—which was little more than an inexpertly shaped and polished rough—made a poor showing in European eyes when compared to a well-cut sapphire, emerald or ruby.

It was not until the development of the knowledge of optics based on Euclid's treatise in the twelfth century that the diamond began its rise to the now preeminent status it holds among precious stones in Europe. Given that the diamond has a uniquely high degree of refraction and reflection as well as clarity, dispersion and luster, only faceting in accordance with the rules of optics could possibly bring out the hidden beauty of the diamond.

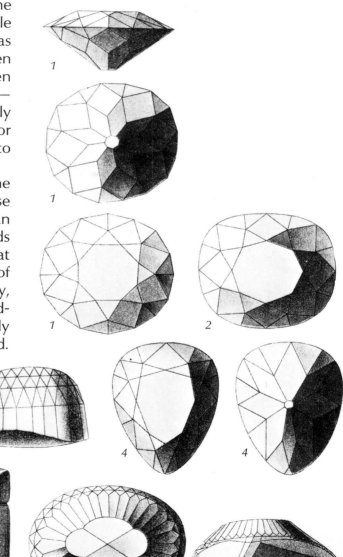

There are records of European cutters in the fourteenth century, but the credit for the first scientific cutting of diamonds is generally accorded to Louis de Berquen of Bruges who in 1476 faceted the three biggest diamonds in the collection of Charles the Bold, duke of Burgundy. It was he who worked on the famous yellow diamond now known as the Florentine, covering it front and back with small triangular facets. The subsequent dramatic history of this stone caused Gardner Williams to pronounce that by unlocking the hidden beauty of the diamond, Louis de Berquen ushered in that period of history when "famous diamonds would pass over the face of Europe like meteors."

The Florentine itself is reputed to have been taken from the body of the duke by a soldier after the Battle of Nancy and sold to a priest for a florin. After that it changed ownership many times until it came into the hands of the Medici family in Florence. It was in that city that the French jeweler and traveler Jean Baptiste Tavernier saw it in 1657 in the possession of the grand duke of Tuscany. He noted in his meticulous manner that it weighed 137.27 carats, was cut in a double rose with 126 facets, and had an irregular nine-sided outline. In the eighteenth century the diamond passed by marriage to the Hapsburgs and the Empress Maria Theresa placed it in the Austrian crown. With the collapse of the Austro-Hungarian Empire in World War I, the Florentine went into exile with the royal family—and into oblivion. Some reports say that the diamond was stolen by an adviser to the royal family who fled with it to South America. Others believe that it was smuggled into the United States in the 1920s, recut and sold. At all events, there can be no certainty as to the present whereabouts of the Florentine. The Kunsthistorisches Museum of Vienna, where the diamond was on display prior to 1918, regards it as "officially" lost.

MARY EVANS PICTURE LIBRARY

ABOVE *Charles the Bold, duke of Burgundy. One of the first of the European nobles to take a fancy to diamonds, the duke encouraged Louis de Berquen in his early efforts to apply scientific principles to the cutting of diamonds and to establish a cutting industry in Europe.*
OPPOSITE *Jean Baptiste Tavernier was a French jeweler with a passion for Oriental travel. He made six journeys to India and Persia, meeting kings and princes and trading diamonds and other precious stones. It was he who first brought to the West the famous Hope Diamond. The stone's reputation for bringing bad luck to its owner is sometimes credited with Tavernier's own death: he is said to have been devoured by wolves on a trip to Russia.*

Nearly all the great diamonds have stories as varied and violent as that of the Florentine, for far from being simply adornments for princes they were very much part of the political and economic scene. By reason of their great value, they were often used as pledges to raise armies or as collateral for foreign loans, and they were frequently given by one ruler to another as tokens of friendship or alliance.

The story of the Regent diamond embodies all the elements of high drama. The huge 410-carat rough was originally found in the Parteal Mine on the Kistna River in India in about 1701

by a slave who smuggled it out of the mine concealed in a self-inflicted wound in his leg. He then made for the coast, where he offered a British sea captain half the value of the stone for a safe passage out of India. The captain agreed, but as soon as they were at sea he killed the slave, took the diamond, and flung the body overboard. He then sold the stone to a prominent Indian diamond merchant named Jaurchund for £1,000, but he seems to have profited little from the deal. Legend has it that the captain squandered the money in the bars and brothels of Bombay and later hanged himself in a fit of remorse.

Jaurchund was now faced with the problem of selling an exceptionally large diamond which had no provenance and which was bound to cause a stir. He let it be known that he had "large diamonds to be sold" and great interest was shown by the British governor of Fort St. George near Madras. This was Thomas Pitt, the grandfather of William Pitt, who was to become Britain's youngest prime minister during the American revolutionary period and after whom Pittsburgh was named. The governor invited Jaurchund to visit him and, knowing the dubious origins of the stone, beat Jaurchund down from his asking price of £85,000 to nearer £20,000. As soon as he had acquired the diamond, Thomas Pitt sent it to

England for cutting. The result was a flawless 140.5-carat cushion-cut brilliant. The cutting took two years and cost him £5,000 but a number of small rose-cut stones were produced at the same time and sold to Peter the Great of Russia for the equivalent of £7,000. The diamond was now known as the Pitt, and its owner as "Diamond Pitt"; it acquired its present title, the Regent, in 1717 after Thomas Pitt sold it to the duke of Orleans, regent of France, for £135,000.

The diamond was worn in the crown of the young King Louis XV at his coronation in 1722, and two generations later Marie Antoinette used it to adorn a large black velvet hat. By this time, the Regent was regarded as the most valuable jewel in the royal treasury—it was valued at 12 million livres or £5 million—and it is hardly surprising that it was the prime target for the robbers who ransacked the treasury in 1792 during the early days of the Revolution. They took the Regent along with a number of other jewels, including the Sancy and the French Blue. The Regent was one of the first to be recovered. It is said to have been found in a hole in a beam in a Paris garret. Back in government hands, the Regent was used to finance Napoleon's rise to power. He carried the diamond set in the hilt of his sword when he was crowned emperor in 1804. After his

exile to Elba in 1814, his second wife, Marie Louise, took possession of the Regent but her father, Emperor Francis I of Austria, insisted that it be returned to France. Once again part of the French crown jewels, the stone was set in the crown of Charles X for his coronation in 1825, and it remained in the crown for the next fifty years until Napoleon III gave it to the Empress Eugénie to wear in a Greek diadem for her hair. Many of the crown jewels were auctioned in 1887 at the time of the founding of the French Republic, but because of its unique historical significance, the Regent was preserved for the nation. It now rests in the Louvre.

Diamonds have always played a major role in the history of France, but none more so than those forming the diamond necklace which some historians believed sparked the French Revolution. Originally commissioned by Louis XV from the royal jewelers Boehmer and Bassange, the necklace was to be a present for his mistress, Madame du Barry. It took two years for the jewelers to amass the 647 flawless stones weighing 2,842 carats needed to complete the necklace, and just when their work was done the king died. Unhappily for Boehmer and Bassange, the necklace had not yet been paid for and they were left with what was literally the most expensive piece of jewelry in the world. The young King Louis XVI and his queen, Marie Antoinette, were great collectors of diamonds. They were tempted, but even they were not prepared to pay the price for the necklace despite the anguished pleadings of the two jewelers who knew they faced ruin if they could not sell it.

An incident from the Diamond Necklace Affair: the court jeweler Boehmer is in despair when Marie Antoinette refuses to purchase the diamond necklace originally commissioned by Louis XV as a present for his mistress, Madame du Barry.

It is at this point that the Count and Countess La Motte come into the story. Poor but ambitious minor nobility, the La Mottes conceived a plan to make a fortune based on three elements. One was the eagerness of the jewelers to sell the necklace, another one was the known interest of Marie Antoinette, and third was the desire of the unpopular Cardinal de Rohan to find favor with the queen. The La Mottes first approached the court jewelers, ostensibly as emissaries of the queen, with the story that she wished to buy the necklace secretly and to pay by installments. They then went to the cardinal, saying that the queen needed his assistance in this delicate matter, and induced him to act as a go-between in the negotiations.

Their scheme was successful and the La Mottes won possession of the necklace, hacked it to pieces, and began selling the stones one by one. However, they soon began to commit the one classic mistake of nearly all nonprofessional criminals. They spent too much too soon, thus drawing attention to their new-found affluence and also making it impossible to pay even the first installment on the purchase price. Boehmer and Bassange went to the palace of Versailles to collect their money—and the whole plot was unmasked.

The king was outraged by the conspiracy

and instead of listening to those of his advisers who suggested that the affair was best forgotten, insisted that the whole story be made public and the guilty punished. Unfortunately, although Louis and Marie Antoinette were totally innocent in the matter, the state of political and social unrest in the country was such that the mere thought that they could have been involved in such frivolous and extravagant actions gave a tremendous boost to the antiroyalist cause. All the grievances of an oppressed people, already nurtured by reports of the luxury and debauchery at Versailles, now centered on this one scandalous incident and on Marie Antoinette's supposed part in it. She became, in the words of Carlyle, "the symbol of the sin and misery of a thousand years."

The fact that Madame du Barry, for whom the necklace was originally made, and Louis XVI and his queen all died on the guillotine might have been expected to give further currency to the belief that diamonds were unlucky for their owners. And yet despite their tragic fates and those of so many of the owners of other famous diamonds, the legend of ill fortune attaches to remarkably few of the world's great stones. Perhaps the most celebrated exception is the Hope diamond. A unique violet blue diamond of 44.5 carats, the Hope is believed to have been cut from the 112.5-carat stone which Tavernier brought back from India for Louis XIV in 1668. The king had the stone recut into a 67.5-carat heart shape for his mistress, Madame de Montespan, and renamed it the Blue Diamond of the Crown, although it soon became better known as the French Blue. It subsequently passed into the hands of Louis XVI and was often worn by Marie Antoinette. After the revolution the diamond was among the royal jewels placed under guard in the Treasury, from where it was stolen in the famous robbery of 1792. It did not appear again until 1830 when it was put up for sale in London and was purchased for the collection of the banker Henry Philip Hope for £18,000. The intervening years have never been convincingly accounted for, but a portrait by Goya of Queen Maria Luisa of Spain, painted in 1799, shows her wearing a diamond remarkably like the French Blue. Subsequently renamed the Hope, the blue diamond was shown at the Great Exhibition of 1851, where it was a great attraction along with the even more famous Koh-i-Noor.

It was not until the diamond passed out of the hands of the Hope family in 1906 that the stories about its bringing bad luck began to be told. The first new owner was a Parisian gem

dealer, Jacques Celot. In 1907 he committed suicide and the Hope was bought from his estate by a Russian playboy called Prince Kanitovski, who was engaged at the time in a tempestuous affair with a beautiful French actress. He gave the fateful diamond to her to wear for one of her performances at the Folies-Bergère and then from his box shot her dead in the middle of her act. Two days later the prince was stabbed to death by exiled Russian revolutionaries.

Tragedies continued to dog successive owners of the stone with monotonous regularity. The next owner was a rich Egyptian merchant, Habib Bey, who drowned together with his whole family in a steamer collision off Singapore. At first it was thought that the diamond had gone down with the ship, but it later turned up in the possession of a Greek broker named Simon Montharides, who sold it to the sultan of Turkey, Abdul Hamid II, for a reputed $400,000. The broker's brief period of possession of the Hope was not enough to save him from what was rapidly becoming known as its curse. Just after the deal had been completed, he and his wife and child were killed when his car drove over a precipice. Nor did the diamond bring any luck to its new owner, the sultan. Known as Abdul the Damned because of his corrupt and tyrannical rule, he gave the diamond to his favorite, Salama Zubayba. In 1908 a group of army officers staged a successful revolt and the desperate but still jealous sultan shot her dead as the rebels broke down the palace gates. The eunuch in charge of the royal jewels, including the Hope diamond, was hanged from the Galata bridge, and the sultan was deposed and exiled.

Cartier of Paris then bought the Hope and later sold it for $154,000 to Edward B. McLean, son of the millionaire publisher, as a gift for his bride, the celebrated Evalyn Walsh McLean, who was also the daughter of a millionaire. It

Queen Maria Luisa of Spain, a portrait painted by Goya in 1799, showing her wearing a necklace containing a large blue diamond. Some historians believe this to be the Hope Diamond, the whereabouts of which were unaccounted for between 1792, when it was stolen from the French Treasury, and 1830, when it reappeared in a London salesroom. TAFT MUSEUM, CINCINNATI

was the misfortunes that then began to occur to the McLean family which caught the imagination of the American public in the 1920s and 1930s and established the Hope's reputation as a stone of ill luck. Their eight-year-old son was run over and killed by a car; one of their daughters and a granddaughter both died of an overdose of barbiturates; and Edward McLean had a nervous breakdown and eventually died in a mental hospital. On the death of Evalyn McLean in 1947, the mysterious blue diamond was bought by Harry Winston, the New York gem dealer, for $180,000 and subsequently presented by him to the Smithsonian Institution in Washington, D.C., where it is now on permanent display. The curse is popularly supposed to have ended there and then, but Harry Winston relates that among the thousands of letters thanking him for his donation was one from a woman begging him to take the diamond back. The country, she insisted, had gone to pieces from the moment the Hope had arrived at the Smithsonian.

But even when enclosed behind bullet-proof glass and protected by electronic alarm systems in museums and royal treasuries, the great diamonds of the world are still able to stir the passions of governments, if not of princes. The latest diamond to cause an international incident is the Koh-i-Noor, the oldest known diamond in the world and probably the most famous gem in the British crown jewels. In 1976 the government of Pakistan demanded its return on the grounds that it was part of the country's heritage and had been illegally removed by the British in the last century. The British government rejected the claim saying that the stone had passed through so many hands in its long history that no one could establish a right to it superior to that of Britain's, and that they had no intention of handing it back to Pakistan or to India.

The Koh-i-Noor in one of its original Indian settings. It was in this form that Runjeet Singh, the Lion of the Punjab, constantly wore the diamond.

The known history of the Koh-i-Noor begins in 1304 when it was first reported as being in the possession of the rajahs of Malwa, the territory which has since been split into Indore, Bhopal and Gwalior. Following the Mogul invasion, the diamond passed into the hands of Sultan Baber, a descendant of Tamerlane and founder of the Mogul Empire in India. A much treasured possession of his, Baber refers to it in his diary in 1526 as "the famous diamond" of such value that it would pay "half the expenses of the world." It remained in the ownership of his descendants for the next two centuries, thus giving some substance to the legend that "he who owns the Koh-i-Noor rules the world." In 1739, however, it was lost to the Persians who, under their ruler Nadir Shah, invaded India and sacked Delhi. There is a story that for fifty-eight days the stone could not be found because the conquered Mogul emperor Mohammed Shah had hidden it in the folds of his turban. Told the secret by a member of the ex-emperor's harem, Nadir Shah invited him to a feast and, observing an ancient Oriental custom, proposed an exchange of turbans. Mohammed was in no position to refuse. Once he had the turban, Nadir Shah ran to his tent and on seeing the great diamond among the silk of the unrolled turban, cried "Koh-i-Noor," which means Mountain of Light, thus giving it the name it has borne ever since.

DIAMOND INFORMATION CENTER, NEW YORK

Recutting the Koh-i-Noor. England's royal family took a great interest in the operation. Here Mr. Voorsanger, the cutter brought over from Amsterdam, watches as the duke of Wellington personally puts on the first facet.
NEW YORK PUBLIC LIBRARY PICTURE COLLECTION

Over the next two hundred years, the Koh-i-Noor changed hands many times. Shah Rokh, the son of Nadir Shah, died under terrible torture rather than reveal the diamond's hiding place to his conqueror, the Aga Mohammed, and its bloody history continued once it passed to the Afghan princes. Imprisoned and blinded by his brother Shuja, Shah Zaman defiantly hid the Koh-i-Noor for years in the plaster of his prison cell, and Shuja, now blinded in his turn by a third brother, Mahmud, yielded his prized possession to Runjeet Singh only to save his family from torture and death. Runjeet Singh was enormously proud of his new acquisition and had the diamond set in a bracelet which he wore constantly. On his death the gem descended to his son, the rajah Dhulip Singh. It remained in his possession until the seizure of the Punjab by the British after the Indian Mutiny when it was among the jewels in the treasury at Lahore that were confiscated and taken as reparations. Two officers carried the "famous diamond" to London and on June 3, 1850, the Koh-i-Noor was presented to Queen Victoria at a great reception held in St. James's Palace to mark the 250th anniversary of the founding of the East India Company.

The Koh-i-Noor may have been "coveted and hoarded with insane passion" in India, but Queen Victoria was not all that impressed. Used to well-cut diamonds full of fire and brilliance, she was positively disappointed with the rudely cut 187-carat stone, as were the people who viewed it at the Crystal Palace Exhibition in London in 1851. Finally, the queen decided to have it recut. A special area was set aside in the workshop of Garrard's, the crown jewelers, and for a fee of £9,000 a cutter from Amsterdam was induced to undertake the task. The Prince Consort took a keen interest in the proceedings and is said to have spent many hours "assisting" in the cutting of the stone. Indeed one report says

that "Her Majesty herself and nearly all the members of the royal family personally assisted at putting on the facets, which for perfection are unequalled; the Duke of Wellington personally putting on the first." When they had finished, the Koh-i-Noor had been reduced to a 108.93-carat oval—and still lacked fire and brilliance. To what extent this was due to the inability of the Dutch cutter to check the enthusiasm of his royal helpers is impossible to say, but no one was pleased with the result. In fact, the Koh-i-Noor lay neglected in a strongbox in Windsor Castle for many years, but in 1911 it was placed in the crown of Queen Mary. There it remained until 1937, when it was made the central ornament in a new crown for Queen Elizabeth, consort of George VI, for their coronation.

No one can doubt the role that the Koh-i-Noor played in the history of India and that, initially at least, it was insufficiently appreciated by its new owners. However, for the British government to return the stone would set a precedent which could strip the treasuries and museums of the world of some of their most prized possessions, all too many of which came originally from the hoards of Delhi.

Another such diamond is the 200-carat Orloff, now in the Kremlin Museum in Moscow. It is shaped like half an egg and many believe that it could be the legendary Great Mogul diamond seen by Tavernier which disappeared after the sack of Delhi. Another and more colorful account of its history records that it was once an eye of the Hindu god Sri Ranga in the temple at Mysore, and that it was stolen by a French deserter who had disguised himself as a Brahmin in order to gain access to the inner shrine. The soldier then fled to Madras where he sold the "eye" to a British sea captain for £2,000 who carried it to London and in turn sold it to a Persian jeweler called Khojeh for £12,000. Khojeh

Catherine II of Russia was a great collector of diamonds. Her most celebrated possession was the 200-carat Orloff which she had mounted in her imperial scepter.

took the diamond to Amsterdam where it was seen by Count Gregory Orloff, a once powerful Russian nobleman who had been dismissed from the court by Catherine the Great. Thinking that a present of such magnificence would restore him to the queen's favor, the count bought the diamond for £90,000 and returned to Russia. Catherine accepted the gift, but instead of wearing it had it mounted on top of the double eagle in the imperial scepter where it has remained ever since. Despite the lavishness of his present, Count Orloff was not reinstated in his former position of power and influence at court.

All the tales of blood and thunder told so far have concerned the older Indian diamonds, but it would be a mistake to think that the great diamonds produced from the South African mines over the past hundred years are without interest. Their stories may be less violent and bloody but they are nonetheless dramatic, and there is little doubt that in earlier centuries they would have rivaled their Indian predecessors. Take the Cullinan, for example. Found in the Premier Mine in 1905, it weighed 3,106 carats and is the largest rough diamond yet discovered. It provided nine major gems, all of them now either in the British crown jewels or in the personal possession of the royal family. The two largest are, in fact, the two largest cut diamonds in the world. One weighs 530.2 carats and is set in the Imperial Scepter, while the other weighs 317.4 carats and is mounted in the band of the Imperial State Crown.

This huge diamond was acquired by the Transvaal government for £150,000 and presented to King Edward VII on his sixty-sixth birthday on November 9, 1907. The task of cutting the largest diamond in the world was entrusted to the famous Asscher Diamond Company in Amsterdam. The senior member of the firm, Joseph Asscher, studied the great stone for two months before deciding the best

The diamond-encrusted Crown of St. Edward, with which all British monarchs are crowned. This ceremonial crown is worn only once in the lifetime of a sovereign for only a few moments during the act of coronation.

DIAMOND INFORMATION CENTER, NEW YORK

way to cleave it. On February 10, 1908, he was ready to begin. He placed his blade in the V-shaped groove he had made in the top of the diamond and struck it with a heavy steel rod. Nothing happened, and the diamond remained intact. The second attempt was a complete success and the Cullinan cleaved exactly as Asscher had planned. There is a popular story that the whole operation was carried out with a doctor and nurse in attendance and that Asscher fainted as soon as his work was done. His son Louis, however, reports that "no Asscher would faint over any operation on any diamond." All his father had standing by, he claims, was a bottle of champagne.

Until the discovery of the Cullinan, the Braganza, weighing 1,680 carats, was the largest rough diamond in the world. It was reputed to have been found in Brazil in about 1790, but its claim to fame is somewhat tarnished by the fact that its present whereabouts are unknown; the Portuguese government disclaims all knowledge of it. Most commentators believe that it is a topaz and not a diamond, but no one has ever seen the Braganza—even to verify that it ever existed.

There is no doubt about the two Brazilian diamonds purchased by the young Archduke Maximilian of Austria, later to become the ill-fated emperor of Mexico. One was a 42-carat cushion cut, now known as the Emperor Maximilian. It had a strange violet fluorescence in daylight, and Maximilian was so attached to the stone that he wore it in a little bag around his neck. He was wearing it at the time of his execution in 1867, and after his death it was sent to his wife, the empress Carlotta in Europe. The diamond later passed into the hands of Ferdinand Hotz, the Chicago gem dealer, and on his death in 1946 it was sold to a private collector.

The other diamond that Maximilian bought

The Emperor Maximilian of Mexico and the Empress Carlotta. One of the emperor's most prized possessions was a 42-carat diamond which he was wearing round his neck at the time of his execution in 1867.

DIAMOND INFORMATION CENTER, NEW YORK

in Brazil was a greenish yellow stone weighing 50 carats which he then had refashioned into a 33-carat cushion cut as a present for his bride, Princess Carlotta of Belgium. It is known as the Maximilian and also as the Carlotta. The stone disappeared after Maximilian's execution, but turned up again in 1901 when two Mexicans were caught trying to smuggle it into the United States. Confiscated by the United States Customs authorities, the stone was put up for auction and fetched $120,000. Its subsequent history comes to an abrupt and undignified end in 1961. Then owned by New York jeweler Morris S. Nelkin, the diamond was hidden in a garbage pail by his daughter, who suspected that there was a burglar in the house. Unfortunately, no effort was made to retrieve the stone until the following morning by which time the sanitation men had already called. The Carlotta has not been seen since.

The great diamonds of the world all have their romantic and historical associations, but so too do the small ones. Ever since 1477 when Archduke Maximilian of Germany ordered a betrothal ring set with a diamond for his bride-to-be, Princess Mary of Burgundy, a diamond ring has become the accepted symbol of enduring love. The custom of giving betrothal rings is an ancient one and occurs in Roman, Egyptian, Greek, and Hebrew civilizations, but the combination of the ring with a diamond remained for a long time a comparative rarity outside court circles.

The first commoner to wear diamonds is reputed to have been Agnes Sorel in the mid-fifteenth century. She was the young and beautiful mistress of King Charles VII of France and is widely credited with inaugurating the change in the role of the diamond from a symbol of royal power and wealth to one of simple feminine adornment. She may also have been responsible for the slightly risqué image that diamonds have which runs parallel with their ultra-respectable role as a token of everlasting love and fidelity when set in a betrothal ring. There may be more than a little truth in the saying that a man buys three diamonds in his life: the first for his bride-to-be, the second for his mistress, and the third for his wife when she finds out about his mistress. Agnes Sorel may have been a commoner but she was still a king's mistress, a position that placed her above the laws forbidding both the wearing of jewelry except by nobles and clergy and trading with the infidel in the East who supplied the diamonds and other precious stones. Diamond rings enjoyed great popularity in England during

ABOVE LEFT *Queen Victoria on her wedding day in 1840. She is wearing a necklace of large round diamonds.* **RIGHT** *This same necklace was to be worn over a century later by Princess Margaret when she married Anthony Armstrong-Jones.* **OPPOSITE** *Agnes Sorel, the beautiful but low-born mistress of Charles VII of France, loved diamonds and is widely credited with being the first commoner to wear them.*

the reign of Henry VIII and in France under Francis I. Both kings were amorously inclined and used their rings to inscribe flirtatious messages on the windows of castle and chateau, a habit their courtiers were quick to emulate.

It was not until the discovery of the huge deposits in South Africa in 1870 that diamonds began to reach a much wider market. Cecil Rhodes, the great architect of De Beers, was quick to spot the potential for expansion and deliberately encouraged the romantic appeal of diamonds. The relationship between man and woman, Rhodes insisted, was the foundation of the diamond's worth, and as long as men fell for women, diamonds would be in demand. Or as Barney Barnato's nephew, Solly Joel, put it twenty-five years later, "Women are born every day and while women are born, diamonds will be worn."

This has remained the consistent theme of the marketing policy of De Beers and others ever since. Emphasis on the romantic appeal of diamonds managed to extricate the industry from the terrible privations of the 1930s and in subsequent years has provided it with a degree of stability and growth that is the envy of every other trade. But in order to achieve such signal success for so long, De Beers had to satisfy two preconditions. One was to have a unique product to sell. The other was to appeal to a basic need in its customers. That the diamond is a unique product is unquestioned. No more than forty tons of gem diamonds have been excavated since the beginning of time, and each single stone loses as much as 50 to 60 percent in the cutting. The end result may be a crystal of 20 points or .5 carat, 1 carat, or 10 carats, but each one is different and distinguishable from another. A diamond, as one advertising copywriter claims, is "Nature's limited edition."

As for the idea of appealing to a basic need, De Beers had a head start thanks to roughly two thousand years or more of tradition. The ring or circle is probably the oldest of man's symbols. Suggested by the appearance of the sun, it has always been imbued with an aura of mystery and magic. With no beginning and no end, it was the natural representation of eternity, and its ability to surround or enclose caused it to be popularly invested with protective powers.

Rings or circlets were almost certainly the first objects ever to be so used, initially for protection and later for decorative purposes as well. Whether worn on the finger, around the neck, on the wrist or the ankle, in ears or in the nose, the ring soon became the most popular single means of personal adornment throughout the world. After a time, the ring may have lost many of its magical connotations, but it has never lost its symbolism. As we have seen, the ring has been used in betrothal and marriage ceremonies through the ages and it was an inspired, if natural, step to encourage the combination of a diamond with the ring. After all, by reason of its virtual

The fulfillment of the American dream circa 1870: the husband presents his young wife with her first diamond necklace. Diamonds were soon to become the status symbol par excellence in American society of the last quarter of the nineteenth century.

indestructibility, the diamond symbolized eternity too, and for good measure it also represented courage, virtue and purity. A ring on its own meant a great deal, but a ring with a diamond was an unbeatable combination.

It is therefore not surprising that the idea caught on with remarkable rapidity, particularly in America and in Britain where the diamond engagement ring has become so much a part of tradition that one is given to between 80 and 90 percent of young women marrying for the first time. The habit is catching on in France and Italy, and even in Germany and Sweden where the diamond ring has had to contend with a traditional engagement ceremony involving the exchange of plain gold rings. Instead of trying to establish a new custom, diamond promotion has aimed at adding a diamond ring to the gold bands as a further present for the woman. In Japan, too, where even the ring by itself had little place in traditional betrothal ceremonies and the diamond had no special significance, sales of diamond engagement rings have leaped dramatically over the past decade.

But despite the growing popularity of diamonds throughout the world, the impact of the great diamonds has never waned. Few have captured the public imagination more in

OPPOSITE *The significance of the diamond depicted in one of the series of popular postcards, "The Language of Precious Stones," published in about 1910.*

recent years than the beautiful pear-shaped 69.42-carat diamond bought by Richard Burton as a birthday present for his wife, Elizabeth Taylor. Originally owned by Mrs. Walter Ames, sister of Walter Annenburg, the publisher and one-time US ambassador to Britain, the stone had been cut from a 240.8-carat rough found in the Premier Mine in 1966. It had been bought at auction in November 1969 by Cartier of New York for $1,050,000— at the time the highest price ever paid for a diamond at auction— and immediately sold to Richard Burton for a rather higher figure. The Taylor-Burton diamond, as it came to be called, was in good company. The year before, Richard Burton had bought the 33.10-carat Krupp diamond from the estate of the German munitions king for $305,000 and two years later he also acquired the engraved heart-shaped diamond, now known as the Taylor-Heart. This diamond had been purchased in India in 1971. It had once belonged to Queen Mumtaz, wife of Shah Jehan, in whose honor the Taj Mahal had been built as a tomb. There

LEFT *Famous diamonds are often featured in motion pictures. Here Jane, played by Dorothy Hart, wears the Transvaal Diamond, a 68-carat champagne-colored stone, in* Tarzan's Savage Fury. *Lex Barker plays Tarzan.* **OVERLEAF** *Shah Jehan (right), Mogul ruler of India from 1628 to 1658, and Mumtaz Mahal (left), his beautiful queen.*

is a story that at a Hollywood party, an elderly gentleman complimented Elizabeth Taylor on her striking pendant and asked her what it was. "You stupid xxxx," replied the actress, "that's the Taj Mahal diamond."

It may be a far cry from the court of Shah Jehan to a film star's mansion in Beverley Hills but the contrast emphasizes the point that the story of a great diamond is never closed. Many have been lost, only to appear centuries later to take on a new and often more magnificent life. And few have ever actually been destroyed like the Pigott diamond which the dying Ali Pasha ordered to be crushed to powder before his eyes. Diamonds outlast dynasties. Or, in the words of Gardner Williams once again:

> A jewel may rest on an English lady's arm that saw Alaric sack Rome, and beheld before—what not? The treasures of the palaces of the Pharoahs and of Darius, or the camp of the Ptolemies, come into Europe on the neck of a vulgar proconsul's wife to glitter at every gladiator's butchery at the amphitheatre; then pass in a Gothic ox wagon to an Arab seraglio at Seville; and so back to its native India to figure in the throne of the Great Mogul; to be bought by an Armenian for a few rupees from an English soldier— and so at last come hither.

OPPOSITE *One of the most beautiful diamonds in the world, the famous and historic 140.5-carat Regent, which now rests in the Louvre.*

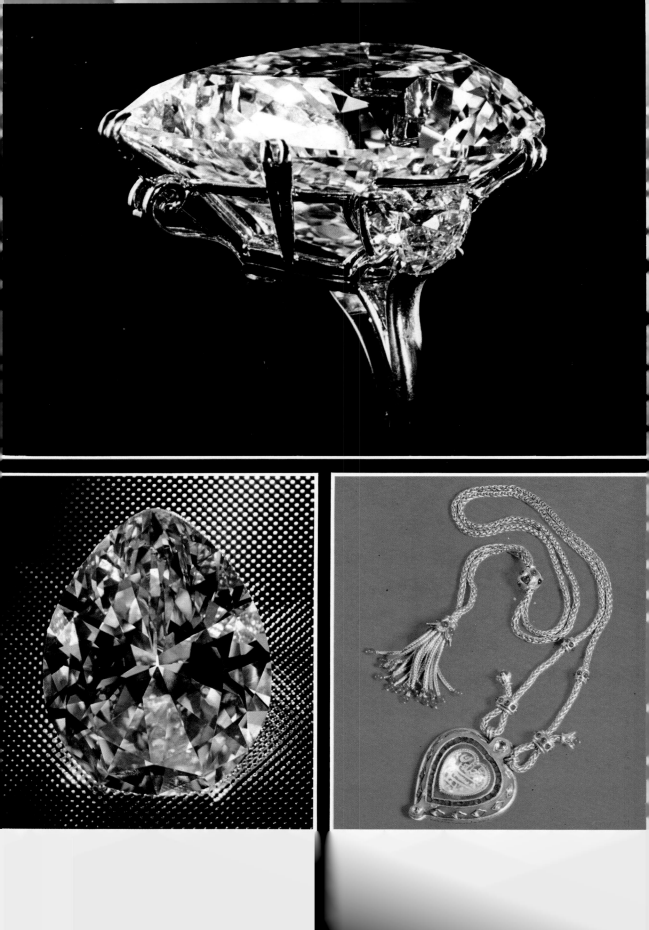

OPPOSITE: ABOVE The Taylor-Burton—this pear-shaped flawless 69.42-carat gem, previously known as the Cartier, was cut by Harry Winston in 1967 from a 240.8-carat rough found in the Premier Mine in 1966. In 1969 it was bought by Cartier of New York for $1,050,000. One of the conditions of the sale was that the buyer could name the stone, but since it was almost immediately resold to Richard Burton as a present for his wife, Elizabeth Taylor, it was known only briefly as the Cartier. **BELOW LEFT** The Transvaal—cut from a 240-carat rough found in the Premier Mine, this champagne-colored pear-shaped diamond now weighs 67.89 carats and has 116 facets. It has featured in many Hollywood films. **BELOW RIGHT** The Taylor Heart—one of the largest engraved diamonds known, the stone was originally given by the great Shah Jehan to his twenty-one-year-old wife Mumtaz shortly before her death in 1653. Cartier acquired the diamond from a royal European collection and sold it for a reputed $50,000 to Richard Burton as a present for Elizabeth Taylor on her fortieth birthday.

THIS PAGE: ABOVE The Eureka—this diamond holds a special place in South African history. Picked up by a small boy on the banks of the Vaal River in 1866, the 21-carat rough yellow diamond sparked the diamond rush which was to transform the country's economy. It was later cut into a 10.73 brilliant and acquired by a London dealer. The Eureka was purchased by De Beers in 1966 on the 100th anniversary of its discovery, and returned to South Africa. **CENTER** The Jubilee—found in the Jagersfontein Mine in 1895, the 650.8-carat rough diamond from which the Jubilee came was originally named the Reitz diamond after the then-president of the Orange Free State. In 1897, after being cut into a 245.35-carat cushion-shaped brilliant of the purest white, it was renamed the Jubilee in honor of Queen Victoria's Diamond Jubilee which was celebrated in that year. A star attraction at the Paris Exhibition of 1900, the Jubilee was then acquired by the Indian industrialist Sir Dorab Tata. After his death, it passed to Paul Louis Weill, the French millionaire. **BELOW** The Tiffany—the largest and finest canary-yellow diamond in the world, this superb diamond was found in South Africa's Kimberley Mine in 1878. Purchased by Tiffany and Co. in 1879, it was taken to Paris where a 128.51-carat cushion-shaped brilliant was cut from the 287.42-carat rough. The great yellow stone has been on continuous display at Tiffany's in New York for nearly a century and is still exhibited there today. It is valued at $5,000,000. TIFFANY AND CO.

The Sancy—the known history of the Sancy began in Constantinople in about 1580 when it was bought by a French nobleman, Nicholas de Sancy, and taken back to France. Sancy later lent the 55-carat diamond to his king, Henry III, to wear in the cap he always wore to conceal his baldness. Reputedly Sancy sent the diamond to the king by the hand of one of his most trusted servants, who was set upon and killed by robbers. Finding nothing of value on his person, the robbers threw the body into a ditch, where it was found some days later. Knowing the devotion of his servant, Sancy directed that the body be cut open. As he had suspected, the diamond was found in the dead man's stomach; the fellow had presumably swallowed it just before being killed.

In 1596 Sancy became ambassador to England and sold the diamond to James I in 1604. The diamond then passed to Charles I, and in 1644 during the Civil War, his queen Henrietta Maria took many of the crown jewels, including the Sancy, to France in order to raise money to carry on the struggle against Oliver Cromwell and the Parliamentarians. When the queen was unable to repay the loans, the diamond remained in France and passed into the hands of Cardinal Mazarin, who subsequently bequeathed his diamond collection to the French crown.

A hundred years later, in the early days of the French Revolution, the Sancy, together with many other famous gems was looted from the Treasury, but while no mention was made of its recovery, in 1795 a diamond of much the same weight was pledged by the directors of France for a loan from Spain. The diamond was never redeemed and passed to the Spanish Bourbons. It then reappeared in 1828 in the hands of a French merchant. He sold it to a Prince Anatole Demidoff of Russia, who in 1865 disposed of it to a Bombay merchant. The Sancy did not remain in India for long, and two years later it was offered for sale by the French jeweler Bapst. It reached its present owners, the Astor family, in 1906 when William Waldorf Astor bought the diamond as a wedding gift for his son's bride, Nancy Langhorne.

WHAT IS A DIAMOND?

The nature of the diamond had puzzled scientists for hundreds of years, and it was not until nearly the end of the seventeenth century that its relationship to carbon was even suspected.

The first well-documented experiment on a diamond was carried out by two Italian academicians in the presence of the Grand Duke Cosimo III in Florence in 1694. They set up a large burning glass, focused the beam on a small diamond and saw it "crack, coruscate and finally disappear," leaving a minute quantity of blue ash. But it was the French physicist Babinet, along with eminent colleagues like Lavoisier, who proved beyond reasonable doubt that a diamond was carbon in exceptionally pure form. This apparent paradox caused Babinet to observe:

> And what is a diamond? The most precious thing in the whole world. And what is carbon? The most common material that is known. It not only exists in vast quantities in the bowels of the earth, but plants and trees of every kind contain it in an inconceivable quantity. . . . And yet the diamond and carbon are identical. Diamond is crystallized carbon.

One of Lavoisier's most celebrated experiments was to place a diamond in a bell jar filled with oxygen which rested in a basin containing mercury. The rays of the sun were then focused on the diamond by means of a large burning glass. After the diamond had been consumed, the bell jar was found to contain great quantities of carbonic acid, indicating to Lavoisier that the diamond was composed principally of carbon. Later experiments by Humphry Davy in England prompted him to conclude that the diamond was composed of carbon and nothing else, a view that was first contradicted in 1841 by Dumas and Strass, whose numerous experiments revealed minute traces of other elements, notably nitrogen and aluminum. It is these slight impurities that deform the perfect crystalline structure of the ideal diamond, and can have a marked effect on the physical properties of a stone. This knowledge is now being used in the production of synthetic diamonds to "tailor" them for particular applications in industry (see "Harder than Steel").

It would be an exaggeration to say that not much more is known about the origin of diamonds today than two thousand years ago when they were believed to be splinters of stars. Nevertheless, it is true that there is still no unanimity among geologists about exactly how and where diamond is formed. As late as

OPPOSITE *The apparatus used by Lavoisier in his diamond combustion experiment. This was one of the earliest experiments to prove that diamond was composed principally of carbon.*

the nineteenth century, theories about the origin of diamonds had been shaped by the fact that the stones had always been found on or very close to the surface, either in riverbeds or in the beds of rivers that had dried up ages ago. And given the unique qualities of the diamond together with its rarity, it is perhaps not surprising that the "heaven-borne" theory should have been the most enduring. Even as late as 1869 the *Gentleman's Magazine* of London reported that a "Continental experimentalist" had declared that the intense cold of stellar space disassociated and crystallized carbon from "masses of meteoric nature coursing through space" and caused diamonds to fall from the sky. The editor went on to comment that "the location of diamonds upon the earth agrees much better with the hypothesis of a sky-source than an earth-source," and that "those Cape specimens now attracting so much attention are found on the surface of the ground only; it is of no use to dig for them." Still, the "Continental experimentalist" may well have a point. Diamonds have been found in meteor craters at Novo Urei in southeastern Russia and at Canyon Diablo in Arizona, although most scientists believe they were created by the heat and pressure of impact and not carried to earth in the meteors.

It was not until the discovery of the "dry diggings" at Kimberley in 1870, coupled with the determination of the miners to excavate every inch of their dearly bought claims, that it became clear that diamonds came from below and not from above. It was also clear that diamond was invariably associated with one particular type of rock, and that this rock was only to be found in clearly delineated areas. Since the rock—and the diamonds—persisted at depth, it was soon suggested that these "pipes" were volcanic in nature and that diamonds had been formed out of carbon under intense heat and pressure deep in the bowels of the earth. They had then been forced toward the surface when those long-extinct volcanoes had erupted millions of years ago. This strange diamond-bearing rock—soon to be called kimberlite—was assumed to be nothing more than solidified lava. But as mining progressed at Kimberley, it was discovered that the pipes were not great volcanic funnels plunging into the earth's core. Rather, they were like irregularly shaped carrots, decreasing in area and petering out in a number of fissures at varying depths from a few hundred to several thousands of feet. Furthermore, relatively few of them contained any diamonds at all.

A great deal has since been learned from

the making of synthetic diamonds, and perhaps the most widely accepted current theory is that since diamond forms at pressures and temperatures between 0.5 million pounds per square inch at 700°C and 1.3 million pounds at 2,500°C, the formation must have taken place at depths of at least 120 miles. Chemical studies pointed to the ultra-basic rock peridotite in its molten form as the most likely to have provided the right conditions for the creation of diamond from carbon. The process of crystallization is assumed to have been long and slow, and the theory goes that conditions remained stable for a considerable period as a result of the pressure of carbon dioxide gas below the peridotite layer being equal to the pressure from the earth above. When the pressure below became too great, the balance was changed and the diamond-bearing magma (molten rock) was driven explosively toward the surface. On the way it picked up other rocks and minerals, forming itself into the "geological plum pudding" that we now call kimberlite, eventually erupting through the surface of the earth and solidifying.

The violence of the eruption toward the surface is believed to account for the fact that so many diamonds are chipped or cleaved. In the De Beers Mine, two large and unusually

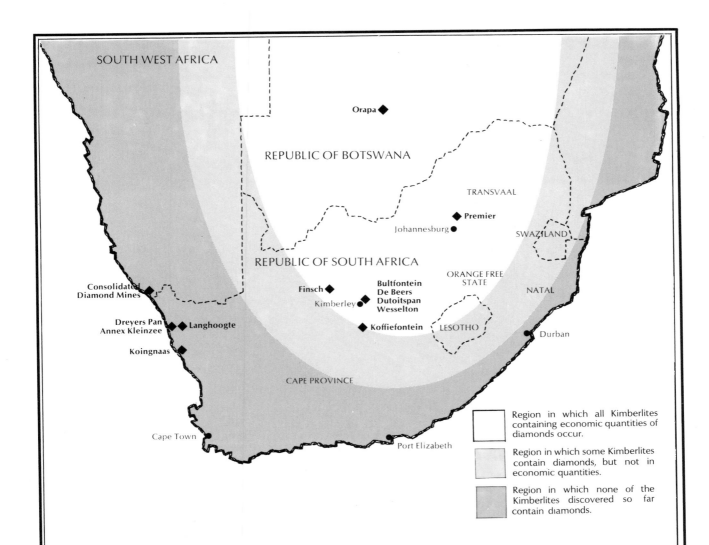

SOUTH WEST AFRICA

Orapa ◆

REPUBLIC OF BOTSWANA

TRANSVAAL

◆ Premier

Johannesburg ●

SWAZILAND

REPUBLIC OF SOUTH AFRICA

ORANGE FREE STATE

NATAL

Consolidated Diamond Mines

Finsch ◆

Bultfontein
De Beers
Dutoitspan
Wesselton

Kimberley ●

Dreyers Pan
Annex Kleinzee ◆ Langhoogte

◆ Koffiefontein

LESOTHO

Durban ●

Koingnaas

CAPE PROVINCE

Cape Town ●

Port Elizabeth ●

☐ Region in which all Kimberlites containing economic quantities of diamonds occur.

☐ Region in which some Kimberlites contain diamonds, but not in economic quantities.

☐ Region in which none of the Kimberlites discovered so far contain diamonds.

WHY IS SOUTH AFRICA SO RICH IN DIAMONDS?

The pattern of distribution of diamond sources throughout the world shows that they are limited to continental areas with a long history of geological stability. This means that diamond-bearing kimberlite bodies are only to be found in areas of maximum stability where they postdate crustal formation by at least 500 million years. The interior plateau of South Africa is such an area, and it is literally riddled with kimberlite. The yield of the pipes tends to diminish the farther they are away from the central area, and of the nine major pipes and some fifty or more minor kimberlite bodies which are, or have been, economically mined, all fall within the boundaries of the central area. In the outer area, the kimberlites found so far have been barren of diamonds, and in the intermediate area their content was such as to make mining uneconomic.

MAP ADAPTED FROM *INTERNATIONAL DIAMONDS NUMBER TWO*

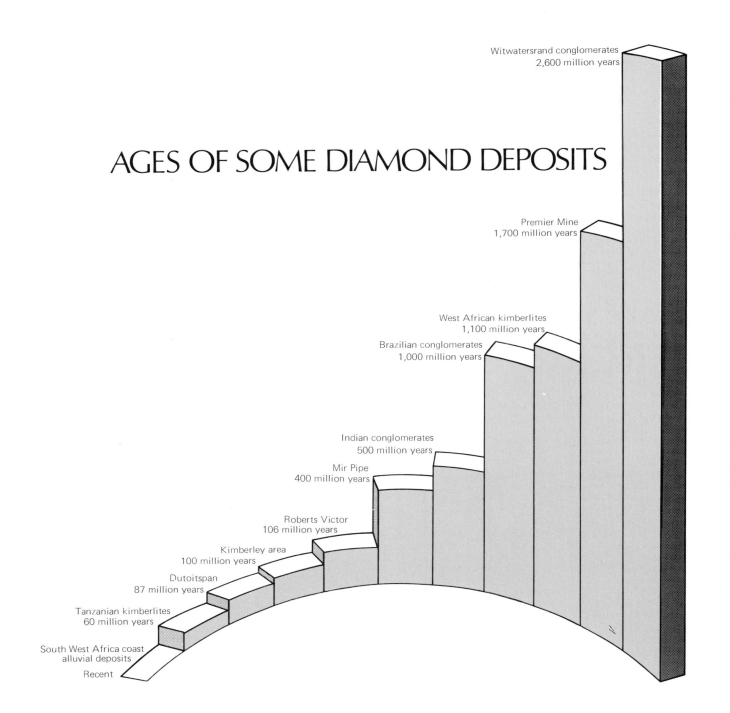

AGES OF SOME DIAMOND DEPOSITS

Witwatersrand conglomerates
2,600 million years

Premier Mine
1,700 million years

West African kimberlites
1,100 million years

Brazilian conglomerates
1,000 million years

Indian conglomerates
500 million years

Mir Pipe
400 million years

Roberts Victor
106 million years

Kimberley area
100 million years

Dutoitspan
87 million years

Tanzanian kimberlites
60 million years

South West Africa coast
alluvial deposits

Recent

shaped pieces of diamond called cleavages were found simultaneously in different parts of the mine, and yet fitted together exactly. Even the huge Cullinan is a cleavage, and there is still a hope that one day the Premier Mine will disgorge the other half of the biggest diamond ever found. Other curious items have been found in kimberlite pipes including pieces of fossilized wood, ancient ostrich eggs, and even a headless human skeleton with the skull discovered fifty feet away at half the depth.

Another puzzling phenomenon is the diminishing yield and average size of diamonds as a mine gets deeper. In the Premier mine, for example, the blue ground down to the 400-foot (125-meter) level yielded between 0.80 and 1.29 carats a load (1,600 pounds), whereas the next 100 feet (33 meters) yielded barely 0.19 carats. The natural assumption from this fact is that far more diamonds have been dispersed across the surface of the earth by erosion of the top of the pipes than have been extracted from, or remain in, the pipes. The South African pipes are estimated to be 120 million years old, and geologists believe that since then a slice of earth (and kimberlite) between half a mile and a mile (800 to 1,500 meters) has been eroded from the Kimberley region. If this is the case then it is calculated that some 3 billion carats of diamonds have been ''lost'' over the ages.

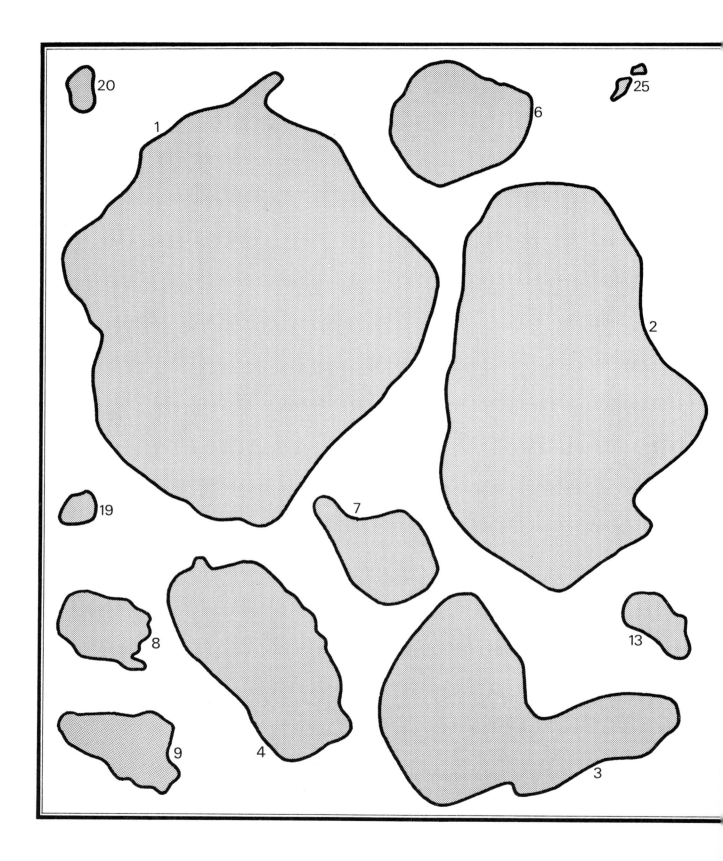

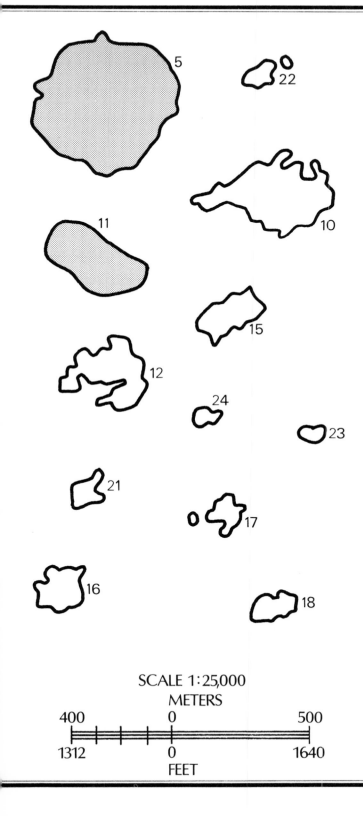

THE WORLD'S LARGEST KNOWN DIAMOND PIPES

Order	Name	Country	Acres
1	Mwadui	Tanzania	360.77
2	Orapa	Botswana	261.93
3	Talala	Congo	235.53
4	Premier	South Africa	79.07
5	Zarnitsa	Siberia	53.13
6	Finsch	South Africa	44.23
7	Koffiefontein	South Africa	27.43
8	Jagersfontein	South Africa	24.71
9	Camatue	Angola	22.98
10	Leningradkaya	Siberia	22.24
11	Mir	Siberia	17.05
12	Dalnyaya	Siberia	13.34
13	De Beers	South Africa	11.86
14	Kimberley	South Africa	8.90
15	Nevidimka	Siberia	6.18
16	Dolgodjdannaya	Siberia	6.18
17	Ossennyaya	Siberia	3.95
18	Molodejnaya	Siberia	3.71
19	Blaauwbosch	South Africa	3.71
20	West End	South Africa	3.46
21	Geophysitchskaya	Siberia	2.97
22	Polyarnaya	Siberia	2.47
23	Sosyednnyaya	Siberia	1.24
24	Malyutka	Siberia	0.99
25	Roberts Victor	South Africa	0.99

Illustrated at the left are the relative sizes and shapes of some of the world's largest known kimberlite pipes, all of which occur in Africa (opposite page) and Siberia (this page). For ease of reference, the figure at the side of each pipe corresponds to the ranking in the table above. The pipes which are tinted are producing mines.

In general, diamond pipes tend to be irregular in shape. It will be noted that many of the Siberian pipes represented here are considerably more irregular than their South African counterparts. Several other Siberian pipes have been discovered, but the Soviet government has not yet released information on their sizes. It is believed, however, that the Zarnitsa pipe, the fifth largest in the table above, is still the largest Russian pipe.

ADAPTED FROM *INTERNATIONAL DIAMOND ANNUAL* (1971)

SCALE 1:25,000

METERS

400	0	500
1312	0	1640

FEET

This dispersal theory could go a long way toward explaining another diamond mystery—the remarkably high proportion of fine gem-quality stones among diamonds found in the marine terrace deposits of South West Africa. The fact that only about 3 percent of the stones found there are of industrial quality compared with 20 to 30 percent in the pipes has caused some geologists to suggest that the marine terrace diamonds come from a different source than other alluvials, perhaps even from pipes under the seabed.

There is no reason why diamond-bearing pipes should not exist under the sea. A more obvious explanation, however, would seem to be the merciless pounding the diamonds would have received at the hands of the waves on this storm-swept coast over millions of years. The larger crystals would have settled more rapidly than the smaller ones, many of which would have been swept out to sea, while the irregular, the fractured and the poorer-quality stones would have simply disintegrated. Laboratory tests simulating wear and tear have shown decisively that a good-quality gem stone will survive unharmed the sort of treatment that can totally destroy a poorer-quality stone.

Probably the best-known quality of the

diamond is its exceptional hardness. The mineralogist Mohs devised a scale, now known as the Mohs scale, in which minerals were ranked from 1 to 10 according to their relative hardness, which was determined by a scratch test: a given mineral on the scale will scratch those below it and be scratched by those above it. Diamond comes right at the top of the list, with no other natural mineral even approaching it in hardness. The scale is not a linear one, and the hardness gap between diamond and corundum, the next hardest mineral on the scale, is much wider than the gap between corundum and talc, the softest:

10. Diamond	5. Apatite
9. Corundum	4. Fluorspar
8. Topaz	3. Calcite
7. Quartz	2. Gypsum
6. Feldspar	1. Talc

Only a diamond will scratch another diamond. It is this quality of exceptional hardness that makes it so valued as an industrial material used, for example, in the heads of rock drills and in the tips of cutting tools.

But although diamond is the hardest substance known, its hardness is directional because, like wood, it has a grain. This was first discovered by the early diamond cutters, who looked upon the knowledge as one of the great secrets of their trade. Since the variation in hardness may range from ten times in one direction to a hundred times in another, appreciation of the fact was clearly vital to successful cutting. For the same reason the diamond is also relatively brittle and can be shattered by a misplaced blow. The cleaver, for example, may study a large stone for days or even weeks in order to establish the exact direction of the grain before attempting his task.

Once it has been cut and polished, the diamond has a number of unique optical properties which account for its superior ranking to colorful and brilliant gems such as rubies, emeralds and sapphires. An exceptionally high degree of luster and brilliance are the most important of these qualities. Luster refers to the quality of light that is reflected from the surface of a material; it is graded from practically nil on certain materials up to a uniquely high level in the case of the diamond, when it is called "adamantine luster." Brilliance is concerned both with the "life" of a stone (the degree of light that is reflected from the surface and interior of the diamond) and with its "fire" (the amount of refraction and color dispersion that is achieved). The more that light is refracted

WHY IS A DIAMOND SO HARD?

The diamond is an atomic crystal whose carbon atoms are held together in a strong and rigid space lattice. This accounts for the diamond's extreme hardness and resistance to deformation but the fact that the carbon atoms are not packed closely together means that the diamond possesses a very high degree of thermal conductivity. The density of the atomic structure varies directionally and this is why the diamond is harder in some directions than in others. In fact it is the nature of the crystal lattice that provides the diamond with many of its unique physical properties.

and split into the colors of the spectrum, the greater the amount of fire a stone is said to have. It is the job of the diamond cutter to achieve a fine balance between the fire and life of a diamond, as maximum fire is not consistent with maximum "life." The early cutters were well aware of these qualities. As the *Sir John Mandeville Lapidary* observed in 1561, the diamond "seems to take pleasure in assuming in turn the colours proper to other gems."

A further distinguishing feature of many diamonds is that they will glow or fluoresce when exposed to ultraviolet light; they may also phosphoresce, or continue to glow, after the removal of the light source. Every diamond is different both in the color and intensity of its fluorescence and phosphorescence, a fact which can make for positive identification of two apparently identical stones of pieces of jewelry. The Hope diamond, which is blue, fluoresces red, for example; while the Maximilian, which is also blue, fluoresces violet even in daylight.

However, despite this unique catalogue of the optical attributes possessed by the diamond, the fact remains that in the rough state in which it is found, a diamond is often not recognized for what it is. It does not sparkle and flash. On the contrary, it is a rather dull,

A rough diamond in its natural state, embedded in kimberlite.

ordinary-looking pebble whose principal distinguishing feature is its shape. The reason is that many diamond crystals are coated with a thickness of inferior quality and badly formed diamond. The coating may be gray, green, brown or black and is usually found to contain many small inclusions of foreign material. It is not necessarily indicative of the standard of the rest of the stone and a dull, dirty coat can cover a diamond of the highest quality—or one almost as dull and dirty as itself.

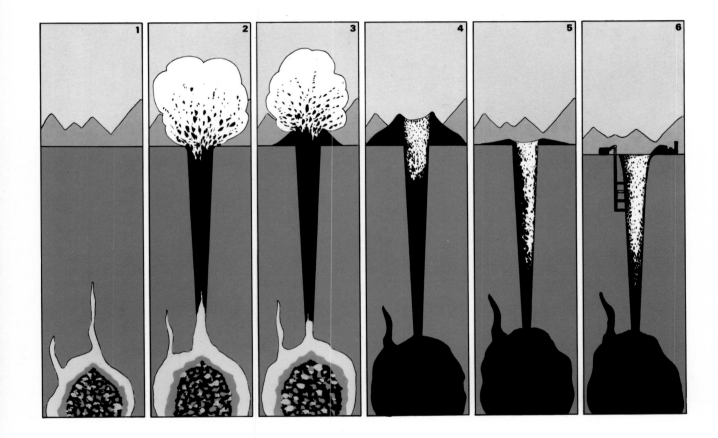

THE BIRTH OF A KIMBERLITE PIPE

1. The pressure of the molten magma begins to crack the surrounding rock at least 120 miles beneath the surface of the earth.

2. The crack reaches the surface and the magma is forced explosively toward the surface.

3. The violence of the eruption causes a cone to form on the surface of the earth.

4. The eruption is complete and the cone cools.

5. The cone begins to weather and gradually becomes almost undetectable on the surface.

6. The pipe is mined.

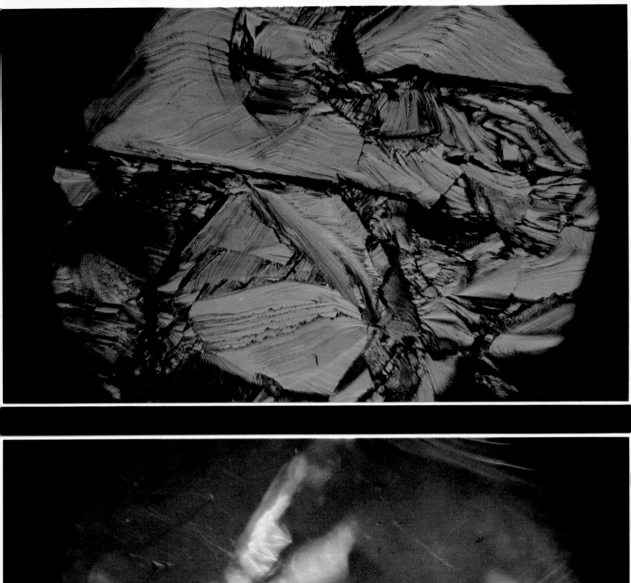

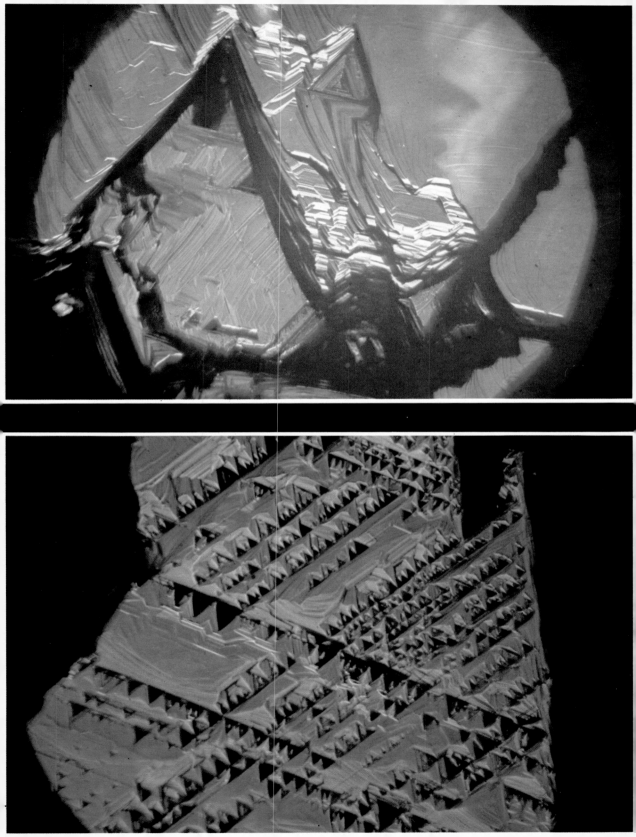

D. DRUKKER AND SONS

PRECEDING PAGES *Four rough gem diamonds photographed by a modified Nomarski differential interference contrast technique. Variations in lighting are used to show up different features of the diamond. At the top left, a cleavage is shown: the uneven growth pattern is much in evidence. The picture at the bottom left has been described as a "Diamondscape"; the surface of the diamond has, in effect, become an art form. At the top right, the striations demonstrate the growth layers of the crystal. In the picture at the bottom right, the characteristic triangular pits called trigons can clearly be seen.* DIAMOND GRADING LABORATORIES, LONDON

ABOVE *One of the most unusual diamonds ever found, the Amsterdam is jet black and totally opaque. Initially classified as just a large piece of mine boart, the stone was very nearly broken up into smaller pieces for industrial use. Fortunately, the cleaver was so impressed by the intensity of the blackness of the splinters that a decision was made to cut and polish the stone as a gem. The Amsterdam is now a 33.74-carat pear-shaped stone with 145 facets, and unlike all other black diamonds, it remains completely opaque, even when submitted to the strongest light. Named in honor of the 700th anniversary of the city of Amsterdam, the diamond is in the possession of its discoverers, Amsterdam diamond merchants D. Drukker and Sons.*

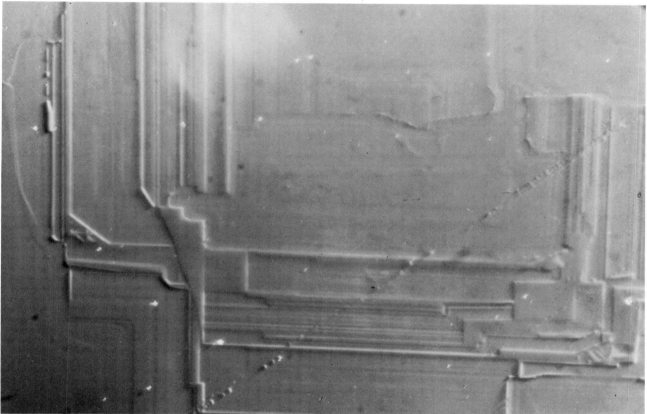

DIAMOND GRADING LABORATORIES, LONDON

Diamonds, like most minerals, are crystalline with a regular internal structure that is not necessarily reflected in the external form. Growth occurs in layers but it is by no means uniform. Some faces may be underdeveloped and others overdeveloped; the whole crystal may change its orientation during growth; or two or more crystals may grow locked together. As a result the diamond appears in many more forms than is suggested by the popularly depicted eight-sided crystal called an octahedron. It appears in other single crystal shapes as well as in formless crystalline masses.

Of the seven main systems of symmetry into which crystals are divided, diamond falls into the cubic system, the most symmetrical of all. The possible forms of regularly shaped diamond crystal are illustrated on pages 66 and 67 along with their number of faces.

The pattern of crystal growth is unique to every single diamond. Additional characteristics are provided by the polishing lines which are superimposed upon the natural pattern, and the two together can be photographed to reveal a crystalprint. Since the pattern of natural growth persists even after drastic recutting, the crystalprint provides a valuable means of identification. The technique illustrated here was devised by Diamond Grading Laboratories of London.

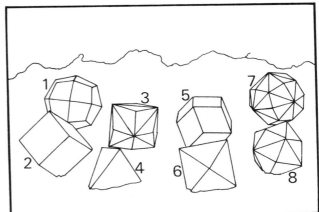

The eight possible ideal forms of regularly shaped diamond crystals (the figure in parentheses designates the number of faces, or sides, each crystal has): 1 Icositetrahedron (24); 2 Cube (6); 3 Triakis octahedron (24); 4 Tetrahedron (4); 5 Rhombic dodecahedron (12); 6 Octahedron (8); 7 Hexakis octahedron (48); 8 Tetrakis hexahedron (24).

The octahedron is the most common of these crystals of regular shape. Even more common than the octahedron, however, are the pieces of no recognizable form. These may be distorted crystals or pieces that have been broken or worn into irregular shapes. It is these diamonds that provide the real challenge to the cutter. Once he has studied them and found the crystal directions, he can often make a higher recovery than he would on a regular crystal. The huge Cullinan was such a stone.

There are literally thousands of divisions into which rough diamonds could be classified as they come from the mines, but in order to simplify the process they are restricted to four main shapes. In order of value and importance to the gem cutter, they are as follows:

1) **Stones** unbroken crystals of regular formation.

2) **Cleavages** broken or irregularly formed pieces.

3) **Macles** twinned crystals, flat and triangular in form.

4) **Flats** irregularly shaped pieces with flat parallel sides.

This is the practical working division and, of course, it cuts right across any academic or scientific one based on ideal crystal types.

The classifications of diamonds already mentioned refer only to gem crystals, but since 80 percent of production is destined for industrial use, there is a broader grouping that divides diamonds into:

1) Gem diamonds
2) Industrial stones, including:
   a) shaped stones
   b) whole stones
   c) boart

The difference between gem and industrial diamonds is purely one of quality and color. The imperfections that affect quality and color may take the form of fractures or fissures or of minute inclusions of other minerals that were

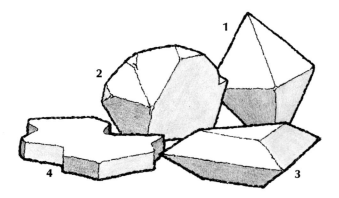

present in the original magma when the diamond was formed. The most popular shape for the gem cutter is the octahedron. For industrial use, the dodecahedron and other more rounded crystals are generally preferred, although octahedrons are still regarded as more suitable for use as truing diamonds for shaping grinding wheels and for setting in the tips of rock drills. Irregularly shaped stones are usually used as glass cutters' diamonds and for setting in stone saws.

Boart (an early Afrikaans word for "bastard") is a minutely crystallized gray or black diamond mass which is not usable in individual crystals for any industrial application. It is therefore crushed to powder for grinding and polishing purposes. Boart has its own numerous classifications, one of the most interesting of which is ballas or shot boart. This is found in the shape of a ball and with no crystalline faces or edges and no lines of cleavage, it is virtually indestructible. The Brazilian name for boart is carbonado.

It would be a mistake, however, to think that boart or carbonado is dull and uninteresting. There was a case in 1927 of what was apparently a 33-carat piece of boart being found to contain a small red diamond of exceptional quality at its heart. It eventually produced a 5.05-carat gem when cut.

On rare occasions boart exists in a form that enables it to be cut to create a truly unique gem. The best-known black diamond is the celebrated Black Orloff, a 67.5-carat stone cut from a 195-carat rough of Indian origin. But a better and much more recent example is the beautiful stone known as the Amsterdam. While the Orloff is more of a dark gun-metal color and partly translucent, the Amsterdam is totally black and impervious to light. The stone arrived at the offices of D. Drukker and Sons in Amsterdam in 1972 in a parcel of mine boart destined to be crushed into diamond powder or to be broken up into smaller pieces for other industrial purposes. At the time the 55.85-carat rough would have been valued at no more than $5–6 a carat. Drukkers tried to cleave the stone and immediately became aware both of its exceptional hardness and of the fact that the splinters were not in the least transparent, but of the deepest black. They decided to proceed with cutting and polishing the stone. The result is a pear-shaped 145-facet black diamond weighing 33.74 carats, one of the rarest gems in the world. Both the Amsterdam and the Black Orloff dramatically underline the fact that the diamond is unique in all its many forms.

HERE THERE BE DIAMONDS

The first undoubted diamond discoveries were in India, and it was there that the first systematic diamond mining was carried on. Jean Baptiste Tavernier, the celebrated French jeweler and traveler in the East, recorded intensive mining going on in the 1660s at Kollur, near Golconda, the legendary fortress city that lent its name to the entire mining area and served as the headquarters of the Indian diamond trade. Today all that remains of Golconda is a ruined fort near Hyderabad. Only the name lives on as a synonym for fabulous riches.

At Kollur, Tavernier saw as many as sixty thousand men, women and children laboring under the whips of overseers. The men dug pits to a depth of 12 or 14 feet (3 to 4 meters), and the women and children carried the conglomerate away in baskets to be washed and sorted. It was at Kollur that the most famous Indian diamonds—the Koh-i-Noor, the Great Mogul and the Regent—are said to have been found. One of the last of the great diamonds to be mined there was the Nizam, a massive stone of 440 carats found in 1835 and named after the Nizam of Hyderabad in whose territory the old Kingdom of Golconda had been incorporated. When last heard of in 1934, the diamond was being used by the Nizam as a paperweight.

OPPOSITE *The cover of the Christmas 1898 edition of* Kimberley's Diamond Fields Advertiser, *representing the alliance between white capital and black labor.*

Another celebrated diamond-mining area was farther north at Panna and neighboring villages in the province of Bundelkund. Here the digging was much more laborious since the diamond-bearing conglomerate lay at a far greater depth than in other areas, being buried under a cover of heavy ground which could be as much as 30 feet (about 10 meters) in thickness. Pits had to be dug to reach the diamond strata and the diggers worked knee-deep in water, breaking the conglomerate and loading it into baskets which were then hauled to the surface.

The earliest mines to be worked, the Indian mines were also the first to be exhausted, having produced an estimated 12 million carats during nearly two thousand years of operation. All the diamonds found in India have been of the alluvial variety, originating in conglomerate rocks and in disintegrated surface deposits in riverbeds or in the beds of rivers that had dried up thousands of years ago. Because all the known deposits are nearly worked out, no large-scale mining is carried on here; the recovery methods used are not all that different from those Tavernier witnessed in 1660.

Today India yields no more than a very few thousand carats, despite an intensive three-year prospecting program carried out under governmental supervision. Hopes began to rise when a diamond pipe was discovered in 1958 at Majgawan in the Panna area, but the recovery rate was not high. Geologists believe that the contents of the pipe had become dispersed over neighboring areas many thousands of years ago.

It was not until 1725 that diamonds were discovered outside of India—in Brazil. The news was greeted with so much skepticism and even outright disbelief in Europe that the merchants had to ship their Brazilian stones via the port of Goa so that buyers would accept them in the belief that they had come

from India. The "discovery" was made by a Portuguese adventurer, Bernardo da Fonseca Lobo, who had come to Brazil to join the gold rush in the district of Minas Gerais. Noticing that the bright stones the gold prospectors used when playing cards looked very much like diamonds, he made up a parcel of the stones and sent them back to Lisbon on the first available ship, together with a letter to the king of Portugal. The stones were indeed diamonds; and by royal proclamation the town of Tejeco, near where they had been found, was renamed Diamantina. The gold prospectors were turned off the area and concessions were soon being given to royal favorites to exploit the diamond beds.

Undaunted, though, the prospectors quickly became adept at illicit diamond digging, and by 1740 the problem had become so

A typical scene in a diamond district in Brazil. Note the overseers and the armed guards, a permanent feature of any Brazilian or Indian picture of the period.

acute that the king switched to contract tenancy, leasing the beds for a fixed term in return for a share of the profits. Slave labor was widely used in Brazil and an incentive to diligent working was that a slave finding a stone of more than 17.5 carats could win his freedom.

In 1844 diamonds were found in the state of Bahia and the diggings were mined so intensively that within twenty years they were virtually exhausted. Production still continues from Brazil's widely scattered deposits—there are fifteen well-defined production areas—but as in India, there is little organized mining. The main activity is on the part of independent local diggers called *garimpeiros*, who sell their finds on the unofficial, rather than official, market. After producing as many as 16 million carats since the first find in 1725, Brazil's annual output today is estimated to be something under 200,000 carats.

It is a strange coincidence that the Brazilian diamonds were found just as the supply from India was running down, and that when the Brazilian deposits were nearly exhausted in their turn, huge supplies were discovered in South Africa.

Discovery in South Africa

It had long been thought possible that diamonds would be found in South Africa. Missionaries as early as 1750 had brought back tales of their existence, and an ordinance issued by the British governor of the Cape of Good Hope in 1812 to regulate the establishment of mines in the colony specifically mentioned the exploitation of diamond finds. But the interior of the country remained relatively uninhabited and unexplored until the migration of the Griquas, a people of mixed blood descended from the original Hottentot inhabitants of Cape Colony. Driven out of the Cape by the European settlers, they emigrated northward and settled in the triangle formed by the junction of the Orange

and Vaal rivers. Then in 1836 they were joined by the Boer farmers, descendants of the early Dutch settlers at the Cape, who trekked inland with their cattle and sheep in search of a place to settle well away from British domination in Cape Colony. The Boers, in turn, drove the Griquas across the Vaal River, claiming the territory and declaring their own republic, the Orange Free State. But the early Boers were farmers, not explorers, and they had little interest in geology that did not lead them to fertile soil or abundant water. It was not until thirty years later, in 1866, that the first known diamond was picked up.

The story of the finding of the first stone has passed into South African folklore. It began when a fifteen-year-old Afrikaner farm boy, Erasmus Stephanus Jacobs, picked up a *mooi klip* (Afrikaans for "pretty stone") by the banks of the Orange River in the Hopetown district of Cape Colony on the farm that his father rented from a local landowner, Schalk Van

Eramus Stephanus Jacobs, the discoverer of the Eureka, the first diamond found in South Africa.

Colesberg Advertiser,

AND NORTHERN FRONTIER GAZETTE.

The Wonderful South African Diamond.

There is a story this morning afloat in the village. It has just been told us by a lady, and we give it just as we have heard it. A Mr. John O'Reilly, a hunter, explorer, &c., something of the Dr. Livingstone stamp, though not yet quite so well known, in his travels in the North Country—somewhere about the Orange River, picked up a stone two or three months since, which he thought had something remarkable about it, and brought it down with him. It was shown to several persons here, and was at length sent down to Dr. Atherstone of Grahamstown to be examined, and as the lady told us, a letter has come by this morning's post from the Doctor, saying that it is a Diamond and worth £800.—Now we quite expect that the "Great Eastern" will have a grand laugh at us about the South African Diamond, as he did some time ago about the Orange River Serpent—but we have stated the report just as we have heard it.—Stranger things, however, have come to pass in the world than the discovery of Diamonds in South Africa.

The first news article reporting the finding of the Eureka in South Africa. The cautiously optimistic tone remained until the finding of the Star of South Africa in March 1869, when it changed to one of unabashed enthusiasm.

Niekerk. He took it home and gave it as a present to his youngest sister. The stone caught the eye of Van Niekerk on one of his regular visits to the farm, and noticing his interest, the child's mother gave it to him. Van Niekerk showed it to John O'Reilly, a trader who was intrigued enough to pass it on to Lorenzo Boyes, the acting civil commissioner at nearby Colesberg. After deeply etching a windowpane with it, he confidently pronounced that it was a diamond, but no one believed him.

Then another arbiter in the case was called in. This was the remarkable Dr. W. G. Atherstone, a physician at Grahamstown with a knowledge that stretched far beyond medical matters and embraced a more-than-amateur knowledge of mineralogy. After a series of tests carried out with the cooperation of the local jeweler, Dr. Atherstone pronounced the stone "a veritable diamond," and asked if he might forward it to the colonial secretary in Cape Town, the Hon. Richard Southey, for confirmation of his identification. In Cape Town the stone was seen by Monsieur Héritte, the French consul, and expert in mineralogy and precious stones. "At the distance of six paces," he identified it as a diamond and offered to buy it for £500. This was enough for the governor, Sir Philip Wodehouse. He purchased the diamond for the same sum and showed it at the International Exhibition in Paris in 1867 as part of the Cape Colony's exhibit.

This 21.5-carat rough diamond called the Eureka may have caused something of a stir in Colesberg and Grahamstown but it cut little ice in Paris. Doubts were expressed about its genuiness, and even those who were convinced that it was "a veritable diamond" did not believe that it had come from South Africa. Everyone knew that diamonds came from India and more recently from Brazil; and they had forgotten the skepticism that had

greeted the Brazilian finds in the eighteenth century. Even Van Niekerk, Boyes and O'Reilly began to have doubts when a diligent search of the farm De Kalk failed to turn up any more of the "pretty stones."

In fact, it was not until some months later that other stones were found, this time on the banks of the Vaal River. Local skepticism still persisted, but the stones managed to create enough interest for the London diamond merchant Harry Emanuel (author of the then-standard work on diamonds) to send out a geologist, James R. Gregory, to make a special report.

His findings were laid out clearly and concisely in London's *Geological Magazine* of December 1868. "During the time I was in South Africa," wrote Gregory, "I made a very careful and lengthy examination of the district

Dr. W. G. Atherstone, physician at Grahamstown and gifted amateur geologist who first recognized the Eureka to be "a veritable diamond."

where the diamonds were said to have been found, but saw no indications whatever that would warrant the expectation of the finding of diamonds, or of diamond-bearing deposits, at any of the localities." He then proceeded to set the seal on this forthright opinion by concluding that "the geological character of that part of the country renders it impossible . . . that any could have been really discovered there." He concluded his report by expressing his conviction that "the whole diamond discovery in South Africa is an imposture—a Bubble Scheme."

Dr. Atherstone wrote a spirited reply which appeared in the March 1869 issue of the same learned journal, impugning both Gregory's geological knowledge and his motives, and adding "so far from the geological character of the country making it *impossible*, . . . it renders it probable that very extensive and rich diamond deposits will be discovered on proper investigation."

It was not long before it became clear which of the two protagonists was right. In March 1869 Schalk Van Nierkerk found another diamond. This time it was a massive 83.5-carat stone of the first water which he had bought from a Hottentot witch doctor who had been using it as a charm. The existence of this enormous diamond had been rumored for over a year—even Gregory had heard of it and typically dismissed it as a myth—and Van Niekerk had to make a hefty payment of ten oxen, a horse and five hundred sheep to induce the witch doctor to part with it. The stone was snapped up by Lilienfeld Brothers of Hopetown for the staggering sum of £11,200, and on its arrival in London was soon sold to the Earl of Dudley for the then-record price of £25,000. The stone was dubbed the Cape Koh-i-Noor by a local newspaper, but was officially named the Star of South Africa. The colonial secretary is reputed to have taken the diamond into

Parliament at Cape Town, placed his hand upon it and said, "Gentlemen, this is the stone on which the future success of South Africa will be built." In fact, there is no evidence that he said any such thing—but he might just as well have done. The misapprehension appears to originate from a contemporary press report in the *Cape Argus* (March 27, 1869) in which a writer speculates on the potential importance to South Africa of the discovery of the diamond. He goes on to make a comparison with Napoleon placing his hand on his sword—in the hilt of which the great Regent diamond was set—and pronouncing that this "was the rock on which the French Empire was built."

In the face of such headline-making news— there were crowds at the docks hoping to catch a glimpse of the stone when it first arrived in Cape Town—doubts about the authenticity of the South African finds soon evaporated. Harry Emanuel virtually disowned James Gregory's report and set off for South Africa himself. Suddenly everyone else seemed to have the same idea. The great diamond rush had begun.

A report of the finding of the huge Star of South Africa, the 83.5-carat stone which really started the diamond rush. The reference to "that fellow Gregory" is to the geologist sent from London who poured scorn on the idea that diamonds would ever be found in South Africa. Gregory was no favorite of the South African press. In his original report on the diamond finds he had blamed the local editors for encouraging the stories "by publishing any communication whatever that is sent to them." At the same time he had speculated that perhaps the diamonds had been brought to the locality by ostriches. Hence the wry comment. For a long time afterwards any doubtful stone found was known as "a Gregory."

DIAMONDS! DIAMONDS!!

ANOTHER DIAMOND FOUND, 83½ carats!

HOPE TOWN.

The following extra to the *Colesberg Advertiser* reached us on Thursday, and was immediately issed as an extra to the *Cape Argus*:

18th March, 1869, 4·15 p.m.

The whole place, I mean the inhabitants, are in a great state of excitement. Schalk van Niekerk has just come in, and brought with him the largest diamond that has yet been found in South Africa. The gem weighs 83½ (eighty-three and a half) carats—first water —and is said to be worth between £25,000 and £30,000. Found *in* the Colony, somewhere below the "Kalk." Mr. Niekerk is the gentleman who was the finder of, or who brought to notice, the first diamond, which was sold to the Governor for £500. That brought in by him to-day, he purchased from the Hottentot or Kafir doctor, of whom we heard about a year ago, using it as a charm in his profession. Niekerk gave him 500 sheep, ten head of cattle, and a horse for it. I wonder what that fellow Gregory would say now, were he here. Perhaps in this instance it was also dropped by an ostrich (?)

19th March.

The diamond has just been disposed of to Messrs. Lilienfeld Brothers for £11,200 (Eleven Thousand Two Hundred Pounds Sterling.)

P.S.—This news is confirmed by dispatch from the Civil Commissioner of Hope Town.

A diamond of unusual symmetry and beauty reached the Colonial Office on Thursday morning, weighing 7·25 carats, and valued at £200.

ABOVE *A scene at Colesberg Kopje in the early days of the diamond rush. The diggings are still shallow enough to be worked by hand.* OPPOSITE, ABOVE *One of the earliest known photographs of an encampment at the Vaal River diggings, probably taken toward the end of 1869.* BELOW *A typical group of Vaal River diggers, about 1871.*

The South Africans were, of course, the first on the scene, and the roads from all the towns and villages in the country were alive with all sorts and conditions of men bound for the newly discovered Eldorado on the Vaal River. They used every means of locomotion from a wagon to wheelbarrow, and many simply walked; but most of the would-be diggers formed themselves into small parties and trekked up in the old-fashioned ox wagon. It was a long and hazardous journey—especially from Cape Town, which meant a trek of nearly a thousand miles, most of which was across the sun-baked Karoo, a virtual desert—and the arrival at the Vaal River was a great event. To quote a contemporary report, "Tossing of hats and continued hurrahs were frequently indulged in at a first view of the Vaal River with its well-wooded banks of

willow, and all expressed genuine satisfaction at the end of the monotonous journey, and at being at last within reach of those prospective fortunes which were to make glad the hearts of wives and sweethearts at home."

The first arrivals made straight for the sites of the original finds, and digger communities were established in the Hopetown district and on both sides of the Vaal River, particularly at Klipdrift and Pniel. The camps increased daily in size, and the pioneer diggers were soon joined by those from overseas, often men from the gold fields of Australia and the United States who had already tried their luck in the diamond fields of Brazil. By the end of 1870 the population of the diggings had risen to about ten thousand. And there were as many individual claims bearing the sort of names familiar to mining districts the world over:

Bosman's Folly, Meyer's Luck, Poorman's Kopje and Forlorn Hope. Diamonds were found in abundance, but the haphazard distribution of alluvial deposits meant that a fortune was more a matter of luck than judgment and eluded all but a handful of diggers.

One of the most remarkable aspects of life in the diamond diggings was the relative lack of violence and lawlessness associated with the opening up of the American West and the Australian outback. All the ingredients were there, with men of a dozen nationalities infected with diamond fever and living in disputed territory away from all the constraints of normal civilized life.

The system for preserving law and order was simple but effective. A Diggers' Committee was elected under the presidency of Stafford Parker, a man of immensely strong character who was widely respected by the whole community including its rougher elements. The rules and regulations were drawn up by Stafford Parker himself and were based on his experience in the Californian gold-mining camps and his service in Her Majesty's Navy. They had to be read and signed by every incoming digger. Two members of the committee were on duty daily in rotation, hearing and settling disputes and complaints in a summary manner. The judgments of these magistrates for the day were invariably accepted. They may have been harsh in some cases—theft, for example—but they were certainly effective. Crime of any sort was a rarity in the diggings, as indeed might be

One of the first to arrive in the Klipdrift diamond fields, Stafford Parker (in the center of this group of diggers), an Englishman, was quick to spot the possibilities. He became official adviser and agent to the local Griqua chief, Jan Bloem, a move which meant that he had established sole trading rights in the area by the time the real rush was under way. He appointed himself landdrost and local governor, and in 1870 he was named president of the short-lived Diggers' Republic.

expected when a convicted thief was liable to being flogged, or dragged across the sharp and stony bottom of the Vaal River, or staked out on the ground and left to the mercy of the insects.

The ownership of areas where diamonds were subsequently found had been disputed for years between the Griqua chiefs; and when the land was shown to be of immense value, the disputes grew more bitter. Soon both the British colonists and the Boer republics of the Transvaal and the Orange Free State began to take a greater interest in the conflicting claims. The British wanted to halt Boer expansion in the west as well as gain control of the diamond fields, and this they succeeded in doing by supporting the claim of the Griqua chief Waterboer and then annexing the territory. Even the carefully delineated limits of the area were "stretched" to the east toward the Free State when diamonds were found at Kimberley. However, the Boers were no match for the British at the time and reluctantly went along with the decision, accepting £90,000 as compensation for the loss of the richest diamond fields in the world.

During the course of these disputes, the Diggers' Protection Association, although mainly inclined toward the British cause, had to manage its own affairs and became so adept at doing so that the members were tempted into declaring a Diggers' Republic. Stafford Parker became the first (and only) president. Its principal aim seemed to be the stopping of any interference by the Boers, and force of arms was resorted to on more than one occasion. But allegiance to the British crown remained strong and the association offered no opposition to the dissolution of their republic when the area was proclaimed British in October 1871.

As more and more treasure hunters poured into the diggings, they soon found that the most promising river claims had already been

OPPOSITE *A close-up of a digger's tent, this one at the river diggings at Gong Gong. The digger is Dan Evans, a one-time president of the Diggers' Union.* **ABOVE** *Adam Kok, chief of the Griquas, who was originally given the land on which the diamond fields were discovered. It was his son, Nicholas Waterboer, who agreed to the annexation of his territory by the British in order to defeat the Boer claim.*

Johannes Nicholas De Beer, owner of the farm Vooruitzicht on which the De Beers and Kimberley mines were discovered in 1871. They had bought this farm in 1860 from the government for £50, and sold out in 1871 to a syndicate for £6,300. The brothers De Beer disappear from history at this point—but not before giving their name to one of the world's biggest and best-known companies.

staked. They therefore had no alternative but to move away from the river banks and try their luck elsewhere. It was their discovery of diamonds in the so-called "dry diggings" that opened the greatest chapter in the history of diamonds in South Africa.

The first "inland" strike was on the farm Koffiefontein in July 1870, reputedly by a transport driver unhitching his team of oxen. After that the strikes came thick and fast, notably at Dutoitspan, Bultfontein, Vooruitzicht and Colesberg Kopje. All became mines that were still yielding diamonds almost a century later. The last two are better known by their later names: De Beers and Kimberley.

Once the news of a strike was out, nothing could stem the rush. Farms were literally invaded by armies of eager prospectors digging up the ground, destroying trees and fences, and generally making farming impossible. Faced with the inevitable, most farmers simply sold out and moved on. Among those were the brothers De Beer. They had bought their farm from the government ten years earlier for £50 and were only too pleased to accept an offer of £6,300 from a syndicate once they had seen the chaos the diggers caused.

The story of the strike at Colesberg Kopje in July 1871 is another one which has passed into

South African folklore, both because it was on the site of what is now the Kimberley Mine and because of the strange manner of its discovery. Under the leadership of Fleetwood Rawsthorne, a group of prospectors from Colesberg (known as the Red Cap Party because of their distinctive headgear) had set up camp near the kopje when they arrived on the farm. Their unruly black servant Damon, thrown out of the camp for drunkenness, spent the night wandering over the yet-unexplored kopje . . . and returned to camp the next morning with a handful of diamonds. Any doubts that incoming prospectors might have had were swept away by the news, and Colesberg Kopje became better known as New Rush.

It was on and around the site of the four discoveries of Bultfontein, Dutoitspan, De Beers and Kimberley, that the first really permanent settlements began to grow up.

A digger's camp in New Rush, soon to be called Kimberley, in about 1871.

Tents and makeshift shelters gradually gave way to more permanent structures of wood and tin; and shops, offices, banks, bars, hotels and brothels sprang up to serve what by 1872 had become a population of more than fifty thousand diggers. Mining camps soon became townships, and places were renamed to mark the change in status: Dutoitspan was changed to Beaconsfield, after the British prime minister and New Rush to Kimberley, in honor of the colonial secretary.

All this time there was still no real knowledge of the origin of the diamonds. James Gregory and Dr. Atherstone had compared the geological environment where they had been found in South Africa with that in India and Brazil, and Dr. John Shaw of Colesberg, in a paper sent to the Geological Society in London in 1871, maintained that there was no distinction in the geographical origin of the diamonds found in the rivers and in the dry diggings. It was left to the persistence of some of the diggers to present the geologists with irrefutable evidence of where the diamonds had come from. It was not until

The diamond market, Kimberley, in about 1880. The offices of the diamond traders centered on one particular street in the town.

the end of 1871 that the pits in the dry diggings broke through the top layer of limestone into soft "yellow ground" where diamonds were to be found in far greater numbers. But when the miners struck rock-like "blue ground" at a depth of between 60 and 80 feet (18–33 meters), many abandoned their claims, assuming that it was barren like the hard bedrock that underlay the diamond-bearing gravels of the river diggings. However, it was not long before the remaining miners noticed that the exposed blue ground in the abandoned pits was beginning to break up. Far from being solid rock, it was nothing more than yellow ground as yet unweathered by the action of air and water. And it yielded even more diamonds. The only possible conclusion was that diamonds originated deep in the earth and found their way to the surface through the medium of vast "pipes," possibly of volcanic origin. Alluvial diamonds were simply those that had been washed away from the mouths of pipes and had naturally been deposited in the rivers.

With this discovery, diamond mining in South Africa entered a new and much more complex era. The shallow pits of the river diggings could be worked by anyone with a shovel and a sieve, but the deepening pits of the dry diggings demanded much greater skills. The individual claims measured 30 feet (10 meters) square (and were often subdivided into halves, quarters and even eighths) and once they had been dug to a certain depth, the weathering action of the air and rain on the walls of the pit meant that collapse, sooner or later, was inevitable. Sensibly it was decreed that a strip of unmined ground of 7.5 feet (about 2.5 meters) should be left around each claim in order to reduce the risk of collapse and also to act as access roads to all claims. This served for a time, but the hazards increased with the depth of working. To quote a contemporary report: "Accidents occurred almost hourly through carts, mules and men falling from the roads into the claims, or buckets of stuff and lumps of rock falling on the heads of the workers below, each disaster being signaled by the frantic cheering of the thousands of natives who seemed to regard a poor unfortunate getting a head or limb broken as a huge joke."

By 1872 there were some 3,600 individual claims in the four big mines with more than 1,600 in the Kimberley Mine alone. And the chaos was indescribable. Instead of the mine laborers trudging up steps cut in the sides of the claim carrying their sacks of blue ground, aerial ropeways were now used and the mines were soon criss-crossed with a spider's web of ropes; each claim or group of claims operated its own haulage system independently of all the others.

If lack of cooperation here made for inefficient working, down below it spelled danger and often death for thousands of diggers. Working with different methods at different levels and with little regard for a neighbor's interests meant that claims were constantly collapsing into each other and burying miners under tons of rock. There was the further hazard of mud rushes. These were caused by water mixing with the huge mass of broken rock, "under great pressure at the level

ABOVE LEFT *The mine at Colesberg Kopje in 1870. The excavations are getting much deeper and wooden staging is beginning to be erected to cope with the haulage system.* **RIGHT** *The Kimberley Mine in the latter half of 1872. Most of the roadways had collapsed and rope haulage was beginning to be used to transport equipment and blue ground to and from the claims below. These ropes were attached to windlasses which were built in tiers so that there would be enough room around the circumference of the mine to cope with all the ropes.* **BELOW RIGHT** *Another view of the Kimberley Mine. By this time all the roadways had collapsed, the stagings now entirely surrounded the mine and an immense network of ropes criss-crossed the crater.* **BELOW LEFT** *By 1879 the Kimberley Mine looked, in the words of Cecil Rhodes, like "a great Stilton cheese."*

of the workings, sometimes bursting through and filling hundreds of feet of level with such velocity that workmen were frequently trapped, and occasionally actually overtaken when fleeing before it."

Flooding, too, was becoming a major problem; the mines were often closed for days while the flood water was pumped out. Pumps were not only expensive, but they were also hard to come by. Even if a digger could find one for his own claim, there was little advantage to be gained if the water continued to seep in from his neighbor's still-flooded workings.

Amalgamations and cooperative effort were the obvious answer to a situation that was rapidly becoming impossible. These had been hindered in the past by the rule that one man should not be permitted to own more than two claims. In 1874, however, the number was raised to ten, and in 1876 the restriction was removed altogether. The way was clear. Syndicates began to buy up great blocks of claims, companies were formed, and what had initially been a free-for-all for individual enterprise gradually acquired the corporate structure necessary for a future major industry. By 1880 the number of claims had fallen from the original 3,600 to a mere 98 and half of these were in the hands of companies. Capital raising was now an easier operation, even if it did involve questionable methods of company promotion and share rigging. But being able to buy a £200 water pump was one thing. To find the thousands of pounds needed to sink shafts through solid rock was quite another. One central controlling body was the only possible solution.

It is at this point that the two great personalities of the South African diamond mining industry take the center of the stage— Cecil Rhodes and Barney Barnato. It is hard to imagine two more totally different men. One, the son of a country parson, shy and reserved.

A little-known photograph of Cecil Rhodes, reputedly given by him to a tennis opponent to whom Rhodes had lost a match and a wager. It is inscribed: "I sign spitefully, C. J. Rhodes."

The other, the son of a poor Jewish tailor from London's East End and a flamboyant extravert. Both made their fortunes out of diamonds independently of each other, but it was the amalgamation of their respective interests that unified the industry and brought into being one of the world's most celebrated and successful companies, De Beers Consolidated Mines.

Cecil John Rhodes arrived in Durban in 1870 at the age of seventeen, intending to join his elder brother, Herbert, on his farm in Natal. The boy had always been in poor health, and his father thought that he would benefit from the warm, dry climate of South Africa. But Cecil arrived to find that his brother had already left to seek his fortune in the diamond fields. He followed him and arrived in New Rush in May of 1871. Initially Rhodes was unlucky. He tried to buy a claim on the De Beers farm but was unable to raise the money, and the claim he eventually bought at Colesberg Kopje turned out to be practically worthless.

In order to make a living, Rhodes decided to use his wits rather than rely on a lucky strike. Noticing that drinking water was in desperately short supply in the mining camps, he arranged to import it together with one of the first ice-making machines. The venture was reasonably successful, but it was water of another kind that gave Rhodes his first real break. With flooding fast becoming a major problem in the diggings, hand pumps were greatly in demand even though they were too small and inefficient. Rhodes had heard of a large steam-driven pump for sale in Port Elizabeth. Joining together with another young Englishman, Charles Rudd, he bought it for £1,000. The pump was to be the foundation of his fortune. It was in constant demand, and Rhodes and Rudd were soon able to order bigger and better pumps to be sent out from England.

Barney Barnato at the height of his fame. A millionaire within ten years of his arrival in Kimberley as a penniless immigrant from London's East End, he went on to make another fortune in gold and property in the Rand.

After a brief spell back in England—which, typically, he used to good advantage by taking a degree in law at Oxford—Rhodes returned to South Africa in 1874 and tried his luck once more at diamond mining. This time he had plenty of capital behind him, thanks to the pumping business, and starting with one small claim in the De Beers Mine, he gradually acquired more and more claims either by outright purchase or by buying into partnerships. By 1880 he was one of the largest owners, and in that year he joined with two other important groups to form the De Beers Mining Company under his control. Only one other group could rival his own in size and power—Barney Barnato's Kimberley Central Mining Company.

Barnato arrived in Kimberley in 1873 at the age of twenty. Like Rhodes, he had come out to join his elder brother, Harry; and, also like Rhodes, he was not an instant success. The year 1873 was a crisis year in Europe and America, and the demand for diamonds had dwindled away to practically nothing. He had little choice but to fall back on the skills he had acquired in the rough and tumble of Whitechapel—boxing, singing and dancing, and dealing in anything that came his way. But even as a successful challenger of all comers in Payne's Circus and doubling as "Barney Barnato, World-Famous Comedian," he could not make a living. Selling notebooks and pencils around the claims was more profitable. It also won him friends among the diggers and made him familiar with the rudiments of diamond digging and trading. For someone with Barnato's quick eye for a bargain, buying diamonds from the outlying claims and then selling them in the towns— "kopje walloping," as it was called—was the obvious trade. The £30 he had saved was not enough to set up in business as a diamond dealer, so Barnato persuaded a young friend, Lou Cohen, to form a partnership by putting up another £60. The shortfall in Barnato's contribution was made up by forty boxes of cigars he had brought with him from London. For a guinea a day, the pair rented a 6' × 9' lean-to at the side of Maloney's Bar, strategically sited midway between the Dutoitspan and Kimberley diggings and, as Barnato noted, the first port of call for diggers from both areas at the end of the day's work.

But business was slow—the diamond depression was still in full swing—until he had his greatest stroke of luck. He bought a horse. Successful kopje walloping meant knowing which claims to visit and which not to bother with. It took many days to ride around the claims, and lost time was lost profit. When one of Kimberley's most successful dealers announced that he was retiring and auctioning all his equipment, Barnato snapped up his aging horse for £27/10s/0d, almost half the partnership's remaining capital. Barnato reasoned that a horse that had carried its master for so many years must know its own way around the diggings that had proved so profitable for its previous owner.

He was right, and his subsequent tours proved so successful that he was soon able to dispense with the services of Lou Cohen. The partnership was dissolved and Barnato joined forces with his brother Harry and his cousin

David Harris, using the stage name he and his brother had used in London, Barnato Brothers. Their diamond-buying business prospered and by early 1876 they had accumulated £3,000 which they staked on buying four holdings in the center of the Kimberley Mine. It was a gamble. The claims had been worked down to the blue ground and the owners believed that there were no more diamonds to be mined. Many others thought the same— the four claims would have fetched £40,000 as a going concern—but Barnato had followed the arguments of geologists who believed in the pipe theory, and was prepared to wager his savings on the blue ground being the beginning and not the end of the rich diamond finds. He was proved right once

A typical diamond buyer's office in Kimberley.

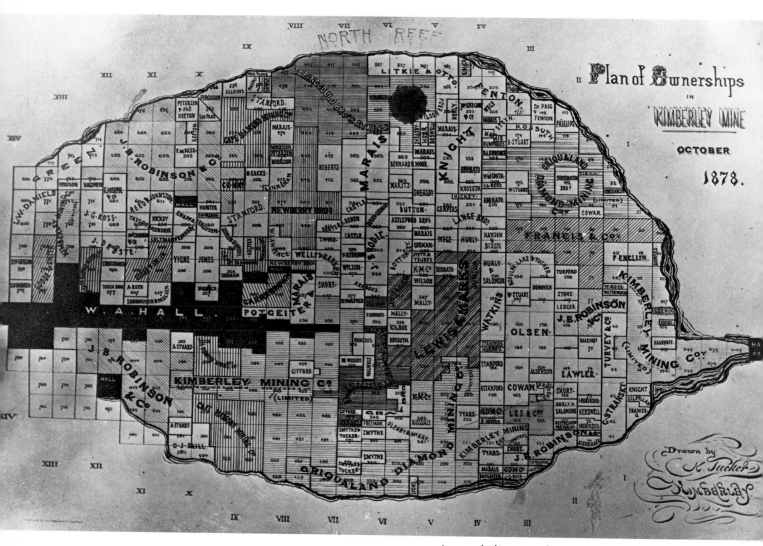

ABOVE *A plan of the claims in the Kimberley Mine in 1878. The original 3,600 claims had shrunk considerably due to amalgamations but they still numbered well over a hundred.* **OPPOSITE** *By 1882 the number of claims was down to about 50. The bid by the Standard Diamond Mining Company and Kimberley Central for the French Company sparked the takeover battle with Cecil Rhodes which culminated in the formation of De Beers Consolidated Mines.*

again and diamonds were soon coming up at the rate of £3,000 every week.

Just like Cecil Rhodes, Barnato bought out his competitors one by one, and in 1880 following the takeover of the valuable claims of the Standard Company and Kimberley Central, he formed the Barnato Brothers Diamond Mining Company. Only the Compagnie Française des Diamonds du Cap, popularly known as the French Company, with a line of claims dividing those of Kimberley Central from those of the Standard, eluded his grasp. In the struggle for control they were to prove critical.

By this time Barnato was quite prepared to

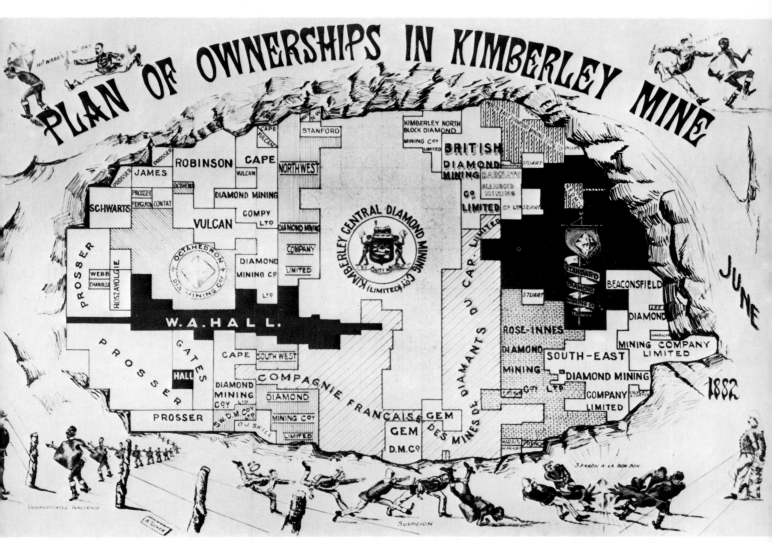

PLAN OF OWNERSHIPS IN KIMBERLEY MINE

settle for total control of the Kimberley Mine for his family company and to leave Cecil Rhodes to look after De Beers. But if Barnato was as much aware as Rhodes of the advantages of central control from the point of view of mining operations, he was a little slow to recognize the other vital reason for overall control of South African production—marketing. The unprecedented flow of diamonds from the Kimberley area was quite capable of overtaking the level of demand, and indeed had already done so in 1873, a year in which diamonds were virtually unsaleable.

Unrestricted competition between the two

mines was clearly against the interests of both companies, but Rhodes had to drive the lesson home. He decided to make a play for the French Company. With the aid of two friends, Julius Wernher and Alfred Beit of Wernher, Beit & Co., and a £1,000,000 loan from Rothschild's in Paris, Rhodes bid £1,400,000 for the French Company. Barnato was furious at what he considered to be trespassing on his particular preserve, and prepared to canvas support for a bid of £1,750,000. Both Rhodes and Barnato were stretched to the limit of their financial resources, but it was Rhodes who accepted the fact and turned it to his advantage. He approached Barnato with the plan that he should be allowed to go with his original £1,400,000 bid for the French Company and then sell it on to his adversary for a combination of cash and a 20 percent stake in the Kimberley Central Mine. Barnato agreed, believing that such a small parcel of shares was no great sacrifice to pay for the consolidation of the French Company into his empire. He was wrong. Rhodes wanted a foothold in the Kimberley Mine and having got it, he intended to make good use of it.

Backed by Alfred Beit, Rhodes began to buy up every Kimberley Central share he could lay his hands on. As the price rose, Barnato was forced to buy too, simply in order to preserve his majority. As the shares went higher and higher, Rhodes prepared to play his master stroke. He boosted production from the De Beers Mine and literally flooded the market with diamonds. As a result the price slumped, leaving the shares of Kimberley Central looking dangerously overvalued. To avoid a crash, Barnato had little choice but to fall in with Rhodes's plans. He sold his shares to Rhodes for a stake in the new amalgamated company, De Beers Consolidated Mines; a life governorship of the company; and something that had been denied him until now, membership in the Kimberley Club. Reputedly this last favor was the most important to Barnato who, despite his outstanding success in business, had found no means of getting elected to the most exclusive club in Kimberley. But even with Rhodes's backing, there were still difficulties over Barnato's election. The story goes that when the club's secretary discovered the voting box rather heavily weighted with black balls, he came downstairs from his office, deliberately tripped on the last step and fell on his face. The balls became all mixed up and the committee had to give Barnato the benefit of the doubt.

The new company was formed in 1888 by

Alfred Beit was one of the great financial brains behind the development of the diamond fields. He assisted Cecil Rhodes in his power struggle with Barney Barnato and became one of the original directors and life governors of De Beers.

liquidating Kimberley Central and transferring all the assets to De Beers for £5,338,650. For many years the check held the record for the largest amount ever written, and it hangs today in the boardroom of De Beers in Kimberley.

With the great battle for control of the diamond fields now over, Kimberley began to take on a more settled air. The rough, tough, mining-camp image gave way to one of Victorian respectability. Rhodes spent more of his time on politics and the fulfillment of his dream of imperial expansion, and became prime minister of South Africa in 1890 at the age of thirty-seven. Barney Barnato too turned to politics. He became a member of the Cape Assembly, and went on to take a major part in the development of the Rand gold fields. But the stormy days of early Kimberley were not over for either man.

Rhodes's respectable political life and his partnership were abruptly ended by his endorsement of the ill-fated Jameson Raid, an attempt to overthrow the Boer government of the Transvaal led by Dr. Starr Jameson, a friend of Rhodes and the administrator of his British South Africa Company whose territory in 1895 had been officially named Rhodesia. The background to the raid was the discontented state of the "Uitlanders" in the Boer Republic. This was the name given by the Boers to the foreigners, mainly British, who had supplied the brains, the enterprise and the money to develop the republic's fabulously rich mineral resources. Yet the Boers allowed them no

This check for £5,338,650 for a time held the record for the largest sum ever written. It was paid by De Beers Consolidated Mines to Kimberley Central Diamond Mining to make effective the amalgamation between the De Beers and Kimberley mines.

electoral rights and gave them no voice in the running of Johannesburg, the city which they had largely created, even though they outnumbered the Boers by four to one. The situation seemed ripe for a coup, and a body of prominent British businessmen in Johannesburg sought the tacit support of Cecil Rhodes and the active assistance of Dr. Jameson. The British inside the Transvaal planned to launch an attack on the arsenal at Pretoria, and simultaneously the Jameson raiders, drawn from the armed forces of the British South Africa Company, would cross the Bechuanaland border and sweep aside the handful of untrained and poorly armed Boer farmers and burghers who might oppose them. The world would have no choice but to recognize a *fait accompli* and South Africa would be united under the British crown.

That at least was the idea. It worked out rather differently in practice. The uprising in the Transvaal was so badly organized that half the would-be insurgents stayed at home; and the other half were so badly frightened that they rode to Pretoria, not to seize the arsenal but to make their peace with the authorities. To cap it all, Dr. Jameson and his men were ambushed at Krugersdorp, eighteen miles outside Johannesburg. It was a great triumph for the tiny Boer Republic and a massive defeat for the Uitlanders and, by implication, for Cecil Rhodes and the British government. The British colonial secretary condemned the raid, and Rhodes had no alternative but to resign. Barney Barnato came into the picture at the subsequent trial of the Johannesburg "rebels" when four of them (including Colonel Frank Rhodes, brother of Cecil Rhodes) were condemned to death. The sentences led to an international outcry, but the Boers refused to budge—until Barnato threatened to close down all his operations on the Rand if the executions were carried out. This would have meant economic disaster for the republic which within two decades had made the transition from a poor agricultural community to a modern and prosperous industrial state, and the president of the republic, Paul Kruger, relented. The death sentences were commuted to hefty fines of £25,000 each, and the two-year prison sentences on the smaller fry in the rebellion (including Barnato's favorite nephew, Solly Joel) to fines of £2,000.

The struggle with the Transvaalers was perhaps the last straw for Barnato. He had achieved so much in so short a time, building first a diamond empire in Kimberley and then one of gold and property on the Rand, that there was little more for him to do. His two nephews, Woolf and Solly, looked after the day-to-day running of the Barnato businesses, and Barnato allowed worrying to become his principal occupation. Signs of mental instability began to manifest themselves, developing into a full-fledged persecution complex. A journey back to England, appropriately enough for Queen Victoria's Diamond Jubilee, seemed the obvious way to make him forget his troubles, and, on June 2, 1897, with his wife and baby son and Solly Joel, he sailed from Cape Town in the SS *Scott*. Four days later he suddenly leaped up from his deckchair and flung himself over the ship's side. He was forty-four.

Cecil Rhodes had one more moment of glory to come. The grievances of the Uitlanders soon broke out again and were directly responsible for the start of the Boer War in 1899. Their appeal for aid from Britain resulted in a large force of British troops being sent to South Africa. The indignant Boers promptly presented an ultimatum to the British agent in Pretoria: withdraw all British troops from the frontiers of the Transvaal and the Orange Free State and return the reinforcements just landed at the Cape—or else.

The British were taken completely by surprise, but within forty-eight hours, the ultimatum was rejected. The Boers promptly attacked a troop train near Mafeking and siege was laid to Kimberley—and to Cecil Rhodes. It was his finest hour. Refusing to defer to Lieutenant Colonel Kekewich, the military commander who had his headquarters in the Kimberley Club, Rhodes set up his own command post at his private house, known as the

The uneasy political status of the diamond fields arising from the conflicting claims over the area prompted the fast-growing population to raise a number of irregular military units. Depicted here is the cap badge of the Diamond Fields Horse formed in 1877 from the Dutoitspan Hussars. The unit served with distinction in the Ninth Frontier War (1878), the Northern Border War (1878) and the Basutoland Rebellion (1880–81). Eventually merging with the Kimberley Regiment in 1899, the Diamond Fields Horse nevertheless operated independently during the Second Boer War and was only fully amalgamated at the end of the war.

Sanatorium. The engineering skills of De Beers were fully employed during the siege. Their workshops turned out an armored train and a huge cannon, immediately dubbed "Long-Cecil," which fired homemade shells filled with mining dynamite at the besieging Boers. The Boers' siege gun, Long Tom, did more damage to Kimberley than Long Cecil did to the Boers, but it was a great morale booster during the four-month siege. Despite the fact that they were running desperately short of food, the townspeople managed to hold out, and when General French broke through the encircling Boers to relieve the city on February 15, 1900, he was greeted by Cecil Rhodes, champagne glass in hand, at the doors of the Kimberley Club.

But like Barney Barnato, Cecil Rhodes's health had suffered greatly from the trials and tensions of the years following the Jameson Raid. Rhodes was seriously ill when he left Kimberley and he died in March of the following year at his seaside cottage at Muizenburg in the Cape.

With the passing of these two great men, the diamond industry of South Africa may have become less exciting but it grew dramatically in importance. By the end of the nineteenth century some 3,250,000 carats were being produced annually from the South African fields. In 1975 the figure was 7,502,000 carats, augmented by the later discoveries at the other pipes around Kimberley and then the alluvial diamond finds on the wild, storm-swept coast which links Namaqualand, the northernmost part of the Cape Province, with South West Africa (now Namibia).

But one of the most exciting discoveries was that of the Premier Mine, near Pretoria, three hundred miles to the north of Kimberley. The discovery of the Wesselton pipe just two miles from Dutoitspan in 1891 had started a new wave of prospecting enthusiasm, and everyone was once again looking for signs of

ABOVE *During the Boer War, the workshops of De Beers turned their hand from the manufacture and repair of mining machinery to more military pursuits. Railway engines and trucks were armored like the one depicted here, and manned mainly by De Beers' employees who were formed into a paramilitary unit known as Scott's Railway Guards.* **BELOW** *Long Cecil, the huge gun designed by an American engineer, George Labram and constructed in De Beers' workshops during the siege of Kimberley. The famous war correspondent Mortimer Menpes said of it, "Of all the things that I have personally seen and read in the annals of war, the most remarkable is the making of this gun in a mining workshop in the center of Africa."*

the yellow and blue ground (now called "kimberlite") which would mean a pipe, diamonds and a fortune. Percival White Tracey who had once worked a claim in the De Beers mine, had moved to the Rand to look for gold and on one of his prospecting trips he came across traces of diamond-bearing conglomerate in the bed of a stream. Armed with the knowledge and experience of his Kimberley days, he argued that it must have been washed down from a nearby pipe. He followed the course of the stream and before long was rewarded with the sight of a small low hill just like the kopjes of Kimberley. But there was one big problem. The kopje was on the farm of Joachim Prinsloo, an old Boer farmer who twice before had been hounded off his land (albeit for a good price) by prospectors, once for gold and a second time for diamonds. The farm, Elandsfontein, was to be his last resting place and he was prepared to defend his privacy with his gun. Tracey made no progress at all with Prinsloo and even after teaming up with a local contractor and self-made millionaire, Thomas Cullinan, the pair of them found any attempt at negotiation rebuffed by a loaded rifle. Tracey and Cullinan had to wait five years until the old man died before they could at last buy the farm from his daughter. What they bought turned out to be the biggest pipe yet discovered. It covered seventy-eight acres and it was fabulously rich in diamonds.

It was in the Premier that the biggest diamond of all time was found on January 25, 1905. The mine manager on a tour of inspection spotted it sticking out of the side of one of the open pits. The massive stone weighed 3,106 carats, roughly 1.5 pounds, and measured 4 inches by 2.5 inches by 2 inches. It was named the Cullinan and was bought by the Transvaal government for £150,000 to be presented to King Edward VII on his birthday in 1907.

So rich was the Premier Mine that it threatened the survival of the whole marketing strategy of De Beers so painstakingly built up by Cecil Rhodes. In fact, it is said that when Sir Alfred Beit visited the Premier in 1903 he suffered a stroke at the sight of the huge workings of the mine, which he believed would destroy everything he and Rhodes had achieved. The Premier remained out of De Beers' camp until 1911 when it was forced into its arms simply because its own unrestricted production had caused diamond prices to slump to such an extent that the Premier had nearly ruined itself.

The second big challenge to the supremacy of De Beers came when diamonds were found in South West Africa, at the time a German protectorate. The area had been prospected

The huge Cullinan, the largest diamond ever found, in the hands of the general manager of the Premier Mine, Mr. M. W. Hardy. Sir Thomas Cullinan is on the left, and the finder, Mr. F. G. S. Wells, is on the right.

intermittently since 1864 but no one was looking for diamonds and after a brief and unprofitable period of lead mining, all interest in the area had evaporated. It was a former employee of De Beers who had moved to the South West as a railway laborer who first noticed some small diamonds in the sand. He informed the German railway official in charge of the region who promptly obtained a group of claims from the German Colonial Company. Attempts to raise finance in Berlin led to the news of the find leaking out, and another diamond rush began. Within four months the whole area had been pegged. In some parts the diamonds were so plentiful on the surface that mining was unnecessary. The Germans employed African laborers to cover areas systematically by crawling on their hands and knees in a line to search for the crystals. So rich was the whole area that the German administration decided in 1908 to protect its interests by declaring the whole area *Sperr-gebiet,* "forbidden territory." From the north of the Orange River to latitude 26° north and inland for 60 miles (100 kilometers), no prospecting was permitted to anyone except the German Diamond Company whose marketing arm was the Diamond Régie of South West Africa. The régie operated independently, selling the unrestricted production of the South West in Antwerp, and thus creating a rival market to London's.

Once again the stability of world diamond prices was threatened. The original Diamond Syndicate, a vertical monopoly from production to marketing, had been formed soon after the founding of De Beers Consolidated Mines in 1888, and it worked reasonably well in the interests of producers and merchants alike. The diamond industry was prone to slumps just like any other industry, but many were unnecessary and simply created by

So rich were the first diamond finds in South West Africa that it was unnecessary to actually dig for them. Here the African laborers and the German officials are exploring an area systematically on their hands and knees, picking up the diamonds as they go.

unrestricted production. There were quite enough uncertainties on the demand side without the producers themselves adding to them. The Premier Mine had provided one such example. Now it looked as if the German South West was to provide another.

It was left to Ernest Oppenheimer to finally establish the measure of control over diamond production and marketing which Cecil Rhodes had dreamed of. It was to take him nearly twenty years. Starting in Kimberley as a diamond buyer with the famous firm of A. Dunkelsbuhler & Co. of Hatton Garden, the young Oppenheimer had his first taste of negotiations during the Premier crisis in 1907 and he was prominent in the talks that brought the Diamond Régie and the Syndicate to terms. Unfortunately, the deal was concluded in 1914, just a few weeks before the outbreak of World War I, and the agreement was frozen. In fact, all the diamond mines in Kimberley closed down for the duration of the war. Ernest moved to Dunkelsbuhler's Johannesburg office to assist in the running of the firm's gold mining interests. He quickly saw the possibilities for expansion and the source of new finance— America. The result was the formation of the Anglo American Corporation of South Africa in 1917 and for a time it became a formidable rival of De Beers. In 1921 the corporation gained control of the principal producers of South West Africa under the nose of De Beers, combining them into Consolidated Diamond Mines of South West Africa, better known today as CDM. Stakes were to be acquired later in diamond producers outside South Africa, principally in Angola, the Congo and West Africa.

Unhappy with the performance of the original Diamond Syndicate, which was not as effective as it should have been in providing a single channel for diamond selling, Oppenheimer made a bid on behalf of Anglo

American for the total production of CDM and then followed it up with a further bid for the output of all the South African mines. The Diamond Syndicate riposted by expelling both Anglo American and Dunkelsbuhlers from membership. It seemed that the situation had rebounded on Oppenheimer. There were now two selling channels in existence and in competition. But this was just a short-term tactical incident in a long-term strategic plan. Oppenheimer's next step was to convince the producers that his new syndicate could do a better job than the old one, backed as it would be by powerful banking interests in New York and London. He was a persuasive advocate and by 1926 the new syndicate was in operation.

All that remained for Oppenheimer to do was to link the production and the selling of diamonds much more closely by unifying them in a single huge operation. De Beers seemed to him to be the obvious vehicle and he set out to gain control of the company. He had already been elected to the board of De Beers when his efforts were rudely interrupted by another crisis in the industry. In 1926 and 1927 two new areas of alluvial diamonds were found, one at Lichtenburg in the Transvaal and another in Namaqualand on the Atlantic coast just below the border of South West Africa.* The strikes were large and rich, and they underlined even more dramatically the need for one central body to regulate production and marketing.

The diggers who rushed into both areas were not concerned with long-term visions of a regulated industry. They simply wanted to make as much money as they could in the

*In the latter area, the geologist Dr. Hans Merensky had noticed that a number of fine diamonds were found in association with a line of fossilized oyster shells running parallel to the sea. The diggings soon became known as the "oyster line," and although the line was only a ledge or terrace where diamonds as well as oysters had been trapped millions of years ago, a rumor was current at the time that diamonds had been found in oysters just like pearls.

OVERLEAF *When diamonds were discovered at Lichtenburg in the Western Transvaal in 1926, the area was proclaimed public diggings. Pegging of claims was carefully organized and as many as 25,000 people took part in a single rush. This picture is of a rush underway at Vaalbosputte, one of the diamond fields in the Lichtenburg district.*

shortest possible time. The position was further complicated because the new diamonds, especially from Namaqualand, were of remarkably high quality and as they came onto the market, world prices plunged. Seeing the effect that these new discoveries were having on prices, buyers in Europe and America decided to hold off—and prices plunged again. The new syndicate was buying stocks from Lichtenburg alone at the rate of £40,000 a week and was horrified to learn that forecasts put future production at as much as £100,000 a week. With no control over production, all the syndicate could do was try to regulate the sales, but the only way they could do so was by buying up all of the production—and their reserves were not limitless. It would be cheaper and more effective, Oppenheimer argued, to purchase the new fields. By the end of 1927 an Oppenheimer-Joel combine had bought into Lichtenburg, and in cooperation with Barnato interests, he had acquired a key stake in "the Aladdin's Cave" of Namaqualand.

The final step was the enlarging of the new syndicate into a Diamond Corporation, to include both producers and the members of the existing syndicate. De Beers would control it and have the right to appoint and remove its chairman. The logic of the move was inescapable. In order to avoid the slumps caused by unrestricted competition from new diamond finds, a supreme controlling body had to be created. At last all the parties involved saw that any short-term advantage they might be able to gain from temporary market conditions would be insignificant when set against the long-term stability and security that Oppenheimer's plans provided for the diamond industry. The effects of the Great Depression dramatically reinforced his arguments. All agreed and the Diamond Corporation was formed in 1930 with Sir Ernest Oppenheimer (he had been knighted in 1921) as chairman, first of De Beers and then of the new Diamond Corporation.

The dream that Cecil Rhodes had nurtured in Kimberley in the 1880s, had at last become a reality fifty years later. Sir Ernest Oppenheimer had set the seal on the life's work of Cecil Rhodes and Barney Barnato. The foresight and vision of one man and the raw energy of another had built a diamond empire, but it took the patience, skill and meticulous planning of a third man to secure those early achievements. Sir Ernest found a worthy successor in his son Harry, the present chairman of De Beers, under whose leadership the group's interests have been further extended and strengthened.

This remains very much the shape of the production and marketing organization today, save that the Diamond Corporation is now a subsidiary of De Beers; and while it still guarantees minimum purchase prices to producers, marketing was taken over in 1934 by a new organization, the Diamond Trading Company. At the same time, the Diamond Producers' Association was formed to lay down policy and to set production quotas. Its members are the producers in the De Beers group in South and South West Africa, the Diamond Corporation and the South African government. After World War II, Industrial Distributors Ltd. was formed to market industrial diamonds, and it too became a member of the association.

The diamond finds in South Africa may be the best known to the world at large because of the human interest involved and the part they played in building a great nation, but they are by no means the only finds in Africa or even the biggest. The fields discovered in the Belgian Congo in 1907 are now recognized to be the largest single source of diamonds in the world (although the vast majority are only suitable for use in industry). Mining has been carried on at two main centers, on the Kasai River at Tshikapa, and at Bakwanga, 60 miles (100 kilometers) east of Luluabourg. The former

WORLD PRODUCTION OF DIAMONDS
1945 - 1975

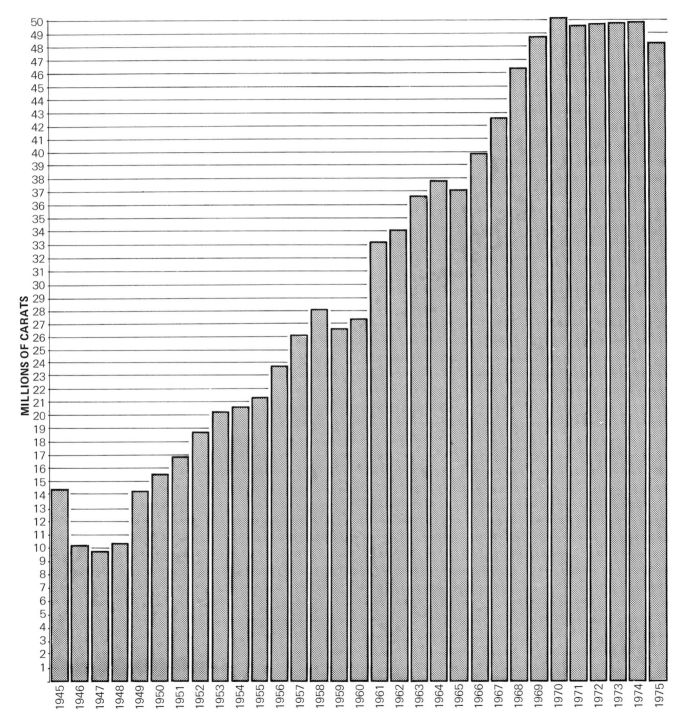

source, now in Zaire, was forced to close down during the anarchy that followed the granting of independence in 1960. Where there had once been thirty-seven active diamond areas operating on an organized basis, there were soon nothing but marauding tribesmen indulging in illicit digging and then in the smuggling of the diamonds across the Congo River to sell them in Brazzaville. The authorities are making strenuous efforts to clamp down on illegal activity, and their task has been aided by helicopter and hovercraft patrols in unprotected areas.

The Bakwanga region is still producing at a high rate as befits an area that has been described as at least one hundred times richer than any other yet discovered. There are thirteen known kimberlite pipes in Zaire and ten of them occur within the fenced mining concession of the Société Minière de Bakwanga. Covered with overburden to a depth of up to 100 feet (30 meters), they represent a veritable hill of diamonds. Such a rich concentration of diamondiferous material has become partially dispersed throughout the region's vast and complex river systems, and here too illicit digging is a major problem. Armed soldiers are on twenty-four-hour patrol of the pipes and the river deposits, but as one commentator wryly remarks, "The soldier is as wont to put aside his rifle for a shovel as he is to fire a shot."

The Congo deposits stretch into Angola but more than twenty kimberlite pipes have been found in the north of Angola itself. Only one, the Camatue pipe, is being worked extensively. The others are uneconomic and are assumed to have dispersed their diamond product along the river system. Until the outbreak of the civil war, there were forty-two active mining areas, all related to one or other of the five main rivers and their tributaries and streams. The mining methods used are simple but effective. The streams are diverted for a distance of a mile or two (two or three kilometers) and the new dry riverbed is mined. In the case of the biggest rivers, which can measure about 1¼ miles (200 meters) across, one side is closed down while the search for diamonds is conducted in the dry half. The process is then repeated on the other side of the river. The concession for the whole of Angola had been in the hands of the Companhia de Diamantes de Angola (better known as Diamang), since exploitation first began in 1917, but the accession of a Marxist administration in Luanda is bound to lead to changes in the present system.

A later discovery in South Africa was made in the semidesert region of Postmasburg, 100 miles (166 kilometers) northeast of Kimberley, by an independent prospector, A. T. Fincham, in 1958. Called the Finsch Mine, it was a huge forty-five-acre pipe and its rate of production quickly attracted the attention of De Beers who eventually bought out Fincham and his partner for £2¼ million.

The biggest diamond pipe yet known was found at Mwadui in Tanganyika in 1940 by Dr. John Williamson. Alluvial deposits had been known in the country since 1910 and Dr. Williamson, a Canadian geologist, deduced the approximate location of the pipe from the distribution of the deposits. After nearly ten years of intensive search he found it. It was eight times larger than the Premier pipe and spread over 361 acres. Known as the Williamson Mine, it still produces around half a million carats annually, and is now owned and operated by the Tanzanian government in partnership with De Beers.

The second largest pipe in the world was discovered at Orapa in Botswana (formerly Bechuanaland) in 1967. Diamond production began four years later and has now reached an annual rate of 2.4 million carats, a figure which makes Botswana the third largest producer in Africa. Situated on the eastern edge of the Kalahari desert, Orapa posed many problems to its developers. The

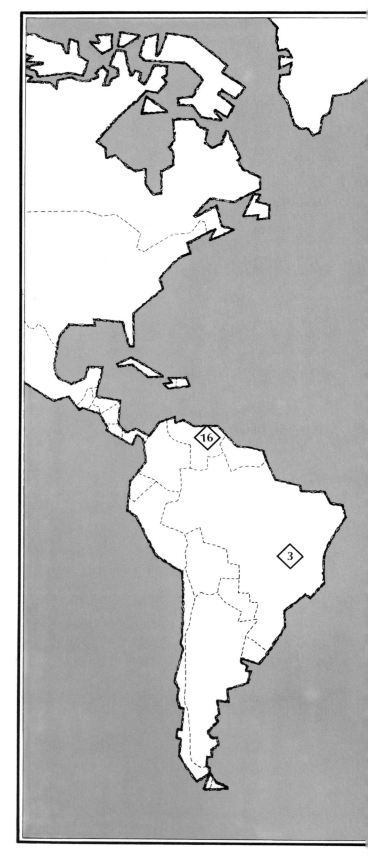

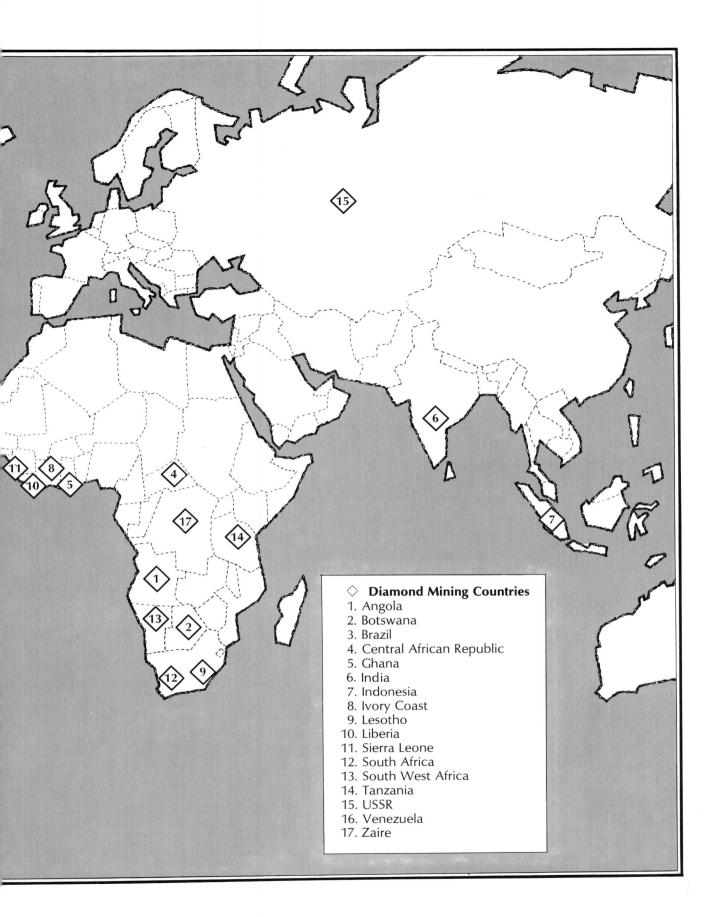

◇ **Diamond Mining Countries**
1. Angola
2. Botswana
3. Brazil
4. Central African Republic
5. Ghana
6. India
7. Indonesia
8. Ivory Coast
9. Lesotho
10. Liberia
11. Sierra Leone
12. South Africa
13. South West Africa
14. Tanzania
15. USSR
16. Venezuela
17. Zaire

site was 144 miles (240 kilometers) away from the nearest railroad depot at Francistown, and was totally without power, water or communications. An all-weather road was first constructed, and then a private rail depot was built just outside of Francistown to handle the huge quantities of equipment and supplies needed for the development of the mine. Water was an even greater problem since the fact that the mine would eventually require 1.5 million gallons a day for mine operations and domestic use meant that a large and permanent source would have to be found. A 25-billion-gallon reservoir was therefore established in the Mopipi salt pan 30 miles (50 kilometers) away and carried by pipeline to the mine. The reservoir itself is filled by water pumped from the Botletle River, which comes down from southern Angola. A second mine, Letlhakane, came on stream late in 1976, and Botswana aims to expand production to 4.5 million carats by 1979.

Elsewhere in Africa, perhaps the best-known diamond production area is Sierra Leone, if only because of the notoriety gained as a result of widespread illicit digging and smuggling activities. From 1934 production had been in the sole hands of the Sierra Leone Selection Trust, a subsidiary of the London-based Consolidated African Selection Trust

(CAST), which was in turn controlled by the huge Selection Trust mining combine. In 1955, however, the extent of illicit digging prompted the government to make a virtue of necessity by restricting the company's concessions to two lease areas only, and licensing the illicit diggers. In 1969 the government went further and acquired a 51 percent interest in the Sierra Leone Selection Trust. The moves did nothing to curb illicit digging or to protect the company's lease areas, despite the employment of a virtual army of over 1,000 security men complete with helicopters and hovercraft. To quote an official report:

Immediately before the government's nationalization announcement, the audacity of the gangsters reached a climax—on November 13, 1969—when a daylight armed robbery took place, and a month's production of diamonds, valued at $3,441,480 was stolen from the security officers of the company who were escorting the diamonds from the mine at Yengema to the SLST sorting office in Freetown. Lawlessness in the mushroom town of Koidu, with its 40,000 ruffians, had become uncontrolled. A fine new two-lane highway that had been built in the lease area became a derelict diggings within ten days; stealing and robbery were everyday occurrences. Illegal diggers, composed of Hausas from Nigeria, Foulahs, Mandingoes, and Konos from Sierra Leone itself, would flock out at nightfall carrying picks, sieves, hoes and torches for a night of raiding the company's reserves. Large parts of the very extensive Yengema lease areas came to look like a battlefield of the First World War, scarred and pockmarked as if by a heavy artillery barrage.

Great interest has been taken recently in South America as a source of diamonds since the reports of fabulously rich finds in the Guaniamo River area in the state of Bolivar in Venezuela. While these discoveries are estimated by some observers to have a dramatic impact on Venezuela's production figures, there can be little certainty about their size. Venezuela has long been known to be rich in diamond occurrences but systematic prospecting and exploitation has always been hampered by the impossible nature of the terrain. The jungle is virtually impenetrable, the river banks are choked with thick and unyielding undergrowth and river weeds, and the places where diamonds have been found are described as "uninhabited and uninhabitable." Nevertheless, a number of diamond rushes, or *bombas*, have occurred since 1970 and as many as 30,000 or 40,000 diggers have hacked their way into this inhospitable territory. The situation has been complicated by the fact that the finds have been close enough to the border of Colombia to attract diggers from that country too. Not surprisingly, tensions were soon running high between Venezuelan diggers and the Colombian "intruders" in the primitive mining camps, and a number of murders and robberies have been reported.

The great unknown quantity in the world of diamond production is Soviet Russia. Diamonds had been found in placer deposits in the Urals by gold prospectors as early as 1829, but later exploration showed no sign of pipe formation. It was not until just before World War II that intensive prospecting began in the huge territory that lay beyond the Lena River in Siberia after a leading geologist, Vladimir Sobolev, had noted the similarity between the geology of the region and that of the diamondiferous "platform" zones of South Africa and India. The war interrupted prospecting activity but the search was resumed in 1947 when a large geological party was landed by aircraft on the western borders of Yakutia. The party barely survived the experience and members were too intent on staying alive to mount a successful diamond search. Later expeditions had greater success but the real breakthrough came in 1953 when a woman geologist in Leningrad, Larissa Popugaieva, was led to the first diamond pipe as a result of realizing the significance of pyropes, the deep red garnets which are usually found in association with diamonds in South Africa.

Statistics are not published by the Soviet authorities, but it is clear that a large-scale diamond-producing industry has been established in the Siberian Arctic under almost impossible climatic conditions. A Western diamond-industry publication refers to the achievement as "one of the technical marvels of our generation, presenting a picture of Soviet courage and perseverance deserving acknowledgment outside all ideological considerations." With temperatures as low as −70°F for seven months of the year, conditions at the Mir pipe in Yakutia, the principal production area, are unbelievably harsh. Under cold of such intensity, "ordinary machinery and ordinary oils become unuseable. Iron bars snap like matchsticks and rubber breaks like brittle crockery. Frozen bread has to be chopped by axe." Aikhal, which is the second main producing region, is some 300 miles (500 kilometers) nearer the Arctic Circle and conditions are described as "far worse." There, the permafrost, which is the freezing of the ground below the ice, is reported to extend as deep as 1,000 feet (300 meters), making the earth as hard and as difficult to penetrate as solid rock. A third source is the Udachnaya pipe, just 18 miles (30 kilometers) to the east of Aikhal. It is a much smaller pipe than the other two but is reported to yield a higher proportion of stones of gem quality.

The high rate of production from Soviet Russia tends to reinforce the view that the Mir pipe is of a phenomenally high grade, and thus able to counterbalance the delays and disruptions of production arising from the extreme cold and blizzards of Siberia. Entirely new mining methods have had to be developed to deal with the extraordinary climatic conditions. Steam heat is used to sink piles into the permafrost and also to drill blasting holes, but later reports suggest that the hot air from jet engines set up near the drilling points is now harnessed and directed into adapted drills. It seems likely that the whole of the working section in the open-cast pipes is being continually "softened up" by the hot air treatment. Similar apparently insuperable problems must have been overcome to establish the recovery plants. One of the problems of building on permafrost is that the warmth from the new structures will gradually thaw the ground beneath, causing subsidence and fracture. The only way to avoid this happening is to build on steel piles driven into the ground which project some feet above it so that any warmth can be quickly dissipated. This is difficult enough to do when constructing simple housing, but because of the huge weights involved and the need for absolute stability, the construction of recovery plants must have presented enormous problems. And yet the Russians claim that the Aikhal plant is the most modern in the world and uses the latest electronic equipment. There is also the point that all known recovery plants employ wet extraction processes requiring large volumes of continually flowing water. All that Western observers can conclude is that either an underground hot water source is being tapped or that natural gas is being piped into the diamond fields to heat the water. Most discount the idea that the Russians have developed a new dry extraction process. As for the quality of diamonds produced in Russia, the ratio of gem stones to industrials is generally put at a little over 20 percent, with the industrials comprising a high proportion of boart and grit. Of those sold to the West, the gem diamonds are mainly very uniformly cut 20-pointers (.2 carat) which compare very favorably with mêlée cut elsewhere. No industrial material is exported, however, since all of it is destined for domestic consumption. Russia has been described as the most diamond-conscious industrialized country in the world, applying industrial diamonds to every possible process in precision engineering with special emphasis on astronautical and military requirements.

There are a number of other diamond-

producing areas but in most cases the current yield is not significant. Borneo, for example, used to be a relatively important source a century ago, and some large and important stones have been discovered there, including the almost legendary Matan diamond, found in 1787. Large stones are now a great rarity in Borneo. The traditional diamond-producing areas are worked by the local population still using the most primitive methods, but some effort has recently gone into modernizing both production and marketing methods. Production is thought unlikely to exceed 25–30,000 carats annually.

It is a source of constant wonderment to

The Mir pipe in Siberia located just 300 miles south of the Arctic Circle.

some Australian geologists that a country as rich in minerals as their own should be a Cinderella as far as diamonds are concerned. Diamonds have been found in Australia in a great variety of locations, but not in any real quantity. Some commercial production was carried out for a time at two adjoining fields at Bingara and at Copeton in New South Wales. The diamonds found there were mainly industrial quality and noted for their exceptional hardness, but production ceased many years ago. Because all the diamond locations were alluvial, there has been some speculation as to their actual source. The intensive exploration effort following the nickel discoveries of the mid-1960s revealed at least one kimberlite pipe in the extreme north of Western Australia, appropriately enough in what is known as the Kimberley Plateau. However, there have been no reports of diamonds being found in the pipe, and similarly no positive news has come from the company whose geologists embarked upon the search for a pipe in the Walcha district of New South Wales.

America is a much more interesting country for diamonds. Again they are few and far between, but some of those that have been found are of very high quality. The best-known source is the Crater of Diamonds at Murfreesboro in Arkansas. This is a kimberlite pipe, but the occurrence of diamonds is so rare that rather than embark upon the enormous cost of setting up a full-scale mining operation, the owner charges a prospecting fee to tourists and amateur geologists. The largest diamond yet found in the United States was unearthed at Murfreesboro in 1928. It weighed 40.23 carats in the rough and is known as the Uncle Sam. Another diamond, a flawless white stone of 15.33 carats, was found in the crater in 1956 by a Texas rockhound just a couple of hours after paying the $1.50 fee. The diamond has since been named the Star of Arkansas.

DIAMONDS ON THE MOON?

When the Apollo 15 mission to the moon retrieved a number of mineral samples from the lunar surface, there was speculation in some quarters that diamonds would also be found there. Soon after the return of the mission, NASA made the following official statement:

Considering the extremely low carbon content of lunar materials, it is most unlikely that diamonds will be found. There are almost certainly diamonds on the lunar surface within meteorites that landed there—either due to the pressure of impact on the lunar surface or due to impact in the meteorites' past history. Then pressures generated would have been sufficient to produce diamonds from the graphite in the meteorites.

The possibility still remains that there may be carbon-rich zones in the moon at depth, so that diamonds could exist near the moon's center. This question is extremely hypothetical and we shall almost certainly never sample rocks on the lunar surface that have come from such depths.

But even if diamonds are found in abundance, their impact on the diamond industry of planet Earth is not going to be significant as long as the retrieval costs of lunar material run at nearly $1 million per gram.

A diamond clip in the form of a rocket and satellite with platinum wire jets passing through a pavé-set diamond cloud. CHRISTIE'S, LONDON

FROM MINE TO MARKET

Until the discovery of the first diamond pipes in South Africa in 1871, for centuries the only source of diamonds known to man had been the river. Diamonds had been found on the banks of active rivers or in the beds of rivers that had dried up thousands of years before, but all the sources were clearly alluvial. The methods adopted for the mining and recovery of diamonds were therefore simple and labor-intensive. Tavernier provides us with a graphic account of the techniques of the great mine of Kollur in the Kingdom of Golconda in India around 1650:

> After the miners have selected the place where they desire to work, they smooth down another spot close by, of equal or rather greater extent, round which they erect an enclosing wall of two feet in height. At the base of this little wall they make openings, at every two feet, for the escape of the water, which they close till it is time for the water to be drawn off.
>
> They excavate to ten, twelve or fourteen feet in depth, but when they reach water there is nothing more to hope for. All the earth is carried to this place, men, women and children draw water with pitchers from the hole which they have excavated, and throw it upon

OPPOSITE *Beach mining in South West Africa. A back trencher cleaning out a deep gulley in the bedrock after the sand overburden has been stripped away.*

the earth which they have placed there in order to soften it, leaving it in this state for one or two days, according to the tenacity of the clay, until it becomes like soup. This done, they open the holes which they made in the wall to let off the water, then they throw on more, so that all the slime may be removed, and nothing remains but sand. It is a kind of clay which requires to be washed two or three times. They then leave it to be dried by the sun, [and it] is quickly effected by the great heat. They have a particular kind of basket made something like a winnowing fan, in which they place the earth, which they agitate as we do when winnowing grain. The fine part is blown away, and the coarse stuff which remains is subsequently replaced on the ground.

All the earth having been thus winnowed, they spread it with a rake and make it as level as possible. Then they all stand together on the earth, each with a large baton of wood like a huge pestle, half a foot wide at the base, and pound the earth, going from one end to the other, always pounding each part two or three times; they then place it again in the baskets and winnow it, as they did on the first occasion, after which they spread it out again and range themselves on one side to handle the earth and search for the diamonds.

Further to the west, about five days' journey from Golconda, Tavernier noted different methods in use. There the ground was sandy, rock-strewn and covered with coppice, and as he comments, "somewhat like the environs of Fontainebleau." The diamonds were to be found mixed with sand and earth in veins in the rocks, and were extracted by the miners using little iron rods crooked at one end. The earth and sand were

Diamond mining at Panna in India. Pits had to be dug through a thick sandstone layer to reach the diamonds. Note the armed guards.

then washed two or three times in the search for diamonds. Harry Emanuel, the nineteenth-century mineralogist, recorded that in the diamond-producing district of Sumbhulpore near Panna in the north, the diamond-washing trade had been carried on for centuries by two tribes. These were the Thara and the Tora, who by their appearance had traces of Negro blood and were judged to be the descendants of slaves imported by one of the earlier conquerors of India for that very task.

The methods employed in Brazil a hundred years later were similar. The diamond-bearing gravels, called *cascalho*, were excavated to a depth of about ten feet and deposited in heaps outside the washing huts. In these huts were long troughs, called canoes, and elevated seats for the overseers who kept a constant watch on the proceedings. The *cascalho* was then washed in the canoes by means of a stream of water coming in one end and flowing out of the other, often from canals cut into the banks of the nearby river. When a diamond was found, the slave would clap his hands as a signal to the overseer who took it and placed it in a water-filled vessel which hung in the middle of each hut.

The early South African diggers on the banks of the Vaal River in 1869 used much the

Washing for diamonds at Mandango in Brazil, about 1760. The slaves are working under the constant supervision of overseers.

same primitive techniques to recover diamonds. The broken ground was taken from
the pits and pounded with shovels to break it
up even more. It was then placed in a rocking
trough fitted out with sieves (sometimes in
three tiers of varying mesh sizes) to get rid of
both the larger material and any fine sand or
dirt. The remaining collection of pebbles,
crystals and coarse rock grains was put in a
fine sieve and washed in order to concentrate
the heavier portion of the material, which of
course would include any diamonds. The
sieve was then tipped onto a table and the
contents hand-sorted. These rockers or cradles were commonly improvised from old gin
crates. A slightly more sophisticated type was
invented and marketed by an American gun
salesman, J. L. Babe. Inevitably his rocker was
known as the "Baby" or the "Yankee Baby."

*At the sorting table by the Vaal River diggings in about
1870. This scene is very unusual because of the
presence of a woman and children. Conditions were so
primitive in the early days that families were almost
invariably left at home.*

ABOVE *A typical scene outside a mining shack in Kimberley, c. 1871.* **OPPOSITE** *By the end of the century, methods of haulage in the mines had been greatly improved and quite sophisticated cable systems were in use for the transport of men and materials. This is an aerial trolley, in operation in 1903.*

This simple sequence of operations had worked well for centuries, but it quickly became outmoded when mining at the dry diggings began to more than scratch the surface of the earth. As the claims went deeper, mechanical methods had to be employed to bring the yellow ground to the surface. The most common method was the endless rope linked to a pair of pulleys, one in the pit and one at the edge, which carried up the broken ground in hide buckets and took them down empty again. Soon there were literally thousands of such ropes and cables coming up from the claim, and staging had to be erected in several tiers around the edge of the mine to cope with them all. As the claims became deeper still, horse whims gradually replaced hand tackle in the lowering and hoisting of buckets. The first one was introduced at the Kimberley Mine in 1874, and in the following year steam engines began to be used to operate the winding gear.

Increasing activity in the mines at Kimberley meant that more efficient methods had to be employed to haul up the blue ground than simply ropes and hide buckets. These large horizontal wooden drums called whims were introduced in 1875 and were driven by gangs of laborers or by horses.

Today's washing pans are mechanically operated and somewhat larger, but they operate on much the same principle.

What has changed dramatically over the years has been the method of getting the broken ground out of the mine. Because diamond mining has a higher proportion of waste material to product mined than is usual in almost any other mining operation, the emphasis has always had to be on the efficient and economic extraction of diamond-bearing ores in bulk. The open-pit operations of the early days rapidly became uneconomic because of the growing frequency with which the surrounding rock collapsed into the hole. By 1882 no less than three tons of rock and debris had to be removed in order to extract one ton of blue ground from the Kimberley Mine.

Attempts to cut back the sides of the mine proved impractical because of the area involved and the increasing depth of the hole, and an experiment carried out at Dutoitspan in which a protecting wall of blue ground was left around the sides of the pit nearly proved disastrous when all the walls collapsed simultaneously.

OPPOSITE *This is the first rotary washing mashine to be employed at the Kimberley Mine. It was introduced in 1874. Prior to that date, washing machines were little more than cradles with sieves at the bottom.* **ABOVE** *By 1894 the washing machines were arranged in rows with the crushed blue ground being fed into them on conveyor belts.*

Water was not readily available in the semi-desert area of the dry diggings and washing techniques could not be used at first. Instead a hand-operated rotary sieve with 1-inch to 1¼-inch mesh called a trommel (Dutch for "drum") was devised for sifting the broken ground. The finer pieces were further pulverized before being shoveled into hand sieves with ⅛-inch mesh. What remained in the sieve went to the sorting table. In due course, rotary washing pans were introduced. These were circular containers about four feet across and nine inches deep with a series of prongs on arms set into the axle. When the axle was rotated by turning the handle, the mixture of water and gravels was swirled around causing the lighter elements to flow over the top of the pan while the heavier ones fell to the bottom.

The blue ground was left to weather on the depositing floors, large fenced areas of land next to the mines. After some weeks, it was raked with harrows drawn by steam engines like the one depicted here. The keeping of chickens and pigeons was a popular pastime among the mine employees since the birds frequently strayed onto the floors and picked up diamonds. One pigeon is recorded as disgorging from its crop no less than twenty-three crystals weighing 5.5 carats.

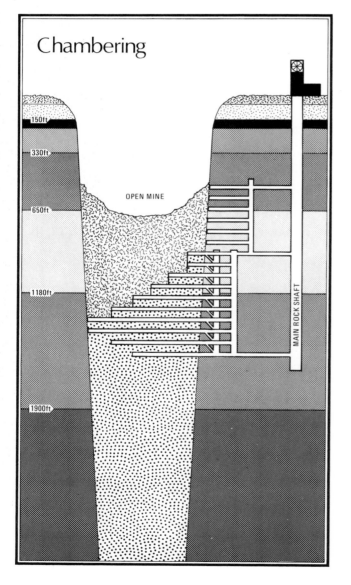

Chambering

150ft
330ft
650ft

OPEN MINE

1180ft

MAIN ROCK SHAFT

1900ft

Today's open-pit mining methods are a far cry from those of the thousands of independent claim holders who crowded into the Kimberley Mine in the 1870s. The whole operation is completely mechanized: towering mechanical diggers and thirty-five-ton dump trucks have replaced the shovels and hide buckets of a century earlier. The problem of the surrounding rock collapsing into the mine, as it did in the early open-pit workings, has been solved by tackling it right at the beginning: the reef is gradually cut back in steps as the mine gets deeper. The result is a much wider and deeper hole. The intention is to take the Finsch Mine down to 1,000 feet (330 meters) before switching to underground mining. In the Kimberley Mine the maximum depth reached in open-pit operations was 800 feet (240 meters); and in the Premier, 600 feet (180 meters). Mining in the Finsch is carried out in 40-foot (12-meter) steps which are blasted along the edges and the broken kimberlite is then loaded by mechanical shovels into dump trucks which transport it to the adjoining treatment plant. It is estimated that the open working will continue for approximately fifteen years.

The gradual consolidation of the many claims into fewer and fewer hands paved the way for the introduction of underground mining techniques at Kimberley from 1883, but these were only partially successful. The real breakthrough did not come until 1890, after all the claims were finally consolidated in the hands of De Beers. In that year an excavation technique called chambering was introduced by Gardner Williams, the American mining expert who was also general manager of the company. In this method, a main shaft is sunk in the rock surrounding the pipe and connected to the pipe by main rock tunnels established at the 600-, 1,000- and 1,600-foot levels (180, 330 and 490 meters).

At 40-foot intervals, chambering levels are established from which a series of parallel tunnels are driven into the pipe leaving 10-foot-wide pillars between. The tunnels on the level below are staggered so that they are positioned immediately under the pillars on the level above. Mining is carried out by blasting the chamber roofs of the top series of tunnels so that the pillars collapse into the tunnel below. The blue ground is then loaded into trucks, transported to the main shaft and hoisted to the surface.

Chambering was used throughout the mines of the De Beers group until 1953 when it was replaced in all except the Wesselton Mine by a more efficient and less labor-intensive technique known as block caving. In this system a series of parallel concrete-lined tunnels called scraper drifts are driven from the main rock shaft into the pipe some 400 to 600 feet (120 to 180 meters) below the top of the blue ground. Openings known as draw points are left in the roof of these tunnels through which raises are cut to form cone-shaped excavations into the blue ground above. The whole block of blue ground above the cone is then mined out to a height of about 7 feet (2 meters) and after a brief interval it begins to crumble and collapse into the cones through the draw points and into the scraper drifts. From here it is dragged out by mechanical scrapers and precipitated into trucks which carry it to an underground crushing plant where it is reduced to pieces of 6 inches (152 millimeters) or less in size before being taken to the surface in skips.

The advantages of block caving over chambering are that all loading is mechanical and much more blue ground can be mined per shift. Furthermore, since all operations are carried out on one level, supervision is much simpler with consequent benefits in the level of safety and efficiency.

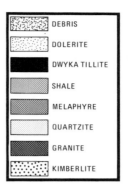

DEBRIS

DOLERITE

DWYKA TILLITE

SHALE

MELAPHYRE

QUARTZITE

GRANITE

KIMBERLITE

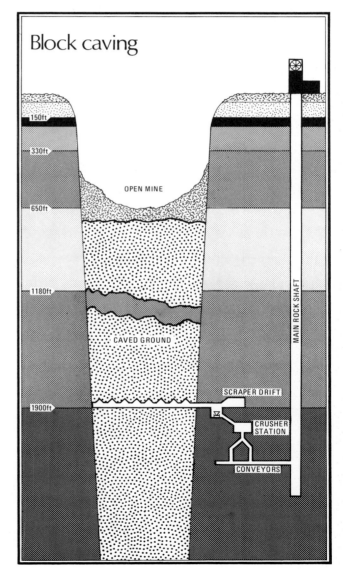

Block caving

150ft

330ft

OPEN MINE

650ft

1180ft

CAVED GROUND

1900ft

SCRAPER DRIFT

CRUSHER STATION

CONVEYORS

MAIN ROCK SHAFT

ABOVE *The Big Hole at Kimberley.*

PRECEDING PAGE *An aerial view of the opencast workings of the Finsch Mine, with the treatment plant in the foreground.* **OPPOSITE, ABOVE** *Removing the sand overburden on the beaches of South West Africa.* **BELOW** *After the removal of the sand, the uneven bedrock is then broken up with compressed air drills and shoveled onto conveyor belts set up on the spot.* **THIS PAGE,** *Drilling holes to prepare for blasting during chambering operations at the Wesselton Mine.*

The earliest known representation of diamond mining, by the sixteenth-century Italian painter Tomas Fedriani. Clearly an oriental scene, the painting presents a rather fanciful idea of how diamond mining is carried on. All the early mining in India was of the alluvial kind requiring only shallow digging in dry riverbeds, but here it looks as if the diamonds are being hacked out of rock formations resembling giant anthills. The portrayal of the miners is very interesting. All are naked and many have one arm tied behind their backs, presumably in an effort to make stealing and concealment more difficult.

Panning gravels in the search for alluvial diamonds on the banks of the River Sewa in Sierra Leone.

ABOVE: LEFT *Gravel and bare bedrock after the removal of sand overburden (piled in the background). The final stage is to sweep the bedrock by hand with small brushes.* **RIGHT** *The grease belt takes advantage of the fact that diamonds cannot be wetted and will stick to grease. The diamond-bearing conglomerate is washed over the moving belt and the diamonds are trapped in the grease while the rest of the material is sluiced away. The belts have superseded the static grease tables which had been in use in the South African mines since 1896. Their advantage is that the treatment process does not have to be stopped at frequent intervals to remove the diamonds and resurface the belt with grease.* **BELOW: RIGHT** *Foreshore mining at the Consolidated Diamond Mines concession in South West Africa. The sand over-burden is stripped and used to build 40-foot-thick walls to keep out the sea while the diamond-bearing gravels are removed.* **RIGHT** *Washing and screening is carried out by passing crushed rock over a series of wire mesh screens. Depending upon the stage of the process, the rejected tailings may, or may not, be the material which passes through.*

ABOVE *Sorting rough diamonds at the mine into basic gem and industrial classifications.* **LEFT** *An octahedron of good color seen under a loupe during sorting.* **OPPOSITE** *Blasting at the Finsch Mine.*

Once the blue ground has reached the surface, it is screened and crushed again, this time to below 1¼ inches (32 millimeters) in size, before being conveyed to the central treatment plant. It is then passed through the rotary washing pans. These pans exploit the high specific gravity of diamonds, which causes them to sink when the blue ground is placed in a state of liquid suspension by mixing it with muddy water called "puddle." On average, about one ton of concentrate is extracted by the rotary pans for every twenty-three tons of waste or "tailings" swept away.

The next step in the recovery process is for the concentrate from the rotary pans to be delivered to the vibrating grease belts. These take advantage of another of the diamond's physical characteristics—its inability to be wetted and its tendency to adhere to grease. The concentrate is sluiced over the grease-covered surface of the belt and the diamonds are trapped while the rest is carried away. The diamonds are automatically scraped off the belt by a heated blade and collected, at which point they are ready for boiling in kettles. This will disperse the grease so that only clean diamonds remain.

An alternative method to the grease belt which is rapidly gaining ground is the X-ray separator. The basis of this method of recovery is that all diamonds fluoresce when exposed to X-rays, whereas all the accompanying minerals in the concentrate do not. The stream of concentrate is fed into the recovery machine, and as it falls toward the collecting bins past the X-ray beams any diamonds present will "light up," trigger a photoelectric cell and activate an air-operated ejector which will blow them into a separate bin.

Another principle method of diamond mining currently in use is beach mining. The richest source of gem diamonds in the world is a stretch of bleak, storm-swept coast in South

OPPOSITE, ABOVE *Underground loading in the Kimberley Mine in 1894.* **BELOW** *Drilling in the Kimberley Mine in 1894.* **ABOVE** *An underground loader in operation in the De Beers Mine at Kimberley.*

West Africa extending 50 miles (83 kilometers) northward from the mouth of the Orange River. The diamonds lie under as much as 50 feet (15 meters) of sand in the clefts and gullies of the marine terraces where they were deposited millions of years ago after being swept down ancient water courses from the inland pipes. Their extraction involves Consolidated Diamond Mines (CDM) in the largest continuous earth-moving operation in the world. Teams of scrapers and bulldozers remove the overburden of sand at a rate of five hundred tons an hour per machine and on occasions as much as two million cubic meters of sand has had to be stripped to uncover a mining area of only 1,000 feet (300 meters) square. Once the ancient marine terrace has been exposed, bulldozers move in to push the gravel into stockpiles, or if it is very deep, it will be loaded by excavators into thirty-five ton dump trucks and transported to the treatment plant. Finally, the uneven bedrock is examined for trapped diamonds by being handswept with small brushes while back trenchers clean out the deeper gullies.

Rather more complicated techniques had to be employed when attempts were made to mine the deposits in the tidal area, the part of the beach between high and low water marks. Huge coffer dams of sand reinforced with concrete blocks were bulldozed into position and it was found possible to keep the sea at bay long enough to mine successfully. The size of the diamonds recovered was disappointingly small, though, and the operation was discontinued in 1971 for marketing reasons.

Another marine operation—one that has captured more imaginations than it has diamonds—is that of mining the seabed by vacuum sweeping. This technique was pioneered by an American oil man, Sam Collins, using one prospecting vessel to map out the payable areas and a recovery barge to do the actual mining. The heavy swell along the coast

Two of the huge scrapers removing the sand overburden during beach mining operations by Consolidated Diamond Mines in South West Africa.

Standard foreshore mining method

High-water mark

Mined out area

Cross wall 130 ft.

400 ft.

Mined out area

Bedrock cleaning

Pump

Stripping direction of advance

Well points

Sea wall

New skew prism wall method

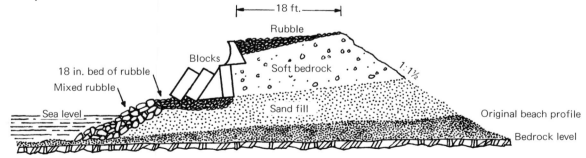

18 ft.

Rubble

Blocks

Soft bedrock

1:1½

18 in. bed of rubble

Mixed rubble

Sea level

Sand fill

Original beach profile

Bedrock level

which could cause the barge to rise and fall by as much as 30 feet (10 meters) presented major technical difficulties and the consequent low recovery rate led to the suspension of operations in 1971.

The recovery process for the diamond-bearing gravels of South West Africa follows much the same pattern as that for kimberlite from the inland-pipe mines, and the diamonds which emerge are sent to the same place for sorting and valuing—the Central Sorting Office of the Diamond Producers' Association in Kimberley. There the diamonds are cleaned in acid, counted and weighed, consignments from the different mines each being dealt with separately.

First of all, the crystals are separated into broad gem and industrial categories with color and clarity being the principal determining factor. There is obviously some overlap between the two groups and it is the balance of demand from the jewelry trade and industrial sources that determines whether the borderline cases should become gems or be consumed by industry. Roughly 80 percent of all diamonds produced fall into the industrial category. The industrials are dispatched to Johannesburg for further sorting and then marketing.

The gem crystals are sorted according to size, shape, purity and color. First the "sizes"— stones weighing about 1 carat or more—are separated from the "smalls." The borderline weight varies around the 1-carat mark according to the state of the market. The next step is to sort the crystals into their basic shapes: stones, which are unbroken crystals of regular or irregular formation; cleavages, or imperfectly formed or fractured crystals; macles, which are twinned stones and triangular in shape; and flats, thin, tabular crystals which look like pieces of broken glass.

Having sorted the diamonds into their distinctive shapes, the sorter now grades them according to purity, or quality. In effect, this means that he assesses them in accordance with what he regards as their value to the cutter. Thus an inclusion or flaw near one point of an octahedron will not detract from the value since it will be bruted away early on in the cutting process. On the other hand, a similar flaw nearer the center of the stone would present a major problem to the cutter and the crystal is given a much lower grading. There are ten classes of quality. Broadly speaking, class one would be a clear, unspotted crystal; class two would have some small spots near the edge; class three, some larger spots, and so on. Beyond class five, gem quality would be in doubt.

Color sorting is a little more straightforward. Most browns are not favored and are rejected, and shade and clarity determine whether yellows and certain very special browns are classified as gems or industrials. There are many famous diamonds in shades of yellow and brown. The Tiffany diamond is a beautiful canary yellow and the 248.9-carat Earth Star is a deep coffee brown. There is no such ambiguity about a blue, a pink or dark green or the very rare red.

The almost infinite shades of white now remain to be classified, ranging from the finest whites through six grades down to pale

yellow. Shade variations will be considered in more detail when the various color-grading systems for polished stones are compared, since at the rough stage color may still be subject to doubt because of the diamond's coating. This is a factor which the chief valuer must take into account at the next stage, which is the valuing of the crystal.

Starting with a basic pricing formula for all the classifications, the valuer adjusts his textbook figure according to his assessment of weight recovery and the problems that the stones may set to the cutters. Such formulae are generally applied to stones weighing up to 14.8 carats; anything over that weight is dealt with individually.

Two diamond sorters at work in Kimberley at the turn of the century. The sieves help them to sort the rough diamonds into size groups.

After the crystals are sorted into their two thousand or more classifications and valued, they are sold by the Diamond Producers' Association (DPA) down the line to the Diamond Trading Company (DTC) and sent then to their sorting office in London. Here they are sorted into individual parcels which cut across a number of categories, and are then offered to diamond dealers and cutters at sales held ten times a year, known as the "sights." The buyers have already had the opportunity to make their requirements known and the parcels are made up to some extent with these in mind. However, the parcels must be purchased as they stand, and a buyer will have to dispose of any unwanted items through the trade at a later date.

The Diamond Producers' Association and the Diamond Trading Company together with the cooperative marketing unit known as the Central Selling Organization (CSO) bring order and stability to the whole diamond industry. The CSO basically adjusts the supply of diamonds to the demand by allocating quotas to its producing members through the DPA and by stockpiling certain categories of diamonds when necessary. Thus a period of temporary oversupply of certain types of diamond will be corrected by holding back both their sales and perhaps even their production. After a time the market is likely to adjust to the new situation and demand will revive. In order to finance such stockpiling, the CSO retains a percentage of the selling prices as a handling and marketing charge, but it has also built up a massive reserve fund totaling some hundreds of millions of dollars.

About 80 percent of the world's diamond production is marketed through the CSO. Ghana has its own diamond marketing board, and grades, values and prices its rough production for sale to licensed buyers, as do the Central African Republic, the Ivory Coast and Guinea. The official production of Venezuela, Guyana and Brazil is also disposed of without the help of the CSO. However, it should be noted that in most of these countries, illicit digging and smuggling is endemic and the only semblance of order to their diamond trade is given by the CSO buying on the open market. The production of the USSR was marketed through the CSO from 1959 to 1963, but the Russians now carry out their own marketing.

Similar arrangements govern the marketing of industrial diamonds. These are sold direct to trade buyers through Industrial Distributors (Sales) Ltd., which is also a member of the CSO. Prices are fixed and stocks are retained whenever necessary to stabilize the market. A separate subsidiary deals with the marketing of synthetic industrial production.

As a result of the degree of control that the CSO exercises over the supply and the marketing of diamonds, it can set the selling prices of rough diamonds in accordance with market conditions. Thus in an adverse economic climate it will hold prices steady, and in a favorable climate it will advance them regularly by small amounts.

In a world in which *monopoly* and *cartel* have become dirty words, the CSO is only too often the object of bitter criticism. The fact remains, however, that it has achieved for the diamond industry a measure of stability that is the envy of commodity producers everywhere.

Having at last emerged from the control of De Beers and the Central Selling Organization and reached the wholesale trade, the diamonds are now ready for distribution to buyers all over the world. The means by which this distribution is effected is a chain of diamond clubs and bourses situated in the world's major diamond trading centers in Amsterdam, Antwerp, London, New York and Tel Aviv. Buyers, sellers and brokers congregate here to bargain over stones in the time-honored fashion of the diamond trade, sealing their bargain with the words *Mazel un*

b'rachah, a Yiddish phrase meaning "Good luck and blessings." Nothing else is needed to create a binding contract. Of course, disputes can and do arise; but when they do, they are settled within the clubs by a board of arbitrators. Rules and regulations are strict, as befits a trade that relies so much on mutual trust; serious violations can result in a member being disbarred and thus effectively excluded from the legitimate diamond trade.

The rough diamonds make their way to the cutting centers of the world: principally Antwerp, Amsterdam, London, New York, Tel Aviv, Johannesburg and Bombay. There are smaller cutting centers in other countries, notably at St. Cloud in France, Idar-Oberstein and Brücken in West Germany, San Juan in Puerto Rico, Lisbon and in Sierra Leone. And since the discovery of massive diamond deposits in Soviet Russia, a growing cutting industry has been established at Sverdlovsk in the Urals. Traditionally the big centers specialize in certain kinds of work. Antwerp works on everything, but especially on cleavages and chips; New York on stones and shapes; and many of the smalls are cut in Amsterdam, Israel, West Germany and Bombay. The cut diamonds now pass into the hands of the manufacturing jewelers to be made into pieces of jewelry and sold to the public via retailers.

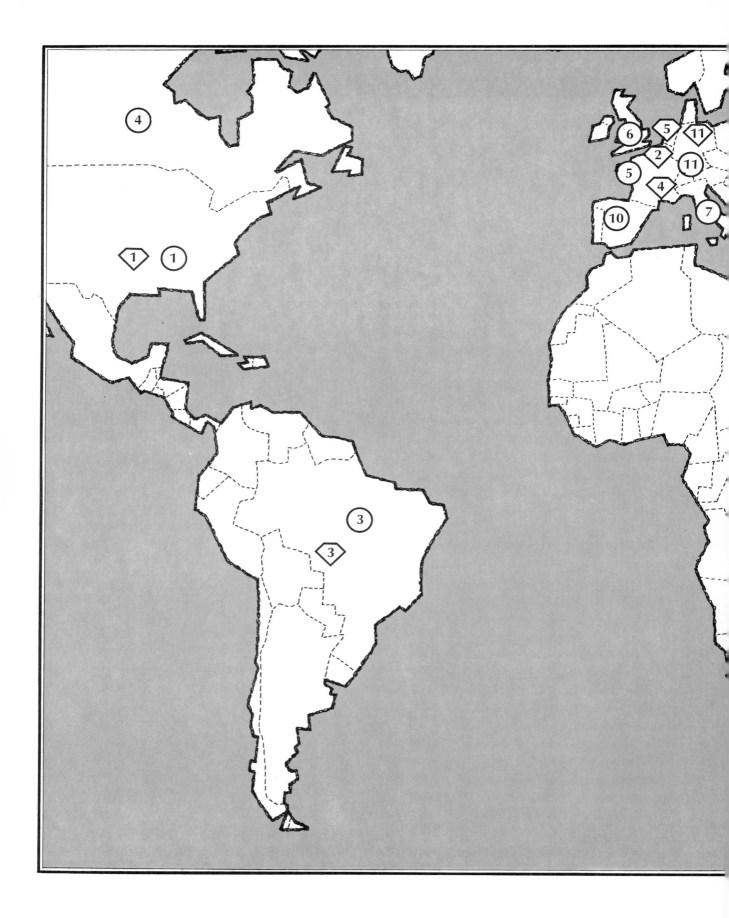

▽ **Cutting Centers**
1. America (including Puerto Rico)
2. Belgium
3. Brazil
4. France
5. Holland
6. Hong Kong
7. India
8. Israel
9. South Africa
10. USSR
11. West Germany

○ **Principal Markets**
1. America
2. Australia
3. Brazil
4. Canada
5. France
6. Great Britain
7. Italy
8. Japan
9. South Africa
10. Spain
11. West Germany

DIAMOND CUT DIAMOND

Since Venice was the gateway to the East, it is not surprising that the first reports of an active diamond-cutting industry originate in that city in about 1330. From there the art quickly spread to Paris, probably because France was very much the principal market for finished diamonds at that time. As early as 1360, an inventory of the jewels of Louis, duke of Anjou, refers to seven faceted diamonds in his collection, and records show that a famous cutter called Herman was working there in 1407. Cutting centers soon began to grow up in other parts of Europe, notably in Bruges in Flanders, in Nuremberg, in Antwerp, in Amsterdam and in Lisbon, all key cities linking trade routes with the market for diamonds. Over the years the importance of some centers grew while that of others declined and new ones emerged.

The unquestioned Jewish domination of the diamond trade began very early. As an international trade of a very specialized nature requiring great skill, it was a natural choice for a people whose culture and experience bridged the gap between Europe and the East. But there was another reason. Diamond cutting was a new trade and not subject to the rules and regulations of the medieval craft guilds which governed so many activities and effectively excluded new

OPPOSITE *Polishing the diamond. An engraving of 1887 showing a cutter at work in the factory of Coster's in Amsterdam.*

entrants. The Jews therefore gravitated toward diamond cutting as it was one of the few trades from which they were not barred. Religious persecution in the sixteenth century led to a further concentration of the diamond trade in Amsterdam as refugees from the tyranny of the Inquisition in Spain and Portugal and from the Spanish raids on Antwerp fled to a country with a long reputation for religious tolerance.

The first great name in European diamond cutting is Louis de Berquen. A native of Bruges, active in the fifteenth century, he is reputed to have been the first lapidary to use diamond powder in conjunction with a wheel in order to cut and polish diamonds with scientific precision. Some commentators believe that the story owes more to legend than fact and doubt that there ever was such a person as Louis de Berquen, but nevertheless a statue of him stands in the diamond district of Antwerp. In any case a Parisian jeweler, Robert de Berquen, writing in 1669, claimed to be a descendant and recounted a number of incidents in his ancestor's life.

A jeweler's workshop, as seen in Diderot's encyclopedia (1770). Note the grille which covers the floor; it is presumably for ease of recovering anything that might be dropped. **OVERLEAF** *Diamond cutters at work, another engraving from Diderot's encyclopedia. Note that the wheel is manually operated.*

Fig. 1.   Fig. 2.

Tavernier reported that the Indians certainly had the facility for cutting diamonds, although their obsession with weight-saving seems to have made them reluctant to indulge in anything more than the most cursory smoothing out of rough edges and polishing pits. Incompetent cutting of the Great Mogul, which reduced its weight from nearly 800 carats to just 280 carats, very nearly cost the life of the traveling Venetian cutter Hortensio Borgio. As it was, the furious owner of the diamond, Aurangzeb, the son of Shah Jehan, fined him 100,000 rupees, his entire fortune.

Tavernier's description of the equipment used at the Indian mines points out the differences between it and that which he must have had in his Paris workshop:

There are several Diamond Cutters at this Mine but none of them have above one Mill, which is of Steel. They never cut but one Stone at a time upon each Mill, to find out the grain of the Stone; which being found, they pour on Oil (not sparing for Powder of Diamonds, though it be very dear) to make the Stone slide the faster; and they lay on more weight than we do; . . . and the Mill was like ours, only the great Wheel was turned by four

Negroes . . . their Wheel does not go as fast as ours, because the Wooden-wheel that turns the Steel-wheel is not above three foot in Diameter.

The famous Italian goldsmith, Benvenuto Cellini described his method of cutting and polishing diamonds as follows:

One diamond is rubbed against another until by mutual abrasion both take a form which the skilled polisher wishes to achieve. With the powder which falls from the diamond, the last operation for the completion of the cut is made. For this purpose, the stones are fixed into small lead or tin cups and, with a special clamping device, held against a steel wheel which is provided with oil and diamond dust. This wheel must have the thickness of a finger and the size of the palm of the hand; it must consist of the finest well-hardened steel and be fixed to a mill-stone so that through the rotation of the latter, it also comes into rapid movement. At the same time four to six diamonds can be attached to the wheel. A weight placed on the clamping device can increase the friction of the stone against the moving wheel. In this way, the polishing is completed.

Cellini wrote his description in 1568, but a diamond cutter of today would feel very much at home in the Italian's workroom. And indeed, if it was Louis de Berquen, a hundred years earlier, who constructed the first polishing wheel to be used with diamond dust and devised the first systematic arrangement of the facets, then he fully deserves his popular image as the father of the diamond-cutting industry. There is, of course, a greater measure of mechanization and a far higher degree of skill as might be expected after five hundred years of experimentation, but the art of the cutter still relies very much on the eye and the hand.

Almost certainly the first regular cut was the table cut. It originated in India and involved taking an octahedron, flattening one point into a table and the opposite point into a smaller table, called the culet, and then bruting or grinding the four ribs above the girdle to provide facets on the upper part, the crown, and the four below to form facets on the lower part, the pavilion. It was this cut, along with its many variations, which dominated the European scene until well into the seventeenth century. The stone's octahedral origins were clearly in evidence, with the angle of the crown and the pavilion to the girdle usually remaining unchanged at 55°.

OVERLEAF *A view of the cutting works of Coster's in Amsterdam, c.1880. The factory was a popular tourist attraction, and in this picture the cutters are surrounded by a crowd of visitors.*

Like the Indian cutters, the Europeans at this time were more concerned with maximization of weight and preservation of the original outline of the stone than with brilliance.

Another early cut that tended to follow the shape of the rough was the rose cut. Flat underneath, the upper and convex part was covered in facets: twenty-four for a Holland Rose; eighteen to twenty for a Half Holland; and six to eight for an Antwerp Rose. Again, there were many variations on the cut, largely depending on the shape of the rough. A Double Rose was a diamond faceted in a dome on both sides, the first use of which is attributed to Louis de Berquen, when he cut the Florentine for Charles the Bold. Rounded stones were suitable for a bead cut and pear-shaped ones would become briolettes or pendeloques.

Depicted here are a variety of the diamond cuts used over the centuries. Because the rose cuts lack "fire," they are rarely used today. Only the emerald and baguette shapes are in current use, together with the three variations of the brilliant cut.

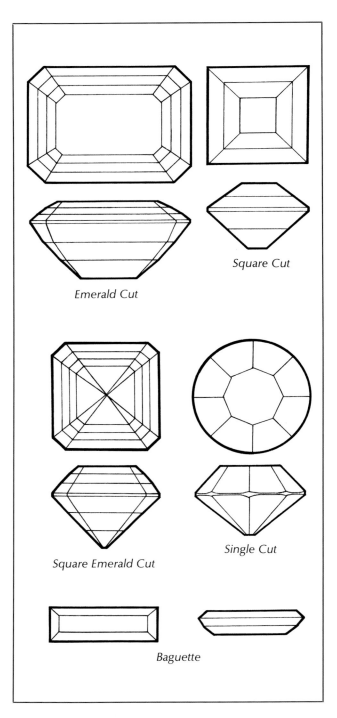

Emerald Cut

Square Cut

Square Emerald Cut

Single Cut

Baguette

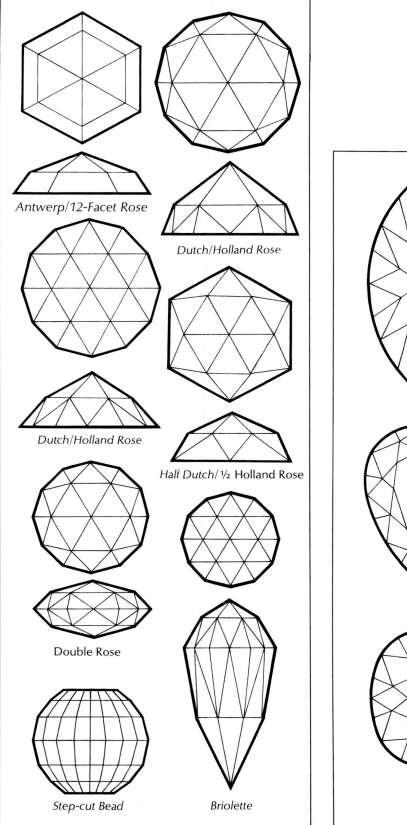

Antwerp/12-Facet Rose

Dutch/Holland Rose

Dutch/Holland Rose

Half Dutch/½ Holland Rose

Double Rose

Step-cut Bead

Briolette

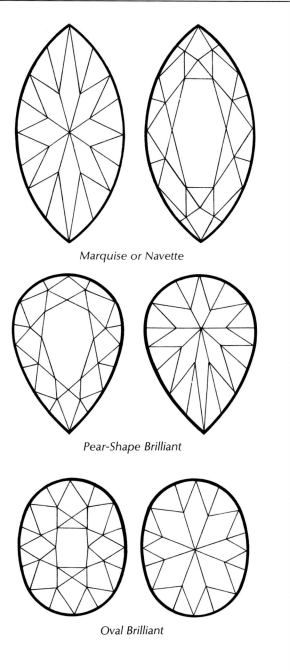

Marquise or Navette

Pear-Shape Brilliant

Oval Brilliant

ENGRAVING THE DIAMOND

Because of the extreme hardness of the diamond, few European lapidaries took to engraving them as they did other precious stones. As a result, the best-known engraved diamonds in the world are Indian diamonds—the Akbar Shah and the Shah, both from the Peacock Throne; and the Mumtaz Mahal, or Taylor Heart, presented to Elizabeth Taylor by Richard Burton in the early 1970s. However, there are a number of examples of this obscure branch of the engraver's art in museums and private collections, all carried out by European lapidaries. The first recorded example is that of the arms of Charles V, engraved by Jacopo da Trezzo in Milan in 1556. His pupil Clement Birago later engraved on another diamond a portrait of the Spanish prince Don Carlos.

According to the Privy Seal records, the sum of £267 was paid to one Francis Walwyn, on January 16, 1628, for "cutting, finishing and polishing a Diamond and engraving upon it the arms of Charles I with the initial letters of his Queen on each side." Francis Walwyn's expertise was obviously in great demand at the English court. The diamond signet ring used by Charles I when Prince of Wales, and engraved with the Prince of Wales's plume of feathers is also his work.

France, too, has produced several engraved diamonds of great historical interest. One is a thin stone engraved with the head of Napoleon. It was on display at the Paris Exhibition of 1867, but its present whereabouts are unknown. Another is a ring that once belonged to Marie Antoinette, which has at its center an oblong diamond inscribed with "Marie."

COLOR SEQUENCE *The stages in cutting the 248.9-carat rough known as the Baumgold Brown into the 111.59-carat pendeloque Earth Star.*

FIRST PAGE: ABOVE LEFT *The rough stone being marked before it goes to the cutting table.* **ABOVE RIGHT** *Alex Diamant, head cutter of Baumgold Bros., examines the stone after the table has been cut.* **BELOW** *The rough stone set in a dop, indicating the first "window" cut.*

CENTER PAGES *The second "window" in the process of being cut on the wheel (left), and the stone on the wheel for brillianteering (right).*

THIS PAGE *Before and after: the original 248.9-carat rough and the finished 111.59-carat pear-shaped brilliant.*

ENTIRE SEQUENCE COURTESY OF BAUMGOLD BROS. AND THE DIAMOND INFORMATION CENTER, NEW YORK

As diamonds grew in numbers and in popularity, the cutters inevitably acquired greater knowledge and skill. They had begun to understand the ability of a diamond to "play" with light and were learning to take advantage of the fact. One of the earliest faceted cuts which marked a step toward the modern brilliant was the Mazarin cut named after Cardinal Mazarin of France in the mid-seventeenth century. It was a cushion-shaped cut with seventeen facets above the girdle and seventeen below, but it still lost a great deal of light through the bottom and the sides.

The next step is generally attributed to a Venetian lapidary called Peruzzi who, in 1700, cut a total of fifty-eight facets on the crown and pavilion, the same number regarded as standard for a brilliant cut today. But if Peruzzi's cut retained much of the light lost by a Mazarin, it failed to demonstrate a diamond's refractive abilities at their best. It lacked "fire." Nevertheless the cut was a great advance, and with the popularity of diamonds boosted by the Brazilian finds, it became very much the standard for the next two centuries. A later variation called the triple cut or the old mine cut was the immediate precursor of what we now know as the modern brilliant.

The credit for the invention of the modern brilliant cut undoubtedly goes to Marcel Tolkowsky who, in 1919 at the age of twenty-one, published *Diamond Design*. In this book he set down for the first time the precise angles and proportions of the brilliant-cut diamond which would give the best optical results for both reflection and refraction. As has already been noted in "What Is a Diamond?", the angles of the facets which give maximum reflection of light back out of a diamond are not those which provide maximum refraction. What Marcel Tolkowsky did was to calculate the best compromise angles to give the greatest refraction or "fire" with the least loss of reflectivity or "life."

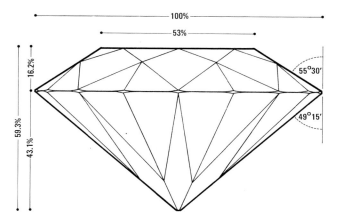

The modern brilliant-cut diamond, which is the result of theoretical calculations of the precise angles needed to provide the best optical effect.

There are two obvious differences between a modern brilliant and earlier brilliant cuts. One is the depth of the stone: the modern brilliant is much shallower than the old mine cut, for example, and involves a major departure from the angles of the original octahedron. The other is the shape of the girdle, which is now completely round instead of simply having the corners of the octahedral shape removed.

There have been some slight modifications to Tolkowsky's angles and proportions since 1919, notably in the Eppler Fine cut of 1940 and the Scandinavian Standard (Scan DN) in 1970, but his work remains the basis for the modern brilliant cut. Variations from the ideal standard occur constantly for a number of reasons. They may concern the positioning of flaws or inclusions, or the stone's color and clarity may be such that obtaining maximum weight becomes the prime objective.

The brilliant cut or round-cut diamond is deservedly popular as a result of its brilliance, its regular shape and standardization, and because most rough diamonds lend themselves to the cut with an average weight recovery of the order of 50 percent. But it is not the only cut. Approximately 2 percent of rough diamonds, because of their shape or flaws, cannot be cut into a round brilliant without an unacceptable loss of weight. It is these stones that are cut into the shapes known as marquise, pendeloques (pear-shaped or tear drop), oval, emerald, triangle and square cuts. As a group these are all classed as fancy cuts. The pendeloque is far and away the most rare. These cuts are more expensive than the ordinary round brilliant cut, because their cost of manufacture is high; but higher weight recovery should more than compensate for this factor. The emerald cut is used for long rough diamonds and although weight recovery is above average at approximately 60 percent, the cut sells at up to 25 percent less than a round brilliant because its long parallel facets fail to show the same degree of brilliance.

For all practical purposes, the smallest stone used today is a ½-pointer, of which there are 200 to the carat (there being 100 points to the carat). On stones up to 2 points in weight, single cuts (with twenty facets) are usually made, although full cuts can be made as small as 3/4-pointers (150 to the carat). The cutting of these very small stones is the basis of a cottage industry in Belgium in the Ardennes, and in France in the Jura mountains. The cutters come into the city to collect a stock of roughs and take them back for cutting on benches set up in their homes.

There are five processes* used in the creation of a polished gem from the rough:

1. Cleaving—splitting a stone along the cleavage plane.

*Because many of the words used in the diamond trade are taken from the Dutch, their adaptation to other languages often results in a variety of spellings; and, indeed, words used in one country may be totally unknown in another. For example, *brillianteer* is used in Britain, while in the USA and on the Continent *brilliandeer* is more common, and *girdling* may be preferred rather than *bruting* as the proper term for the rounding process. The word *scaife* is from the Dutch word for wheel, and is still used in traditional centers, but *wheel* is now commonly used.

2. Sawing—dividing a crystal by using a diamond saw.

3. Bruting—shaping a diamond by removing part of it by rubbing against another diamond.

4. Grinding or Blocking—making a flat surface by holding the crystal against a rotating wheel applied with diamond powder.

5. Brillianteering or Polishing—preparing the finished gem by a more refined application of grinding techniques.

But before anything at all is done to the stone, it is studied carefully by the cutter. Using a magnifying glass (usually a 10x loupe), or even the new polariscope in potentially difficult cases, he will examine the diamond in order to determine the direction of the grain, and the location of any inclusions or imperfections. He can then decide exactly how to cut the stone to produce the maximum value in its finished state.

The factors the cutter has to take into account are many and varied. For example, cleaving or sawing may not be necessary; very many diamonds are placed on the wheel exactly as they are. It is up to the cutter to decide whether he has to take away a large enough piece to warrant either cleaving or sawing. He may also be tempted to compromise on the ideal proportions by cutting the stone to gain weight. This he would do by reducing the height of the crown and adding to the width of the table. Cutting in this fashion can be worth as much as 10 percent in weight, and is commonly done to a diamond that would weigh just under a carat if cut to ideal proportions. However, as in everything to do with diamond cutting, the cutter's judgment is a fine one. He cannot deviate too far from the ideal proportions in his effort to gain weight, because the value of the additional weight may be more than offset by

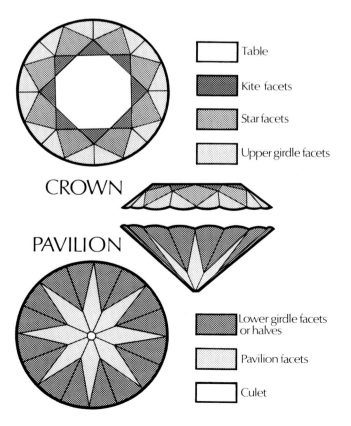

CROWN

PAVILION

Table

Kite facets

Star facets

Upper girdle facets

Lower girdle facets or halves

Pavilion facets

Culet

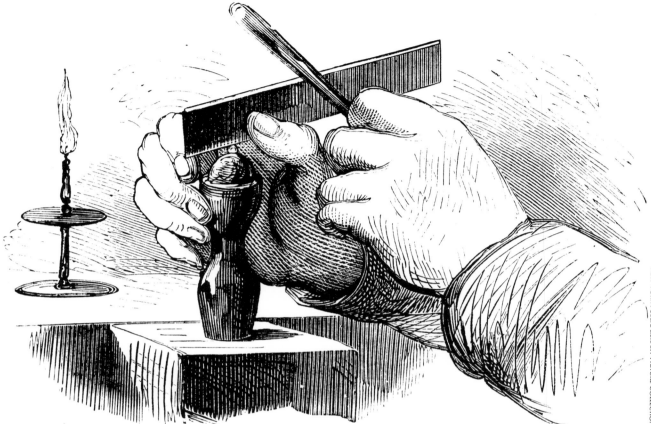

ABOVE *A diamond about to be cleaved, 1880.* **OPPOSITE** *Cutting the 601.25-carat Lesotho, the first diamond ever to be cleaved in public in front of television and movie cameras.* **ABOVE LEFT** *The cutter prepares to cleave the stone into two pieces.* **ABOVE RIGHT** *Operation a success.* **BELOW** *Before and after: the rough Lesotho (center) surrounded by the eighteen gems that it eventually provided. The aggregate weight of the stones recovered was 242.5 carats, a loss of about 60 percent.*

the loss in value attributed to a bad "make." (The closeness of the finished brilliant to the ideal proportions is known as its "make.")

Having decided what shape the stone is to be, the cutter will mark it with India ink to show where the first division is to be made, either by cleaving or by sawing.

Cleaving: This is the method used for dividing large irregular stones without crystal faces. It is done with the grain. The diamond is placed in the little cup, called the dop, at the end of an eight-inch wooden stick, and set there with a cleaver cement made out of a mixture of shellac, rosin and brickdust. The cleaver then makes a small notch, or kerf, in the stone using another diamond to do so and sets the stick holding the diamond to be cleaved upright in

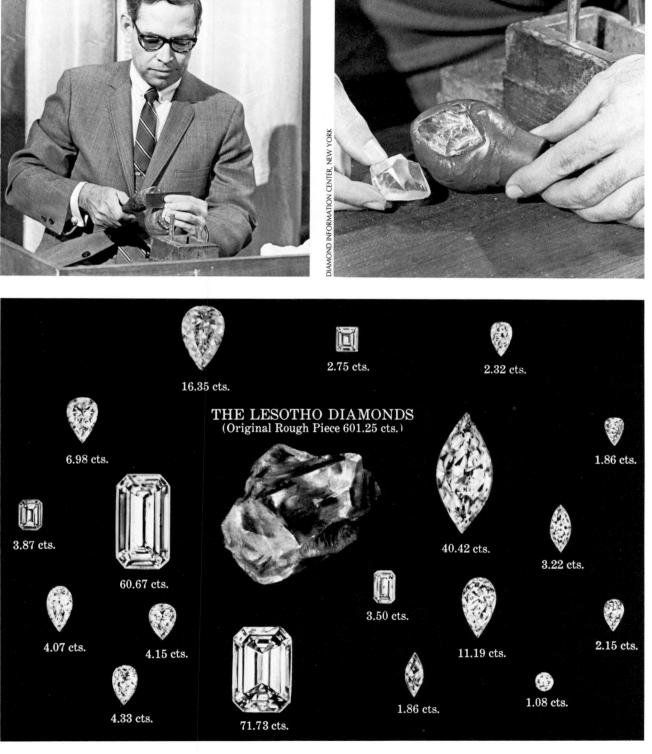

2.75 cts.

16.35 cts.

2.32 cts.

6.98 cts.

THE LESOTHO DIAMONDS
(Original Rough Piece 601.25 cts.)

1.86 cts.

3.87 cts.

60.67 cts.

40.42 cts.

3.22 cts.

3.50 cts.

4.07 cts.

4.15 cts.

11.19 cts.

2.15 cts.

4.33 cts.

71.73 cts.

1.86 cts.

1.08 cts.

DIAMOND INFORMATION CENTER, NEW YORK

a tapered hole in the workbench. He then places a knife blade in the kerf, and strikes it sharply with either a wooden mallet or an iron rod. The stone should then split along the cleavage plane.

The art of the cleaver has always been regarded as the greatest talent in the diamond cutting industry. In the early part of this century, the cleavers of Amsterdam would arrive at work in the morning, often in their own carriage, wearing high silk hats. They were the aristocrats of the diamond world.

Because of the existence of stress points in a diamond, there is always some risk involved in the cleaving process. The invention of the mechanical saw has meant that sawing, rather than cleaving, is now done almost exclusively. For large stones, however, there may be no alternative to cleaving; and on such occasions, the cleaver once again takes his place in the sun.

A bank of sawing machines in a modern cutting factory. Because it takes hours to saw through even a small diamond, it is essential that many machines operate simultaneously. The process may appear to be automatic, but the machines are constantly checked to see that the cutting is progressing satisfactorily.

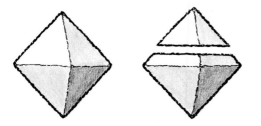

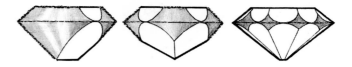

Sawing: Clean regular octahedra are normally divided by sawing. The diamond cutter is said to "saw grain"—that is, he cuts in a noncleaving direction. The diamond to be sawn is set in a holder at the end of a mechanical arm which allows the stone to rest by its own weight against the blade of the saw. The saw itself is a wafer-thin disc of phosphor bronze, the edge of which is coated with a paste of olive oil and diamond dust. The disc revolves at between 4,500 and 6,500 rpm, but it still takes forty minutes to saw through an average .25-carat octahedron, and between two hours and a whole day to divide a stone of 1 carat.

against the scaife, a flat, revolving cast-iron wheel dressed with olive oil and diamond dust. First, he grinds the table of the diamond and then a crown or bezel facet between the girdle and the table, followed by a second crown facet exactly opposite the first and another facet on either side between the first two. The stone is then turned over and four pavilion facets are ground below the girdle. These eight facets are followed by four more on the crown and four more on the pavilion. The next step is to grind the culet facet, at the base of the diamond where the pavilion facets meet. It should be exactly parallel to the table. The blocker then polishes the facets he has cut by swinging the tang across the polishing ring on the scaife.

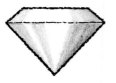

Bruting or Girdling: The next step is to shape the sawn or cleaved stone into a circular outline. This is done by setting the stone to be rounded in a holder on a revolving shaft and holding another diamond against it. The result of this very skilled operation should be a diamond with a perfectly rounded girdle set exactly parallel to the table. The diamond used as a tool is usually itself a rough and will be bruted in its turn.

Grinding or Blocking: The partly finished stone is now ready for faceting. The blocker mounts the diamond in a dop on the end of a mechanical arm called a tang and places it

Brillianteering: The brillianteerer completes the whole operation by adding the remaining forty facets, twenty-four above the girdle and sixteen below it. First of all he cuts eight star facets where the crown facets meet the table, and then sixteen girdle facets where they meet the girdle. Finally he cuts two long facets called halves into each of the pavilion facets. All the facets are then polished.

The cutting process is a long and exacting one and the cutters stop and check the accuracy of their work continuously. An experienced cutter can develop exceptional skill; and working by eye alone, he can achieve the required angles to within a few minutes of a degree by aligning edges and reflections of edges.

HOW TO RECOGNIZE A DIAMOND

Despite the apparent familiarity the general public has with diamonds either as a result of owning them or constantly looking at them in jewelers' windows, the fact remains that not only can very few people distinguish between a good diamond and a bad one, they do not even know if what they are looking at is a diamond at all. It is unhappily true that the average jeweler is not much better informed about what may be his principal stock-in-trade. He relies on the integrity of his wholesaler for the supply of diamonds priced according to their quality, and on a few simple rules of thumb when he acts as an appraiser for a customer.

On the matter of quality and thus the value of a cut diamond, the criteria are known as the "4 Cs." They are Color, Clarity, Cut and Carat. Obviously, it helps to have apparatus like spectroscopes and spectrophotometers, stereomicroscopes, electric balances and also proportionscopes, but a knowledge of the basic techniques enables a fairly accurate assessment of a diamond to be made with nothing more than a 10x loupe and the human eye.

Color

The point of color grading is to mark the degrees of deviation from the whitest possible stone down to the yellowest which is still acceptable as being of gem quality. There are a number of grading systems in use, but the most widely accepted internationally has become that of the Gemological Institute of America (GIA). Their grading letters may seem a little unromantic when compared with the more descriptive and emotive terminology of some of the other systems, but they leave less room for doubt, a fact which can only be of benefit to the trade and the public. For example, the term *blue white*—which is commonly accepted by the public as indicative of the highest quality—is notoriously misleading and while its use is forbidden to members of the National Association of Goldsmiths in the United Kingdom and the American Gem Society, it is still widely used by other jewelers. Strictly speaking, blue white should apply only to an extremely rare type of white stone. As Eric Bruton comments in his encyclopedic work *Diamonds,* "it is probably true to say that 99 percent of the diamonds sold retail as blue-white are not only not blue-white, but are not even in the top five color grades."

The most commonly accepted grading systems at the moment (e.g., see the chart on page 180) are the two American ones already mentioned— the GIA and the Amer-

ican Gem Society—another devised by the Scandinavian countries in 1970 and known as the Scandinavian Diamond Nomenclature and Grading Standards (usually shortened to Scan DN), and that of the National Association of Goldsmiths used in the United Kingdom. It should be noted that the comparison scale may differ markedly in its various versions, simply because the categories are all demarcated by the human eye and thus inevitably subjective.

Color judgment is not easily acquired and a beginner, for example, would detect no trace of color in the grades down to L on the GIA scale and its equivalents. This is particularly true when the diamond is viewed from the front and the eye confused by the spectrum colors. Grading is therefore carried out by holding the diamond in a slim V-shaped piece of white paper or card and viewing it through the side. Long practice will enable the grader to distinguish more and more finely between stones, but to aid the process, many use grading stones of ascertained color as a basis for comparison. Lighting is vitally important. Sunlight, for example, contains ultraviolet light, which can cause the diamond being examined to fluoresce very slightly blue but enough to hide any hint of yellow. This is in part why the windows of the sorting rooms of the Diamond Trading Company in London all face north. (It must be noted, however, that this only serves to minimize glare. Ultraviolet light is, of course, always present in daylight.)

The terms *river* and *Wesselton* refer to two particularly fine types of diamond found most commonly in the river diggings and in the Wesselton Mine. Unlike blue white, they are regarded as legitimate terms to use. Tiffany's, for example, calls its top color grade "extra river."

Clarity
Having ascertained a diamond's color, the

CLARITY GRADING SYSTEMS—A COMPARATIVE VIEW

UK	GIA	SCAN DN	
Flawless	FL	FL	No internal or external flaws.
		IF	Internally flawless, but with minor surface imperfections, which can be easily removed by polishing.
VVS	VVS_1 VVS_2	VVS_1 VVS_2	Very, very small inclusions or spots outside the table and not easily visible, or minor external imperfections.
VS	VS_1 VS_2	VS_1 VS_2	Very small inclusions, but larger and a little more obvious than in VVS_1 and VVS_2.
SI	SI_1 SI_2	SI_1 SI_2	Small inclusions or surface marks which are more obtrusive than in VS_1 and VS_2.
1st Piqué 2nd 3rd	I_1 I_2	1st Piqué 2nd Piqué	Inclusions or surface damage now visible to the naked eye and affecting the table.
Spotted	I_3	3rd Piqué	Larger and darker inclusions which can be easily seen through the table. Scratched table.
Heavy spotted			Very obvious dark spots under table and pronounced surface damage.

next step is to grade it according to clarity by assessing its degree of freedom from imperfections. This can be done simply by using a 10x loupe and examining the stone both internally and externally. Clarity grading is more straightforward than color grading, but arguable classifications can still arise. Once again there is no universally accepted standard despite the apparently close correspondence between the standards used in the United States, in the United Kingdom and in Scandinavia.

The grades range down from "flawless" for a stone which is totally transparent and free from internal marks of any sort when seen through a 10x lens to "heavy spotted," where the marks or inclusions are clearly visible to the naked eye. Contrary to popular opinion,

very few inclusions are actually carbon spots, and many spots which appear black may not be inclusions at all but simply other varieties of imperfection. They may be tiny bubbles or groups of bubbles, called clouds; cleavage cracks, called feathers or butterflies; or naats (from the Dutch), which are similar to knots in wood and arise from the contact point of twinned crystals. Marks on the surface of the diamond are taken into account as well as internal flaws; also included are minor imperfections resulting from cutting. But again, problems can and do arise from the fact that certain flaws are acceptable under some classifications and not under others. The various classifications and their explanation are shown in the chart above.

A number of reputable firms make up their

COLOR GRADING SYSTEMS— A COMPARATIVE VIEW

AGS	GIA	SCAN DN under 0.50 ct	SCAN DN 0.50 ct & over	UK
0	D	RAREST WHITE	RIVER	FINEST WHITE (BLUE-WHITE)
	E			
1	F	WHITE	TOP WESSELTON	FINE WHITE
2	G			
	H		WESSELTON	WHITE
3	I	TINTED WHITE	TOP CRYSTAL	COMMERCIAL WHITE
4	J		CRYSTAL	TOP SILVER CAPE
5	K			
6	L	YELLOWISH	TOP CAPE	SILVER CAPE
	M		CAPE	LIGHT CAPE
7	N			
	O			
	P		LIGHT YELLOW	CAPE
8	Q			
	R			
		YELLOW	YELLOW	DARK CAPE
9–10	S–X			

OPPOSITE AND ABOVE *A certificate of the type supplied by the Diamond Grading Laboratories of London's Hatton Garden. The most advanced laboratory techniques are used to grade the diamond, and a unique feature is the incorporation of the diamond's "fingerprint" which ties the certificate irrevocably to the stone. This "fingerprint" is a photograph taken by interference contrast techniques of the pattern of natural crystal growth individual to each diamond and which remains unaltered after cutting and polishing.*

own classifications. Tiffany's, for example, grades its stones into five types. If no flaws are visible through a 10x lens, the stone is graded "flawless." If a slight flaw is visible, it is graded M_1 or M_2 depending upon it size (M means microscopic). The third class is VS_1 (very small), the fourth S (small), and the fifth and final category is "imperfect" where the flaw can be seen with the naked eye.

Inclusions are tiny crystals of other minerals that crystallized at the same time as the diamond. The vast majority of diamonds have such inclusions, usually crystals of olivine and garnet.

Cut

Diamond cutting is a craft that requires great skill; inevitably though, some cutters will fall short of perfection and turn out misshapen stones. This is not the same as deliberately producing a stone which does not conform with the ideal proportions, since the aim may be to eliminate otherwise awkwardly positioned flaws or to balance weight against quality. In such cases the "make" of the diamond, as the cut is called, may not fit the ideal but it will not be very far off; and the advantages of cutting it in this way will probably outweigh the disadvantages as a result of gains in weight and clarity. A badly cut stone is something else. It may be asymmetrical, or have badly positioned facets of varying sizes, or a culet which is not central. The crown may be too shallow or too deep, the girdle too thin, or the culet too pointed.

With practice it is relatively easy to assess proportions by eye alone, especially by using the reflections in the table of the stone as a guide. A stone with a pavilion that is too shallow will reveal a circular reflection of the girdle when viewed through the table, giving a "fish-eye" effect. Too deep a pavilion, on the other hand, will throw up a black reflection in the center of the table.

Diamond Grading Laboratories Limited

We hereby certify that the following information is a factual record of tests carried out using Diamond Grading Laboratories' systems

Petersham House,
57A, Hatton Garden, London, EC1N 8EX.
Telephone 01-405 8045 or 01-405 7034
Telex 23457

Natural/~~Synthetic~~ Diamond

Certificate No. 7000

The stone was unmounted
for examination.

(Red symbols denote internal characteristics; green, external. Symbols indicate nature and position of characteristics, not necessarily their size.)

Carat Weight	1.10	Cut	ROUND BRILLIANT
Clarity Grade *	23		
Colour Grade *	426	By DGL Spectrophotometer	
		By DGL Calibrated Masterstones	
Finish/Make *	GOOD		
Fluorescence *	SLIGHT, WHITE (4)		

Dimensions	Millimeters	Percentage of Average Diameter	Scan DN* Ideal Percentage
Diameter Maximum	6.78		
Diameter Minimum	6.72		
Average Diameter	6.75		
Total Depth	4.00	59.3	58.0
Table Spread	4.20	62.2	57.5
Crown Height	0.80	11.9	14.6
Pavilion Depth	3.00	44.4	43.1
Girdle Thickness	0.20		
Culet Size	GOOD	*See Overleaf	

IDENTIPRINT from TABLE

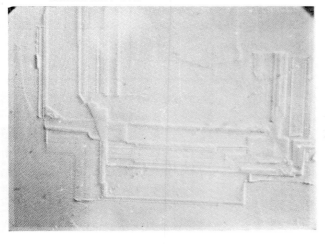

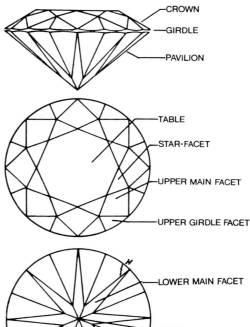

CROWN
GIRDLE
PAVILION

TABLE
STAR-FACET
UPPER MAIN FACET
UPPER GIRDLE FACET

LOWER MAIN FACET
CULET
LOWER GIRDLE FACET

COMMENTS

Director's Signature   *Date*

SPECIMEN   21.1.1975

Carat

The weight of a diamond is measured in carats, an ancient measuring unit derived from the seeds of the carob tree. These small black beans are remarkably uniform in weight, but an international standard metric carat has now been agreed upon which is equal to 0.2 gram. There are 142 carats to the ounce and the carat is commonly divided into 100 points. Diamonds of less than 1 carat in weight are known as "pointers."

A small portable chemical scale can be used to weigh diamonds to within a hundredth part of a carat, although many jewelers now use more sophisticated electric balances. It is possible to judge weights by measurement of standard brilliant-cut stones, but it must be realized that assessments made on the basis of this sort of guide can only be approximate.

Valuation

All four Cs are taken into account in arriving at a value for a diamond, and a flawless 1-carat stone of good color will be worth more than a heavy spotted 3-carat light yellow. Nevertheless, given that a diamond is of good color, clarity and cut, carat weight is the most critical factor in determining price. One reason for this, apart from the scarcity of the bigger stones, is that while fashion and local taste may affect the desirability of color and the extreme rarity of the truly flawless diamond increases the demand for slightly less-perfect stones, weight remains the only constant and easily calculable factor under the grading systems most commonly used today.

The price of diamonds increases sharply as the successive carat barriers are crossed, and the same applies for weights below 1 carat, at the 25-, 50-, and 75-point marks. This has always been the case since Tavernier first published in 1679 the basis on which prices were calculated by the Indian merchants and

VALUE OF BRILLIANTS UP TO FIVE CARATS.

The Prices given below are those of perfectly white and pure Brilliants, free from defects or flaws, of the proportions shown, and liable to variation with the changes of the market.

				Value in 1865.	
				£	s.
A Brilliant weighing	½	of a carat	. . .	6	0
,,	¾	,,	. . .	11	0
,,	1	,,	. . .	21	0
,,	1¼	,,	. . .	35	0
,,	1½	,,	. . .	45	0
,,	1¾	,,	. . .	55	0
,,	2	,,	. . .	80	0
,,	2¼	,,	. . .	90	0
,,	2½	,,	. . .	110	0
,,	2¾	,,	. . .	120	0
,,	3	,,	. . .	140	0
,,	3¼	,,	. . .	150	0
,,	3½	,,	. . .	175	0
,,	3¾	,,	. . .	190	0
,,	4	,,	. . .	220	0
,,	4¼	,,	. . .	240	0
,,	4½	,,	. . .	300	0
,,	4¾	,,	. . .	330	0
,,	5	,,	. . .	350	0

Weight by which Diamonds and precious stones are calculated.

4 grains	. . . . .	1 carat.
151½ carats	. . . . .	1 oz. troy.

The progress of diamond prices over the past century has not been one of uninterrupted advance despite the obvious disparity between those ruling in 1865 and today. In 1874, for example, the vastly increased production from the newly opened South African mines caused diamond prices to slump to less than £1 ($5) a carat, and it is only since De Beers achieved complete control of both production and marketing in the 1930s that a steady advance has been seen. The prices shown here relate to cut diamonds, and a rule of thumb dictates that the cost of cutting doubles the price per carat despite the loss of approximately half the weight. In other words, a 1-carat brilliant would be priced at much the same figure as the 2-carat rough from which it was cut. A "perfectly white and pure Brilliant . . . free from defects or flaws" as described in this list of 1865 would equate with a D (color) and FL (clarity) grading according to the GIA scale, and the medium price in February 1977 (before the 15 percent increase in March) for a 1-carat stone was nearly $16,000 as against £21, or approximately $100, just over a century earlier. The high premium which a top-quality stone commands is shown by the fact that a good but lower quality 1-carat diamond of H-J color and VSI clarity would have a medium price of around $3,500.

OFFICIAL DIAMOND PRICE INCREASES SINCE WORLD WAR II

This table shows (in arithmetic form) the record of official diamond price increases anounced by the Diamond Trading Corporation over the past thirty years. There are two main components behind any price increase: the market factor and the currency factor, the importance of the latter being dramatically shown in the table.

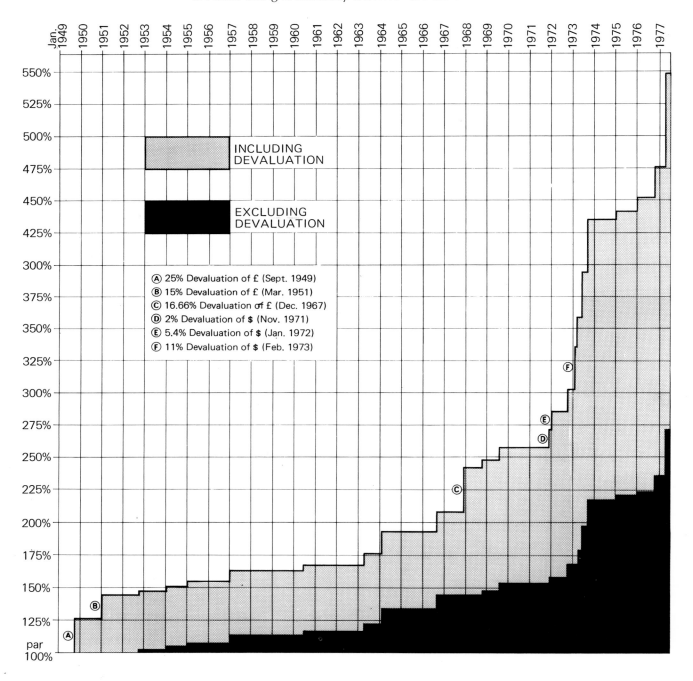

INCLUDING DEVALUATION

EXCLUDING DEVALUATION

(A) 25% Devaluation of £ (Sept. 1949)
(B) 15% Devaluation of £ (Mar. 1951)
(C) 16.66% Devaluation of £ (Dec. 1967)
(D) 2% Devaluation of $ (Nov. 1971)
(E) 5.4% Devaluation of $ (Jan. 1972)
(F) 11% Devaluation of $ (Feb. 1973)

gave us "the rule to know the just price and value of a Diamond of what weight soever . . . a secret known to very few people in Europe." It was a simple squaring rule, whereby the value of a single carat would be multiplied by the square of the weight of the stone to be priced. Thus if a 1-carat stone was worth 150 livres, as it was in Tavernier's day, then a 5-carat stone would be priced at 3,750 livres. The Parisian jeweler Robert de Berquen used very similar calculations in tables published in 1669, as did the jeweler David Jeffries in London in 1750. It should be noted that today once a stone reaches a weight of x plus 0.8 carats (x being any whole number), it is valued as if it were in the whole carat range immediately above it. Thus a 3.8- or a 3.9-carat diamond is valued by multiplying its weight by the figure appropriate to the 4-carat range.

There have obviously been changes in the pattern of demand over the past three centuries, but this rule of thumb remains remarkably accurate until the higher carat weights are reached. For example, with a fine 1-carat stone running at about $8,000 today, a stone of 100 carats would work out at $80 million on the squaring rule instead of the round $1 million it might be expected to fetch.

Colored or "fancy" diamonds are in a world of their own, and the only reasonable guide is what a similar stone may have fetched at auction. A price of almost $1 million was recorded in 1976 for a lilac pink diamond of just 24.44 carats, making the highest price per carat yet recorded. The stone was purchased on behalf of a Saudi Arabian jeweler, a fact that demonstrates how economic circumstances can effect the value of a rare diamond—or indeed any object that is virtually unique.

We now come onto rather difficult ground. At the beginning of this chapter it was stated that "a fairly accurate" assessment of a diamond can be made with nothing more than a 10x loupe and the human eye. But it must also be pointed out that this is exactly how diamonds are most commonly graded and valued even though tens and even hundreds of thousands of dollars may rest upon that judgment. Hence the furor over the colored diamond sold by Christie's in Geneva in 1971 and the one withdrawn from the same saleroom in 1976. One expert's opinion is simply not the same as another's, but while such disputes may be inevitable and acceptable in the art market—is a painting really by Raphael or by a talented pupil?—it is difficult to understand why opinion should be the final arbiter in a case where fact is easily ascertainable if the proper equipment is used. Weight can be measured by the Oertling electric balance to a thousandth part of a carat; color can be determined by a spectrophotometer, using pure barium sulphate powder as the standard of whiteness; clarity or purity can be ascertained by examination under a stereomicroscope; and cut can be judged by using the proportionscope, which throws a magnified shadow of the stone onto a diagram of the ideal proportions etched on a screen.

As far as categorizing diamonds for investment purposes, such a rigid, unequivocal international grading system is essential, and it is the advent of the diamond as an investment

DIAMONDS AS AN INVESTMENT

There is no alternative to a precise system of grading by scientific testing of color, clarity, cut and carat if the diamond is to become an acceptable international medium of investment. Unsystematic and subjective standards up until now have militated against the establishment of the diamond in such a role. However, the picture appears to be changing despite the apparent reluctance of the diamond trade to amend their traditional testing procedures and the move is likely to gather pace as investors become unwilling to hazard ever larger sums of money on arguable opinions.

But apart from the revolution in grading techniques, the diamond trade is also being disturbed by the whole concept of the diamond as a medium of investment. The doubts are very understandable in that the creation of a large pool of diamonds held as investments implies the establishment in due course of a secondary source of supply of diamonds in a trade that relies for its stability on one single source. Fears have therefore been expressed that "investment diamonds" could build up a potential for wrecking the market by disturbing the careful control of supply that De Beers has exercised since the early 1930s.

Such fears are almost certainly greatly overstated. The market for investment diamonds is small and specialized in that it is restricted to high-quality stones within narrow weight brackets (ideally from 0.45 to 1.65 carats) which form far too small a proportion of the total supply to have any significant effect upon it in the future. The possibility exists, of course, that many less-reputable firms will arise, as indeed they already have, with the object of selling lower-quality stones on the basis of subjective grading techniques. But if this happens, the danger will not be to the trade but to the gullible investor. The best firms do not promise a quick return but strictly advise at least a five- to ten-year minimum holding period. On this basis top-quality diamonds have proved an outstanding investment over the past forty years, and given the prospect of growing demand allied with a decreasing supply—all known reserves are likely to be depleted within the next forty years at the current rate of extraction—there is little reason to doubt the investment merits of diamonds over the next decade.

medium that has given a new impetus to fact rather than opinion as a basis for the judgment of quality. There can be nothing but trouble for investors and dealers alike in a system where it is possible to pay $20,000 for a diamond judged as "D" and flawless by an expert in the GIA in New York which a London gemologist might rank as "Fine White" and VVS and thus worth perhaps only $15,000.

Having said that few people, jewelers included, can tell a good diamond from a bad one, it is probably true to say that many do not even know if what they are looking at is a diamond at all. Since diamond has been extensively copied from the earliest days, it is worth listing a few simple tests which anyone can use as a guide to determine whether a stone is in fact a diamond or simply one of its many simulants. The tests may not be decisive but they are useful for someone without ready access to a microscope, a spectroscope or X-ray apparatus. It is a great advantage to be able to examine a stone unset, but in most cases this will not be possible. There is one advantage in seeing a diamond in its setting, however, and that is that the setting itself may provide a valuable clue to the nature of the stone.

The setting
It might be thought that a diamond is not usually going to be found in a cheap gold setting, or even in a good-quality silver one. This is broadly true of modern jewelry but it is not such a good guide for antique jewelry where silver settings were much used to show off the diamond to its best advantage just as white gold or platinum are used today. A diamond may be set open and held by claws, or set close with the rim and base enclosed, but many simulants would be close set. The reason for this is not necessarily the intent to

Simulants versus diamonds

deceive, but the desire to keep the base airtight to prevent tarnishing of the foil backing which is often applied to increase brilliance or give color. In older jewelry, in the days before the brilliant cut was developed, foil was used for diamonds as well as simulants since it provided the brilliance which was otherwise lacking. Painting the backs of stones was another method used to induce extra brilliance or false color. George Kunz, the celebrated nineteenth-century American gemologist, recorded that he discovered by using his fingernail that the famous rainbow necklace of the Romanoffs was nothing but a string of second-rate diamonds with painted backs.

General appearance

A genuine diamond has a degree of luster which is not matched by any of its imitators because its hardness allows it to be polished to a unique finish; but for anyone not familiar with diamonds, it is essential to have an undoubted diamond at hand to give some standard for comparison. The high reflectivity of a brilliant-cut stone also provides a useful standard since the fact that most of the light entering from the front is reflected back means that it is not possible to look right through it from the top. This is not the case with most simulants. A good test for transparency is to hold the stone, culet down, on the page of a book or a newspaper. However, this is not an infallible test both because the simulants may be backed to disguise their greater transparency, and because older, prebrilliant cut diamonds will let more light escape from the back and therefore have a greater degree of transparency.

The amount of wear or chipping on the edges and corners is often said to be another good indication of whether the stone in question is a diamond or not, but this is not really so. Hard though they are, diamonds are very liable to damage, especially when they are allowed to jostle against each other in a jewelry box. The most vulnerable points are at the top and the girdle, and these may show considerable damage.

Hardness
The standard test of a diamond's hardness used to be to hit it with a hammer. As explained earlier, this is a dangerous and a useless test which is not likely to be employed today. Another dangerous practice is to attempt to use a polished diamond to scratch another material. The test may be conclusive if the girdle or the culet scratches a piece of corondum, a ruby or a sapphire, but the edges of the diamond may not survive unscathed. The popular belief that a diamond will cut glass is also founded in fact, but the test is not of much practical value since so do many other materials.

Refractivity
The high refractive index of diamond can be used as a test by placing the stone in a highly refractive liquid in a white cup. A diamond will stand out clearly while many simulants will be much less visible. This is a negative test since a number of simulants also have high refractive indices and will also be clearly visible. Again, it helps to have a known diamond to provide a standard of comparison. The liquid most commonly used is monobromonapthalene; benzene can also be employed, despite its slightly lower refractive index.

Other tests involve:
1. The surface tension of the diamond, whereby a drop of water placed on the table of the diamond will persist as a globule for much longer than on any other type of stone.

2. Its high thermal conductivity, which means that a diamond is colder to the touch than other gems and becomes warm much more quickly when held close to the body.

3. The refractive quality of the diamond, which allows it to present a single image of the culet and back facets whereas many simulants are double-refracting and thus present a double image. This test can be carried out with a normal loupe.

4. The weight of the diamond, since no simulants have exactly the same weight/size ratio. Strontium titanate, for example, is much heavier than a diamond of the same size.

5. Certain internal features, such as cleavage which are not present in any other simulant with the exception of topaz. The cleavage fissure looks like a line edge-on or as a patch when seen from the front.

6. The accuracy of the cut. It might be assumed that the accuracy of the cut could be a giveaway based on the reasoning that more time and trouble would be taken in cutting a diamond than in cutting a simulant. However, the reverse is true. The simulant, being much softer, is easier to cut, and the angles and meeting points of the facets are usually much more precise. By the same token, however, the edges will tend to "burn" during the cutting process and thus appear less sharp.

The principal simulants are:

1. Paste: This is simply high-density lead glass and is far and away the most commonly used material to simulate diamond. It was very popular in the eighteenth century and can be found in very fine settings. It is sometimes called "strass" after G. F. Strass, the manufacturer of a particularly fine type of paste. With a hardness rating of only 5 on the Mohs scale, paste tends to show signs of wear very quickly, and can be detected by the hardness test. It lacks luster.

2. Yttrium aluminum garnet: Also known as YAG or diamonair, this is a synthetic material first created in 1969, and generally considered to be the best simulant yet. It is very hard (8 ½ on the Mohs scale), takes an excellent luster, and is principally distinguishable from diamond by its lower refractive index. Heavier than diamond, were it cut to the size of a 1-carat diamond, it would weigh 1.28 carats. It was used by Elizabeth Taylor to duplicate the 69.42-carat, pear-shaped diamond given to her by Richard Burton.

3. Strontium titanate: Also known as fabulite and starilian, this is another synthetic material first manufactured in 1953. It is relatively soft with a Mohs rating of 6, and thus is liable to show marked signs of wear. Its dispersion is excellent, but this in itself is a giveaway since it creates an effect that has been described as "flashy." It is heavier than diamond, a piece the size of a 1-carat diamond weighing 1.46 carats.

4. Synthetic rutile: Frequently used as a diamond simulant since its introduction in 1948, this titanium compound has a faint yellowish tinge. It can be relatively easily distinguished from diamond by its high double refractivity which shows up clearly in the doubling of the back facets.

5. Synthetic spinel and synthetic sapphire: Frequently used to provide the small stones surrounding a large colored stone, both these simulants are distinguishable by their low refractivity which causes them to almost disappear during the immersion test. This is a useful test for spotting whether these synthetics have been used to replace missing diamonds in a cluster.

6. Zircon: A common simulant, colorless zircon can be very deceptive because of its similarity to diamond in hardness, refractive index and dispersion. What gives it away is its

considerable double refraction, which can be clearly seen with a hand lens. It also has a distinctive steely appearance.

7. Topaz: Often passed off as diamond, especially in the East, the similarity is not as great as that of most synthetic simulants. It lacks fire and brilliance and is also double-refracting, but the simplest test is the immersion one: topaz becomes even fainter than synthetic spinel.

8. Quartz (rock crystal): Commonly mistaken for diamond by the inexpert, quartz is almost the diamond's equivalent of "fool's gold." Like topaz, quartz has no real fire or brilliance, and it also feels tacky to the touch.

9. Doublets: There is little doubt of their intention to deceive, since doublets consist of a crown of diamond cemented to a pavilion of some simulant. Almost invariably close set, they can usually be distinguished by the presence of bubbles in the cement layer and also by the reflection of the table which often appears in the layer of cement. Doublets may even consist of two layers of diamond with the aim of simulating one large diamond.

Colored and irradiated diamonds

The other great problem area in recognizing a diamond for what it really is is that of color, since attempts are frequently made either to give a diamond a rare and distinctive color or to conceal a less desirable one. The latter can be achieved by applying a colored coating to a small area of the stone, usually to the girdle where it will be concealed by the mount. The principle is that the mixing of complementary colors will produce white light, and thus a yellowish tinge can be effectively removed by the application of a small area of violet. Early methods involved the use of dyes, inks and even indelible pencils, where simple washing was enough to remove them. Later coatings, however, are applied in the same way as they are to optical lenses and are difficult to remove save by boiling in acid. The latest ultra-thin coatings are not detectable by normal chemical or X-ray tests and there is little doubt that there are many diamonds in existence looking better than they should.

As for actually coloring stones, this is done by irradiation in a cyclotron or in an atomic pile. This damages the crystal lattice and alters the light absorption capabilities of the diamond. The process usually results in a greenish color of varying intensity depending upon the length of time of exposure, but it is not the apple green of the extremely rare natural stone. Stones treated in this way can be detected by spectrophotometer examination, which will reveal distinctive light absorption bands which would not otherwise be present. In order to get colors other than green, an irradiated diamond has to be subjected to heat treatment for a number of hours at a temperature of between 500° and 900 °C. This will change the color to yellow or golden brown. A certain rare type of diamond known as Type IIb (see p. 263) will become red or purple. The nature of the irradiation determines whether the new color is only skin deep or whether it penetrates right through to the heart of the stone. Only neutron bombardment in an atomic pile could achieve the latter effect.

Detection of a falsely colored diamond can be difficult without gemological laboratory equipment, but the shades of color are usually enough to arouse the suspicions of an experienced diamond man. Furthermore, the very high cost of a large colored diamond will prompt most potential buyers to call for a laboratory examination.

Mistakes were made, however, even in the highest reaches of the trade, when the practice of irradiation was not generally known about. Christie's, the famous London saleroom, in 1971 sold a 104.52-carat golden yellow diamond which was subsequently found to have been artificially colored. And in 1976 the same auctioneers withdrew a "superb" canary yellow rectangular-cut diamond valued at over a million dollars because its authenticity had been challenged. The 39.87-carat stone had been certified as "flawless and of natural color" by the Swiss Foundation for the Research of Gemstones in Zurich, but a potential buyer, M. Jacques Arpels of Van Cleef & Arpels in Paris, insisted that a further expert opinion should be obtained. The diamond has now been sent to the Gemological Institute of America for testing, and at the time of writing, their decision has not been made public. It was Van Cleef & Arpels who had bought the falsely colored diamond in 1971. Cases have recently been reported where the diamond has been irradiated in the rough, and it therefore is no longer enough to claim that a color must be genuine because it was that color in its uncut state. Irradiation of diamonds with the object of changing their color is not illegal, and the process is carried out commercially by a laboratory in New York.

BAUBLES, BANGLES AND BEADS

Diamonds were initially prized more for their magical powers than for their beauty, and worn as talismans rather than as objects of personal adornment. It took over five centuries for them to achieve their present preeminent status in jewelry. The process was a gradual one, moving through four stages.

The first stage came about in the second half of the fifteenth century when the art of cutting and polishing diamonds began to develop in Europe. The art was already well known in India, but it was not until 1476 that it began to make great strides in Europe under the leadership of Louis de Berquen of Bruges. But although de Berquen is popularly credited with being the father of the diamond-cutting industry, the results of his endeavors and those of his pupils were still rudely fashioned stones. There was as yet little understanding of the optical properties of the diamond, and the stones lacked fire and brilliance. Nevertheless diamonds were growing increasingly popular in court circles, particularly in France. They enjoyed a great vogue at the court of King Charles VII whose mistress, Agnes Sorel, encouraged the celebrated French merchant adventurer, Jacques Coeur, to import them from India. She is generally regarded as the first woman to popularize the wearing of diamond jewelry.

It was Cardinal Mazarin of France in about 1640 who launched the second stage. A great

OPPOSITE *Marilyn Monroe wearing the Moon of Baroda. This 25.95-carat pear-shaped canary diamond came originally from the hoards of Delhi looted by Nadir Shah in 1739. For nearly two hundred years it was in the possession of the Gaekwars of Baroda until 1943 when it was purchased by Meyer Rosenbaum of Detroit. The diamond was worn by the actress in the film "Gentlemen Prefer Blondes," the musical which included the song "Diamonds Are A Girl's Best Friend."*

ABOVE *An imperial tiara in seventeenth-century Hungarian style composed of five fleur-de-lys set with cabochon sapphires and rubies enriched with diamonds and pearls.* **OPPOSITE** *A diamond and sapphire necklace from a suite that once belonged to the Empress Marie Louise, second wife of Napoleon. After the exile of Napoleon, the empress returned to Vienna and the jewelry remained in the possession of the Austrian royal family. The whole collection including this necklace was buried in 1945 to save it from the Russian occupying forces.*

lover of diamonds, he sponsored experiments by the Paris lapidaries who used various combinations of facets to discover how to produce the most brilliant result. They resolved upon a pattern not too far removed from the modern brilliant but with only thirty-four facets, seventeen above the girdle and seventeen below. Inevitably, it was called the Mazarin cut. The cardinal is also reputed to have encouraged the development of the rose cut into forms of much greater brilliance.

The immediate effect of these experiments was a dramatic boost in the appeal of diamonds over the colored precious stones that were formerly in favor. No longer were diamonds simply colorless gems desired more for their rarity than their beauty, to be set in gold and enamel and surrounded by rubies and emeralds. They were now brilliant in their own right and could dispense with such settings. A further filip to the popularity of diamonds was given toward the end of the century by the Venetian cutter Peruzzi. He developed a fifty-eight facet cut which is widely regarded as the predecessor of the modern brilliant.

By the turn of the century, diamonds had become firmly established in the world of jewelry, but because of their comparative rarity they were still not greatly used outside the circles of the rich and famous. It was the diamond discoveries in Brazil in 1725 that totally changed the supply picture—and initiated the third stage. For a time the European market was literally flooded with diamonds and they became the stock-in-trade of every jeweler, much more so than any other stone had ever been. They were used for every conceivable item of jewelry, as well as for objects like snuff boxes or miniature portrait frames. But the enormous popularity that they enjoyed during the reign of King Louis XVI and Marie Antoinette was partially responsible for their eclipse during the final decade of the eighteenth century. The wearing of not only diamonds but almost any form of jewelry was to risk being identified with the luxury and idleness of the *ancien régime*, a link that could have had fatal consequences during the years of the Terror.

The seizure of power by Napoleon Bonaparte in 1799 restored order and stability to France and the establishment of his imperial court in 1804 provoked a love of display almost as great as that which dominated the court of his unfortunate predecessor. Indeed, the passion of the Empress Josephine for diamonds rivaled that of Marie Antoinette. It was she who started the fashion for diadems or tiaras which was taken up so enthusiastically during the final quarter of the century by the "queens" of American society. The collapse of the First Empire in 1814 brought a renewed period of austerity to France and even when interest in jewelry reawakened with the return of the Bourbons, the vogue was for the colored stones and enamels of Gothic and Renaissance art. Diamonds had to wait for the accession of Napoleon III and Eugénie in 1852 for their return to favor.

OPPOSITE *A diamond necklace originally made for the French Empress Marie Louise.*
DIAMOND INFORMATION CENTER, NEW YORK

OPPOSITE, ABOVE An unusual bracelet of chased gold set with diamonds, emeralds, rubies and a large baroque pearl shaped like a military helmet. The bracelet is said to have been given to Mme. Emile Pellapra by the Emperor Napoleon on his return to Paris after the Battle of Waterloo. BELOW A diamond tiara with a fleur-de-lys motif. The five larger fleur-de-lys are detachable. THIS PAGE: ABOVE LEFT An antique necklace in the form of three diamond wild rose flowers intersected by diamonds and rose diamond leaves and buds. The necklace also forms a tiara and the three flowers are detachable. ABOVE RIGHT An eighteenth-century necklace composed of fifteen diamond clusters each with a fancy-colored diamond center, with matching brooch and ear pendants. Traditionally this diamond suite was part of the ransom offered by the Empress Catherine of Russia to the sultan of Turkey for the return of her husband Peter the Great after his capture at the Battle of Rusen in 1711. BELOW An eighteenth-century necklace composed of seven diamond festoons with matching ear pendants.

ALL PICTURES ON THESE TWO PAGES COURTESY OF CHRISTIE'S LONDON.

In nineteenth-century England diamonds were much in demand. The young Queen Victoria was a great lover of jewelry and diamonds in particular, and the new rich of Britain's industrial society were quick to follow her lead. The death of the Prince Consort in 1861 was followed by a period of more somber display, but diamonds came back into prominence from the 1870s onward with the discovery of the South African diamond fields.

The South African fields were the richest source of diamonds ever known, but since their discovery coincided with the United States' meteoric rise to wealth and power, the diamonds did not swamp the market as the stones of the first Brazilian finds had done. A whole new market had opened up which, together with the demand from Europe, was capable of absorbing as much as the mines could produce. This was the fourth and final

OPPOSITE *The late Mrs. Cornelius Vanderbilt wearing part of her million-dollar collection of diamonds. Note the fringed corsage garland, a popular Edwardian jewelry fashion.* **ABOVE** *A diamond, ruby, emerald and Lalique enamel brooch in the form of a dragonfly.* **OVERLEAF LEFT** *A diamond necklace composed of a fringe of alternate strands of collet and baton diamonds, and a diamond brooch in the form of a buckle and bow.* **OVERLEAF RIGHT** *A diamond brooch pendant (above) designed as a bow supporting a line of brilliant-cut diamonds at the center of a cascade of alternate sections of diamonds and fine piercing. A Victorian diamond brooch (below) in the form of a sun burst with a diamond cluster center.*

VANITY, VANITY . . .

The flamboyant diamond millionaires like Barney Barnato were very much folk heroes in their native London. They were affectionately lampooned in *The Girl from Kay's*, a popular musical show staged in London in 1902, in which the ambition of the heroine was to marry the leading male character billed as "Max Hoggenheimer, a South African millionaire." This song is from the finale:

> *It's very nice to be*
> *A dame of high degree*
> *With blood and reputation beautifully blue;*
> *But folks with cash can get*
> *Into the smartest set,*
> *And that's what I shall proceed to do!*
> *When driving through the park,*
> *Perhaps you may remark*
> *A silver-mounted perfumed petrol motor trap;*
> *You'll see me on the box*
> *In furs of silver fox,*
> *With just a few big diamonds in my cap.*
> *I'll marry Hoggenheimer of Park Lane,*
> *The money he is winning*
> *I'll set it gaily spinning*
> *And ev'ry one that sees me will explain*
> *That I'm Mrs. Hoggenheimer of Park Lane.*

stage in the diamond's rise to become the world's premier gemstone. Adequate supply matched by permanent demand, coupled with the almost infinite variety of sizes, shapes and quality meant that the jewelers of the world could use diamonds in any piece of jewelry they produced, from the most inexpensive to the almost priceless. Diamonds had, in fact, become the gem of the people in a way that Marat and Robespierre would never have believed possible.

This new era in the world of jewelry received a tremendous boost from the rise of the motion picture industry, which created a totally new category of the rich and famous that people could identify with. Queens and princesses and society millionairesses had been in a world apart, but the new screen goddesses were not. The lives of many of them had been a "rags to riches" story—and they often played exactly the same part on the screen, thus becoming a symbol of the limitless possibilities inherent in a democratic and affluent society. They were not hated or envied. As a result they were imitated in an unprecendented way. Their dress, their hairstyles, their make-up—and their jewelry—set the fashion for the country and for the world.

The history of diamonds in jewelry, especially over the past century, has been very

much bound up with the history of the great jewelry houses. Today their names are synonymous with fine diamonds; and if diamonds are the stock-in-trade of jewelers the world over, to some they are much more than that. To Tiffany's, Cartier and Van Cleef & Arpels, to mention only a handful of the great names, diamonds are part of their history.

Although Tiffany's started life in the midst of the recession year 1837 as a "stationery and fancy goods store," it was an instant success; and as New York society recovered from the slump, the founder Charles Tiffany rapidly increased the variety and improved the quality of his merchandise. Always keen to seek out the latest novelties, wherever they might be found, in 1841 he imported a range of paste jewelry from Paris which the ladies of New York were soon falling over themselves to buy. The success of this line prompted Charles Tiffany to go for the "real thing," and from 1845 onward the store sold only diamonds and ceased to stock paste.

ABOVE *Charles Tiffany, who founded Tiffany's in 1837.*
OPPOSITE *The Star of South Africa.* CHRISTIE'S, LONDON

The British Imperial State Crown, containing the
317.4-carat Cullinan II

The Imperial Scepter, with the 530.2-carat Cullinan I

The diamond-encrusted Sword of State

A diamond-studded tiara, once owned by the empress Josephine, first wife of Napoleon

Diamond and emerald necklace by Van Cleef & Arpels

Earring with a rare blue 6.61-carat diamond suspended from a cluster of white navettes

Watch by Andrew Grima, with a jagged "glass" of tourmeline quartz and pavé set with diamonds GRIMA

Ring by Andrew Grima: a 55.91-carat pear-shaped diamond set in platinum, with a ribbon of baguettes

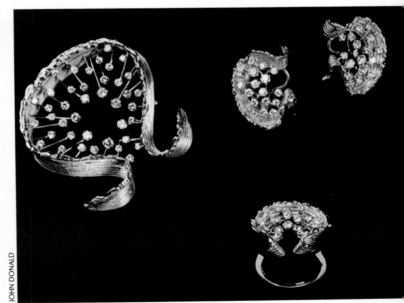

Brooch/pendant with kite-shaped diamonds set in polished and granulated yellow gold

Brooch, earrings and ring. Ribbon design set with small brilliants.

DIAMOND INTERNATIONAL AWARDS

The Diamond International Awards is the largest and most prestigious jewelry design competition in the world. Sponsored by De Beers since its inauguration in 1953, the competition now attracts over a thousand entries from designers all over the world. It is particularly concerned with the role of diamonds in jewelry design, and each entry submitted must contain a minimum of five carats of diamonds. The award-winning designs are selected by a panel of six judges on the basis of their beauty, originality and creative use of diamonds.

Please note: All photographs are courtesy of De Beers. In each case, the name of the designer, his or her country, and the year of the award appears as a credit at the side of each photograph.

Cuff links in diamonds, lapis lazuli and yellow gold

YOSHIRU MOCHIZUKI, JAPAN (1974)

"Diamonds Are Forever"—bracelet with diamonds and yellow gold

RICHARD BONEHILL, ENGLAND (1976)

Ring with alternating diamonds and clusters of stainless-steel ball bearings

NORMAN TEUFEL, USA (1975)

CATHERINE BÖHLER, FRANCE (1975)

Ring with navette and brilliant-cut diamonds in white gold setting

Pendant in gold, enamel, diamonds and rubies

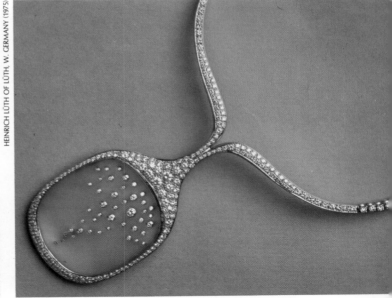

Necklace with diamonds, white gold and rock crystal

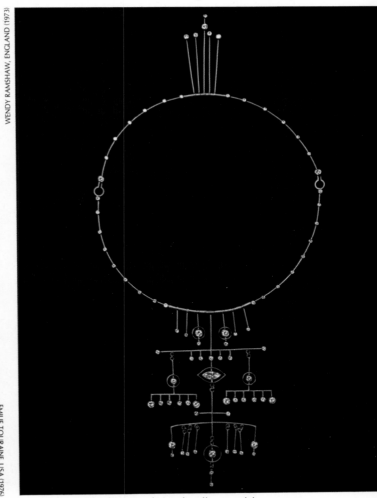

*Pendant of white and brown diamonds set in a fragment
of an authentic Acoma Indian pot*

Necklace with diamonds and yellow gold

Pendant/brooch with white and brown diamonds, yellow gold and platinum

Watch bracelet with diamonds, ivory and ebony

Man's ring with baguette diamonds, white gold and quartz   *Necklace with diamond, ivory and yellow gold*

Brooch with diamonds and white gold

Necklace with diamonds and yellow gold

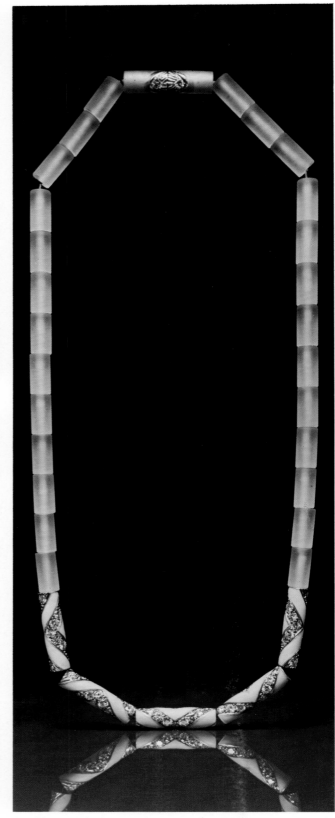

Necklace with diamonds, enamel and rock crystal

It was not until the year 1848 that Tiffany's became one of the great names in the diamond world in a coup that earned Charles Tiffany the title of "the King of Diamonds." The store's annual buying trip to Paris happened to coincide with the collapse of the regime of Louis Philippe and the two buyers, John Young and Thomas Banks, arrived in a city in turmoil. It was a dangerous time to be in Paris—both men were arrested by the revolutionaries on a number of occasions—but it was a great opportunity for two Americans flush with cash. Royalist supporters eager to flee the country were only too ready to sell their jewelry for any price they could get, but apart from these private purchases, the two buyers returned to New York with a slice of the French crown jewels. Just how and where Young and Banks acquired the royal jewels is not certain, but it is known that a number of items were missing from the collection after the mob surged through the Tuileries and before order could be restored. Still, dubious acquisition or not, the American press loved the story, and the resulting publicity secured Tiffany's position as America's foremost jewelry store as well as establishing its international reputation.

The 1880s and 1890s were the heyday of American society and the new millionaires of industry and commerce displayed their wealth with an opulence that rivaled that of the royal courts of Europe. Happily, Tiffany's was there to cater to their tastes, and indeed many of the diamonds and other jewels that were to adorn the wives of the millionaires of the New World came from the royal treasuries of the Old. Tiffany's was always a keen buyer of choice items from the royal collections, so many of which were broken up during the second half of the nineteenth century; but it was the French crown jewels which once again gave the store its greatest coup.

The royal collection had suffered greatly

from the Revolution of 1789, the subsequent fall of Napoleon and later upheavals, but during the Second Empire, the Empress Eugénie had amassed diamonds with an enthusiasm as great as that of Marie Antoinette. By the time the empire collapsed in September 1870, the collection had been restored to its former glory and the Empress Eugénie was determined not to leave it behind. Sensing trouble, she had most of her jewels crated and dispatched to the port of Brest, ready for transportation to England. Some reached London, but a number of crates had to be left behind and these were eventually reclaimed by the new French government and returned to Paris. After long and careful deliberation, the French decided to sell the bulk of the collection and in 1887 a much-publicized sale by auction was held in the Hall of State in Paris. Tiffany's practically swept the board, buying all the most important pieces and accumulating twenty-four of the sixty-nine lots offered. The French press reported that they were destined for "lady millionairesses on the other side of the Atlantic," as indeed they were. The finest piece of all, the so-called "great necklace of Eugénie" with its four rows totaling 222 large diamonds of the first water, was to be seen at a Paris ball the night after the sale, clasped

OPPOSITE *A cartoon of 1887 speculating on some of the new uses that the wives of US senators might find for the French crown jewels.*

Charles Tiffany (left) in the Union Square store in 1899. When it was first opened in 1870, the New York World *hailed it as "A Mine of Wealth and a New Palace of Beauty."*

around the neck of Mrs. Joseph Pulitzer, wife of the millionaire newspaper proprietor.

If there had been any doubt about the transfer of "diamond power" to the New World, the 1887 sale was the clincher. Three women—Mrs. John Jacob Astor, Mrs. Clarence Mackay and Mrs. Leland Stanford—were reputed each to own more jewels than any of the crowned heads of Europe with the exception of Queen Victoria of England and the czarina of Russia. In fact, when the new Metropolitan Opera House was opened in New York in 1883, the first tier was quickly dubbed "The Diamond Horseshoe" because the brilliance of the diamond jewelry of its patrons outshone the house lights. But it was not only the grandes dames of American society who bought diamonds from Tiffany's. The self-made millionaires like "Diamond Jim" Brady and John "Bet a Million" Gates were eager to display their newly acquired wealth and chose to do it with diamonds. Gates regularly wore three diamonds on his shirt-front and three more on each suspender clasp, but Diamond Jim had no less than thirty-one different sets of cuff links, shirt studs, belt buckles, tie pins and watch fobs, all made up in diamonds. His transportation set was his favorite. He had made his fortune in freight, and each piece of this set was a different railroad car. In all, the set contained 2,548 diamonds. The queens of the stage, too, were avid customers. Lily Langtry, the Jersey Lily, made frequent visits to Tiffany's although on one she was reported to have said that she did not want any more diamonds, having already $40,000 worth!

A few decades later it was the moguls of the motion picture industry and the stars of Hollywood who replaced the socialites, the robber barons and the stage stars of the Gay 'Nineties as Tiffany's most-talked-about patrons. In a more democratic age and one where affluence was more widespread, the public was much readier to identify with this new élite than with the old. Tiffany's was quick to spot the trend and to encourage it, recognizing that there have to be more people prepared to spend $200 on a ring than there are those who want to spend $100,000. Today, Tiffany's may still be jeweler to the rich and famous, but they also claim to sell more engagement rings than any other single establishment in the world. In other words, Tiffany's has moved with the times, capitalizing on its exclusive image instead of letting itself be strangled by it. It is not an easy task to transfer the goodwill built up out of servicing a small and wealthy clientele to a much wider market, but that Tiffany's has done it success-

JEWELERS
By Special Appointment
To

King Edward VII of England
The King and Queen of Portugal · 1904
The Emperor and Empress of Russia · 1905
The King of Siam · 1907
The King and Queen of Greece · 1907
King George of England · 1909
The King of Serbia · 1911
The King and Queen of Spain · 1912
The King and Queen of Belgium · 1913
The King and Queen of Italy · 1919
The Prince of Monaco · 1920
The Prince of Wales · 1920
The King and Queen of Rumania · 1921
· 1922

A page from a Cartier booklet of gift suggestions in 1927 listing thirteen of their royal appointments. CARTIER

fully is evidenced by Truman Capote's choice of the store as a key element in his book *Breakfast at Tiffany's*. The heroine, Holly Golightly (played in the film by Audrey Hepburn), recommends a trip to Tiffany's as a cure for the blues, and explains to George Peppard, "It calms me down right away, the quietness and the proud look of it; nothing very bad could happen to you there."

The most celebrated of European jewelers, the House of Cartier, was founded by Louis François Cartier in Paris in 1847, reviving a business started by his grandfather at the court of King Louis XV nearly a century earlier. Louis François's work was an immediate success. It was particularly admired by the Princess Mathilde who introduced him to the fashionable circle around the Empress Eugénie at the Court of Napoleon III.

Louis was soon joined by his son Alfred and when in 1898, his grandsons Louis, Jacques and Pierre came into the business, they established the present Paris House at 13 rue de la Paix. From that point on, the House of Cartier has gone from strength to strength. Jewelers to no less than twenty different royal houses in their time, Cartier continues to serve many of those that still remain, while its unique reputation has attracted the custom of the new society of the merchant princes of the Middle East and the stars of show business.

A truly international house, Cartier first branched out from Paris in 1902 when at the urging of one of their best customers, the Prince of Wales (soon to become King Edward VII), Jacques Cartier opened his first London shop in New Bond Street. Noting the numbers of wealthy Americans who were patronizing

Louis Cartier, grandson of the founder of the House of Cartier and the master jeweler whose artistry remains the inspiration of the Cartier designers today. CARTIER

the Paris salon, Alfred Cartier sent his son Pierre to America in 1907 to investigate the possibilities of opening a branch there. So impressed was Pierre by the growing affluence of the New World that he recommended the immediate establishment of a New York House. It was opened on Fifth Avenue in 1908 and became an instant success.

On the death of Alfred, his eldest son, Louis, took over the Paris house, while Jacques remained in London and Pierre in New York. There is little doubt that the Cartier family created the most remarkable dynasty of jewelers ever known. However, with the death of Louis Cartier in 1942, the company began to slip away from family control and each of the houses came under different management. Then, in 1972, Robert Hocq, the French industrialist, acquired Cartier, Paris, and in 1974 he added Cartier, London. The return to the unity of a family tradition came in 1976 when the New York house was brought back into the fold. Robert Hocq now controls the Cartier International empire and his only daughter, Nathalie, is director of the Paris house. It was thanks to her inspiration that "Les Must de Cartier" were established to bring the brilliant and original Cartier designs to the younger generation.

OPPOSITE *The House of Cartier in New York. This beautiful Renaissance mansion on the corner of 5th Avenue and 52nd Street was acquired in 1917 from Morton F. Plant in exchange for a string of pearls priced at $1,000,000.*

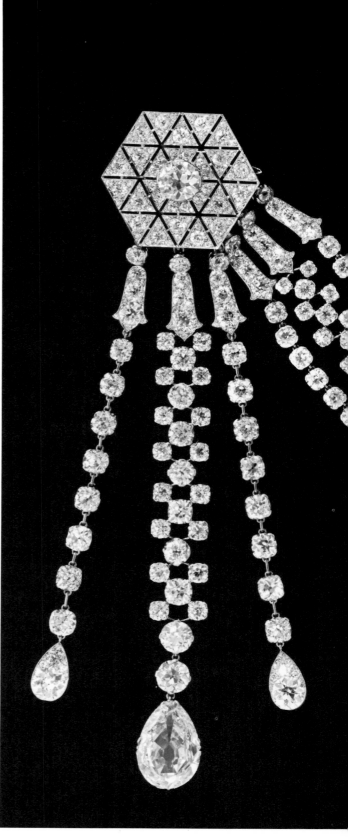

A diamond stomacher designed by Cartier in the 1920s. This was a fashionable item of jewelry in the period and was usually custom-made. The stomacher depicted here contains 424 diamonds weighing 272 carats in all.

PARKE-BERNET GALLERIES AND DIAMOND INFORMATION CENTER, NEW YORK

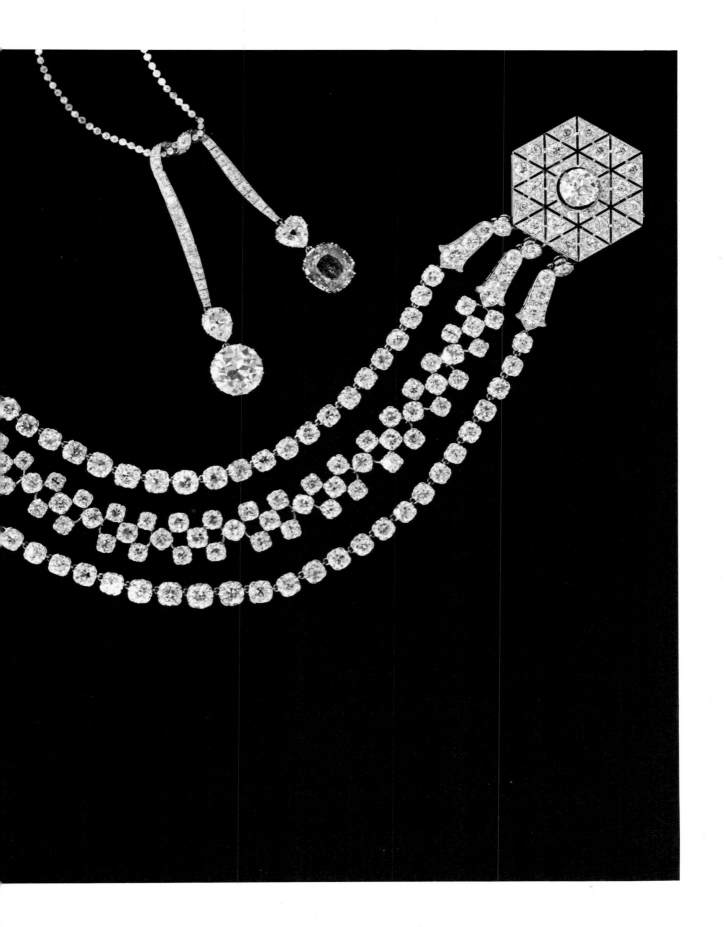

Another great house with its origins in Paris is Van Cleef & Arpels. Founded by Léon Arpels in the late 1880s, like Louis Cartier, he was joined at the turn of the century by his three sons, Julien, Louis and Charles. The business prospered, rapidly gaining a reputation for artistic and technical excellence which remains unrivaled to this day. Still a family firm, Louis heads the whole international operation, while his sons Jacques and Pierre look after Europe. His third son, Claude, is based in New York and controls the Fifth Avenue establishment together with the branches in Beverly Hills and Palm Beach.

All the great jewelers mentioned so far have been established for a century or more, a necessity, many might think, to gain acceptance in a very conservative trade. Andrew Grima of London is a notable exception. As a young designer in the late 1950s, he soon became disillusioned with what he regarded as the traditional and unimaginative jewelry that had characterized the previous fifty years, and deliberately set out to create a renaissance in jewelry design. Dismayed by the soaring prices of emeralds, rubies and sapphires, he concentrated on the beautiful but then neglected semiprecious stones like citrines, amethysts, opals, tourmalines, peridots, aquamarines and topaz. For settings he chose gold predominantly, but created new textures for the metal which combined with the individual shapes of the stones, meant that each piece of jewelry was virtually unique. Always a diamond enthusiast, Grima incorporated diamonds in almost every piece he created, using their icy brightness to set off the warm glow of the gold and the striking color of the semiprecious stones. His store in Jermyn Street in London is now a mecca for buyers all over the world who are looking for unusual and exciting jewelry.

Another London designer who has rapidly established an international reputation for

OPPOSITE *Ring by Andrew Grima, featuring a 25.3-carat round champagne diamond surrounded by six small oval diamonds in a platinum setting.*

himself is John Donald. Like Grima, he prefers to make use of the natural properties of gemstones and precious metals, and often sets uncut crystal shapes in textured gold surrounds. Very much attracted by the cube forms of pyrite crystals, John Donald has made them a consistent theme in many of his designs, creating them in gold and setting them with diamonds. His designs can be complex, but when they are, they have the complexity of nature and not of a formalized man-made structure. As a result, John Donald's jewelry is always dramatic and exciting, never cold and stark.

An American name that is known throughout the world of jewelry is that of Harry Winston. Look at any list of famous diamonds and a remarkable number of them will turn out to have been bought and sold by Harry Winston. As the son of a jeweler, the young Winston learned his future trade early in life. He left school at fifteen to work in his father's Los Angeles shop and rapidly developed his selling skills by peddling suitcases of jewelry around the saloons of the Californian oil towns. By the time he was nineteen he had decided to go into business on his own and with $2,000 saved from his Californian days, he founded the Premier Diamond Company. Knowing the importance of a good address, he established the headquarters of his one-man firm at 535 Fifth Avenue in New York. His skill in dealing soon earned him adequate financing and his business flourished. He specialized in buying jewels from estates, re-cutting and resetting them along modern lines, and reselling them. The estates were a valuable source of jewelry of the highest quality, much of it coming from collections that had been built up in the 1880s and 1890s.

Since these early days, Harry Winston has become one of the leading personalities of the diamond business. Always ready to back his own judgment, he was prepared to spend a million dollars on a diamond without a buyer in sight, secure in the knowledge that he could sell it.

Many of the world's great diamonds have passed through his hands. They include the 726-carat rough Jonker, the Vargas from Brazil of almost identical weight, the Star of the East (94.8 carats), the fabulous Hope diamond (44.5 carats), the Idol's Eye (72 carats), the Nassak (43 carats) and the Niarchos (128.25 carats). His clientele is equally impressive and features many crowned heads. The late King Ibn Saud of Saudi Arabia and King Farouk were great diamond fanciers and regular customers of Harry Winston Inc.

Very much an unconventional figure, even a maverick, in a business which can be very staid and conventional, it is still not difficult to understand the success of a man who can say: "I love the diamond business. It's a Cinderella world. It has everything! People! Drama! Romance! Speculation! Excitement! What more could you want?"

There are many designers all over the world, either working independently or in the workshops of the great jewelry houses, whom it has not been possible to mention here. They range from the young designers who enter the De Beers Diamond Award competitions (some of whose creations may be seen in the color section of this chapter) to the talented individuals and teams employed by such internationally famous houses as the Meisters of Zurich, Bulgari of Rome, Dunklings of Melbourne, Garrard's of London, and Bailey, Banks and Biddle of Philadelphia; and by popular nationwide retailers like the Zale Corporation of Texas, Stern's of Johannesburg and Samuel's of London.

But in every case, the combination of a diamond, however small, with the skill and inspiration of a designer, creates a unique piece of jewelry with a very special significance to whoever wears it.

ROGUES' GALLERY

Crime and diamonds have gone hand in hand ever since the first diamond was discovered, but no murder, mayhem or robbery has caused as much dismay in the diamond industry as the terrible crime of IDB. The initials stand for "Illicit Diamond Buying," a practice which became very widespread in the South African diamond fields from the earliest days and still continues. It was accepted as a simple fact of life that the African laborers would try to steal diamonds and smuggle them out of the mines just as the Indian and Brazilian workers had before them, and the real criminal was regarded as the person, usually a European, who bought the stones from them. So seriously did the diggers regard the offense that they were only too likely to take the law into their own hands when someone was caught in the act. A contemporary report in Kimberley's daily newspaper, the *Diamond Fields Advertiser,* describes one such incident:

> . . . a native runner was detected tampering with some boys at the sorting table. He was promptly knocked down . . .; a crowd was soon attracted by the cry of a "diamond buyer's tout," and if ever a wrongdoer had his deserts, that tout had his. Every man in the crowd hit him with something. Finally he was taken to one of

OPPOSITE *The high tariff on diamonds and other luxury goods imported into the United States led to a great deal of corruption on the dockside quite apart from out and out smuggling. This political cartoon of 1879 does more than hint at the liaison between smugglers and officials.*

the platforms on the roof, where it was proposed to string him up. In the meantime, a report was made to Mr. Commissioner Giddy of what was going on. He hurried up, and pleaded earnestly with the diggers to hand him over to the authorities to be punished, which they finally did.

One of the difficulties in these early days was that diamond trading was totally unregulated. Anyone could buy a diamond from anyone else, save from African laborers, and even this exception was not against the law unless theft could be proved. As a result the traffic in stolen diamonds reached epidemic proportions and involved every section of the population. A visiting English journalist after a tour of the Kimberley jail in 1881 wrote: "Every species of malefactor seemed to be gathered together. There were a great many in for diamond stealing and illicit diamond buying, men as well as women, some of whom were respectable people of the upper class in Kimberley." And yet it was probably true to say that these were only the small fry in the IDB game, and that the real organizers were too clever—or too big—to be touched.

A much more concerted effort to "crush the viper that was gnawing out the vitals of the people" was launched in 1881 with the formation of the Diamond Mining Protection Society. One of the leading lights in this society was J. B. Robinson, a diamond magnate and the mayor of Kimberley. After discussions with an emissary from the London police force, he proposed that Kimberley hire a team of detectives seconded from Scotland Yard and set up a Special Diamond Court to deal with IDB offenses. Both the detectives and the court soon acquired a reputation for rough justice, the former for planting evidence and for setting traps for suspects using agents provocateurs, and the latter for convicting on the most flimsy of evidence. But although large sections of the population of the diamond fields objected bitterly to the harshness of the new system, there was enough support for it to see it enshrined in the Diamond Trade Act of 1882. This was a piece of legislation of unparalleled harshness. It reversed the burden of proof, gave the police sweeping powers of search and arrest, and laid down severe penalties for IDB and related offenses ranging up to fifteen years' imprisonment with fines up to £1,000. Almost the only recommendation of the Diamond Mining Protection Society not taken up by the Cape Assembly was that buyers of illicit diamonds should be flogged as well as the stealers.

One of the first victims of the new legislation was Isaac Joel, licensed diamond buyer and nephew of Barney Barnato. Arrested for illegally possessing three 10-carat diamonds, things looked so black for Isaac Joel that his uncle returned posthaste to Kimberley from London to try to get him off the hook. Despite reputed attempts to bribe the detective in charge of the case and desperate appeals to the influential J. B. Robinson, who was now chairman of the Diamond Mining Protection Society, all of Barnato's efforts were in vain and the case was sent to the Special Diamond Court for trial. It was never concluded. Isaac

Joel had obviously weighed his own chances and decided not to run the risk of facing his accusers. He returned to London and thereafter played his part in the running of the Barnato empire from outside South Africa.

There were reports that after the passing of the Diamond Trade Act, frustrated IDB agents were crowding onto the boats leaving South Africa, convinced that their days were numbered. However, so lucrative was their trade that it was not long before new ways were found to circumvent the laws. That IDB continues to be a real problem is evident from almost any copy of the *Diamond Fields Advertiser*. The following report headed "Policeman choked accused" is from a February 1976 copy of the paper:

> Colonel J. F. Erasmus of the diamond squad in the Supreme Court in Kimberley described how he had throttled the accused to prevent him from swallowing diamonds he was carrying in his mouth. The accused spat out one of the stones and a further five were recovered within the next few days. He pleaded not guilty to seven charges of illegally selling a total of 62 diamonds to a former city diamond buyer.

Thefts from the actual mines were greatly reduced by the introduction of the compound system in 1884. This involved the mine laborers' being confined in security areas for the duration of their contracts and being subjected to searches when they left. Gems would often be found in shoe heels, in canes, or in cans with false bottoms. And there has been at least one instance where a miner has embedded diamonds in his flesh, just as the Regent diamond was smuggled out of the Parteal Mine in India in 1701. A visiting physician to the De Beers hospital noticed that one of the patients was showing signs of tetanus; finding an ugly-looking wound in the man's leg, he cut it open to find a rag containing a number of diamonds. Gardner Williams, who reported the incident, observed dryly, "the native soon recovered, a wiser if a poorer man." The record for the amount of diamonds swallowed in an attempt to smuggle them out rests at twenty-one stones with a total weight of 348 carats, a fortune in diamonds then and now.

The compounds were self-contained communities with all the relevant amenities of a small frontier town and that they were a sensible and successful creation is evidenced by the fact that they are still in use today in all the principal mines and that a high percentage of miners return for further tours of duty. The body searches and the purgative doses of the past have today given way to simple fluoroscope examination of persons and luggage, and successful smuggling requires an ever-higher degree of ingenuity. Attempts, nevertheless, continue to be made and there is always a fund of stories among diamond men of the latest methods. The problem is more difficult to contain in South West Africa (Namibia) because of the nature of the diamond deposits. There the whole town of Oranjemund is itself one vast compound and all the inhabitants need security clearance before leaving its limits.

One of the most dramatic stories concerns the member of a prospecting team who over a period of years stored a cache of diamonds in the desert some way to the north of the town. Efforts to bribe a boatman to pick up the diamonds failed because none could be found who was willing to hazard his boat on the breakers of this storm-swept coast. Eventually the prospector persuaded a private pilot to carry out the operation. First of all, an emergency landing was staged at Oranjemund airfield to pick up enough fuel to enable the trip to the north to be completed. The pilot was given the fuel along with a warning to stay away from the forbidden area, and after a feint to the south, he circled and flew north. He quickly pinpointed the position of the secret store of diamonds and selected his landing place. Unfortunately, he chose the smoothest and nearest strip to the diamond store instead of the area recommended by the prospector. The wheels dug into the soft sand and the airplane tipped onto its nose and was wrecked. Legend has it that the skeleton of the airplane still lies there in the desert.

Other stories tell of attempts to get diamonds out of Oranjemund itself. In one the chief security officer was the unwitting helper—or so he concluded when he went to start his car the morning after arriving in Cape Town and found that the petrol tank was missing. As one of the few men in town above suspicion, his car was not liable to be searched on leaving Oranjemund, and it could only be assumed that someone realizing this had poured a handful of rough diamonds into his gasoline tank ready to be removed by an accomplice in Cape Town. A similar story involved the dining table of the retiring general manager. He too was above suspicion and thus allowed to take his furniture with him when he left, unlike ordinary employees. Nothing was apparently stolen after a break-in some weeks later at his new house in Durban, but his dining table was found to have a leg missing!

Diamonds have always proved excellent raw material for the confidence trickster and none more so than in the case of the Great Arizona Diamond Swindle, described by *The New York Times* as "the most adroit and skillfully managed affair in the annals of fraud." The story began with an ex-gold miner from Kentucky called Philip Arnold who in 1871 decided to cash in on the interest aroused by the new diamond finds in South Africa by "discovering" a diamond field in Arizona.

Already familiar with diamonds of the industrial variety from working with a San Francisco maker of drilling equipment, Arnold set the scene by appearing in that city in 1872, carrying two heavy bags full of poor-quality emeralds, rubies and a mass of industrial diamond pebbles which he claimed to have found in Arizona, deep in Apache country. He left the bags in the custody of another mining man, swore him to secrecy and then departed. By the next day, the story was all over town. A group of local businessmen and bankers sought out Arnold and requested him to allow them to appoint an independent expert to survey the site. Arnold, gambling that no one in the entire country knew enough about diamonds to disprove his claim, readily agreed. However, Arnold insisted that the surveyor be blindfolded and led him on a three-day ride to the diamond claim. It turned out to be in Colorado and not in Arizona; his earlier report, Arnold explained, was to put potential claim jumpers off the scent. The site proved to be as rich in diamonds as Arnold had predicted and the surveyor returned to San Francisco heartily endorsing Arnold's story. The local bankers were beside themselves with delight; but knowing that more money than they could muster would be needed to exploit such a remote claim, they decided to approach some leading East Coast financiers. The financiers were intrigued but not convinced. They insisted that the opinion

of no less than Charles Tiffany be obtained before they would commit themselves.

Once again Arnold was content to let his backers carry out their own tests, confident in his belief that the fact that the stones were really diamonds, though of poor quality, would sidetrack any doubts about the authenticity of the actual claim. As soon as he learned that Charles Tiffany had tested the stones and confirmed that they were diamonds, Arnold decided that it was well worth putting himself to some trouble and expense to ensure the success of his venture. Taking a ship to Europe, he engaged two agents to spend nearly $40,000 on buying up a large selection of small, low-quality diamonds, and returned with them to America. Approaching the claim site from the direction of Denver, which made it just an hour's ride from the nearest railroad instead of the three days it took from San Francisco, Arnold liberally scattered the diamonds over the mesa. A further surveying trip was made under similar circumstances to the first, and when the experts reported more than favorably, $500,000 was forced on an apparently reluctant Arnold for the rights to his claim. Considering that the surveyors had estimated the claim to be worth more than $5 million an acre, Arnold had sold out for a song. Com-

Diamond Mines !

ARIZONA !

Expedition Overland Direct.

An Expedition to reach the Diamond Mines is now organizing. The route proposed is as follows: Denver to Fairplay; Fairplay to Rio Grande; up Rio Grande to Las Animas Park; thence by Rio Manchos, Cottonwood Creek and Colorado Chiquito to Prescott. Expedition not to start with less than 30 men, well armed. Estimated expense of outfit, $250 per man, including animals, guns and provisions. All persons who can furnish this amount, and be ready to start by September 1st, will please address, *at once*, lockbox 579, Denver, giving name, occupation and address. If a sufficient number reply to this advertisement, full particulars will be immediately published.   aug13:2t

ABOVE *An advertisement from the* Rocky Mountain News *of August 13, 1872, attempting to get together an expedition to the Arizona Diamond Fields.* **OPPOSITE** *Three months later the* San Francisco Evening Bulletin *carried this report of "The Most Dazzling Fraud of the Age."*

plaining bitterly that he had been cheated by the Eastern establishment, he went back to Kentucky.

It had been a lengthy and complex operation for Arnold, but his problems were now over. For the new owners of the claim, however, they were just beginning. Doubts about the diamond find had already been expressed in a number of quarters including *The New York Times*. The paper had carried a story from a London diamond broker that an unknown American had bought a great number of rough diamonds "paying no attention whatever to the weight or quality," and that it was their opinion that the stones had been used by the alleged discoverer of the diamond mines in Arizona. Surprisingly, little attention was paid to these disturbing rumors, and one of the new backers, Baron Rothschild of Paris, pronounced that: "America is a rich land. It has given us many surprises. It reserves many more." The evidence that finally exposed the diamond find as a fraud was provided by a young government geologist, Clarence King, who had earlier surveyed the site without coming across any trace of diamonds. A return visit by him to the area did indeed reveal diamonds in profusion, but any thoughts that he might have had about being mistaken were soon dismissed when some stones were found to be partially cut, and others showed distinct signs of having been ground into the earth by heavy heels. One diamond was even found on top of a tree stump. It took a long time for the financial establishment to live down this little episode, but it was not enough to prevent diamonds figuring in confidence tricks again and again.

Not surprisingly, diamonds have been the object of a vast number of robberies over the years, but perhaps none was more unusual or dramatic than the Amsterdam Diamond Raid, which took place on May 13, 1940. It was not strictly a "crime" in the accepted sense of the word, although the commander of the German forces in the Netherlands must have regarded it as one. So rapid had been the German advance in the West in the early days of the war that the Netherlands, Belgium and France were overrun all within the space of six weeks. For the Dutch, the war was over in five days, leaving no time to evacuate the valuable stocks of industrial diamonds lying in vaults in Amsterdam. But so vital were these to the war effort that an immediate decision was made at the highest level in London to snatch them from under the noses of the Germans.

Reputedly on the direct orders of Winston Churchill, a British intelligence officer contacted two Dutch diamond merchants based in London, and within twenty-four hours organized a lightning raid on Amsterdam. A

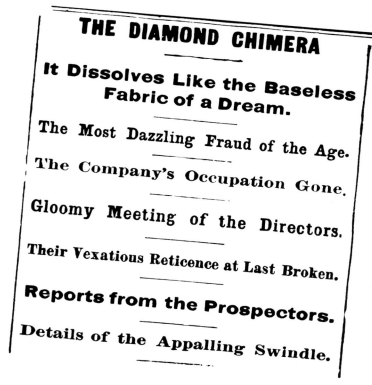

THE DIAMOND CHIMERA

It Dissolves Like the Baseless Fabric of a Dream.

The Most Dazzling Fraud of the Age.

The Company's Occupation Gone.

Gloomy Meeting of the Directors.

Their Vexatious Reticence at Last Broken.

Reports from the Prospectors.

Details of the Appalling Swindle.

British destroyer, HMS *Walpole*, was ordered to land the three men at the port of Ymuiden early on the morning of May 13 and pick them up at eight o'clock in the evening of that day. The port had been heavily bombed and the party arrived in a ruined, smoking town packed with refugees fleeing from the German invaders. All public transport had broken down, but the raiding party commandeered a large American car which a woman was about to drive over the quayside. Once they had convinced her of the importance of their mission, she drove them back into the beleaguered city of Amsterdam. The instant they reached their destination, the diamond men contacted their fellow merchants and persuaded them to hand over the stocks of industrial diamonds in order to deny them to the Germans. The diamonds were stuffed into a naval kitbag and the hazardous journey back to Ymuiden began. When the three men arrived at the port early that evening, they found that it had been bombed yet again and that the boatman who was to take them out to the destroyer beyond the harbor mouth had been killed. At pistol point the British officer ordered the captain of a tug to make the rendezvous with HMS *Walpole*. The next day at eleven P.M. the Dutch government acknowledged defeat, but by then a kitbag full of vital industrial diamonds had arrived safely in London. So secret was the operation that no official record exists and the name of only one of the raiders is known. He was Jan Smit, grandson of the founder of the well-known Amsterdam firm of J. K. Smit & Sons.

Three centuries ago even the crown jewels of England caught a robber's eye. With its massive walls, its deep moat and its permanent guard consisting of the pick of the king's soldiers, no place in England would have been considered more invulnerable in 1671 than the Tower of London. And yet on May 9 of that year an attempt was made to steal the crown jewels which very nearly succeeded. The mastermind behind the conspiracy was Colonel Blood, an Irish soldier of fortune, so bored with the idleness of life in Restoration London that he planned this daring coup as much for excitement as for gain.

While the Tower, by tradition and superstition, may have appeared inviolate, Colonel Blood based his plan on two simple observations. One was that the crown jewels were only lightly guarded by the assistant keeper of the regalia, Talbot Edwards, a man of seventy-seven who had his apartments in the Martin Tower directly above the jewels. The other was that despite its military reputation, the Tower of London was really a small community which necessitated the constant coming and going of a host of civilians. In the guise of a priest, Colonel Blood managed to strike up a friendship with the Edwards family and soon became a frequent visitor, and thus

"While he was being questioned at the Vercelli police station, S. Sandro Oicci of Milan began to make a strange whistling noise. After several minutes of this, Inspector Kasar reached over and tweaked his nose. Out popped a diamond. S. Oicci said he kept his diamond in his nose because he feared pickpockets."—A report from the True Stories feature of Private Eye, *the English satirical magazine.*

a familiar face, to the guards at the Tower. On the day set for the robbery, he called upon Edwards early in the morning in the company of three confederates. As soon as they were inside the Martin Tower, they struck the old man over the head with a wooden mallet and set to work to seize the royal regalia from its resting place. Fortunately for them the jewels were kept in a recess in the thick wall of the lower chamber and were protected by nothing more than an iron grille. Once they had ripped away the grille, the choice before them was which items to take and which to leave. Colonel Blood knew that getting out of the Tower would not be as simple as getting in, especially if they were seen to be carrying large objects. He therefore decided to leave such weighty pieces as the crown of England and to go for only those which could be compressed or cut up and concealed about their persons. His choice fell on the scepter, the orb, plus the light but diamond-studded state crown, which also contained the famous balas ruby of the Black Prince. Seizing the same mallet he had used to stun the luckless Talbot Edwards, he battered in the arches and flattened the band of the state crown. At the same time, one of his fellow thieves set about filing in two the unwieldy scepter, while another wrapped the orb in his cloak.

It was at this point that Colonel Blood's luck began to run out. Talbot Edwards's son, a soldier newly returned from Flanders, appeared suddenly and the robbers froze in their places. To cries of "treason and murder," Colonel Blood and his associates fled from the Martin Tower, shot down the guard at the Byward Tower and reached the outer defenses of the fortress. There they were quickly overwhelmed by a mixed company of soldiers and civilians and the crown jewels recovered.

In an age when sheep stealing was a capital offense, it would have seemed inevitable that Colonel Blood would have been a prime

MARY EVANS PICTURE LIBRARY

Blood & his Accomplices making their Escape after Stealing the Crown of CHARLES the SECOND

A contemporary engraving showing Colonel Blood and his accomplices making their escape after stealing part of the crown jewels from the Tower of London.

A New York diamond broker transfers diamonds to a safe from the specially designated garment which he wears between his coat and his waistcoat.

candidate for hanging, drawing and quartering at Tyburn Tree at the very least. But the king, Charles II, is reputed to have laughed uproariously when told of the attemped theft of his regalia and to have insisted on passing judgment on Colonel Blood himself. What passed between them as they talked alone in the king's chamber no one knows, but Colonel Blood emerged as a member of the king's bodyguard with a salary of £500 a year for life, an enormous sum in those days.

Armed robbery is a constant worry for any jewelry store and security systems are constantly being tightened. But no system can be regarded as watertight until it has been tested in the field. Some years ago Tiffany's had to change their 5/8-inch thick, and supposedly shatterproof display windows after two dawn raiders smashed them with sledgehammers and got away with $163,000 in jewelry. The new toughened glass managed to withstand another onslaught some months later, this time by bullets, but in any case the windows are now wired to a central alarm system.

An $800,000 robbery at Tiffany's newly

opened Chicago branch in 1966 provided the incentive for still further refinements in security precautions. At 8 A.M. on a Saturday, the first seven employees to enter the building were surprised by four hooded gunmen and locked in a storeroom. When the manager arrived a few minutes later, he was ordered to deactivate the night alarms and open the vault before being forced to join his staff in the storeroom. Since then the alarms cannot be switched off unless a coded signal has first been received by the office of the security agency, and all the windows are covered by electronic beams.

But no doors or locks or electronic eyes can be guaranteed to foil the true artists of crime who always seem to have one more new idea up their sleeves. Relying on psychology more than simple trickery or sleight of hand, they know that for themselves more than for the guards, "eternal vigilance is the price of freedom." One simple but effective ruse which would probably work as well today as it did in 1893, is that employed by the notorious Sophie Lyons with her husband and partner in crime, Billie Burke. The incident, which took place at Tiffany's, is described in a contemporary report:

Sophie swept regally into the store and demanded to be shown an assortment of rubies and diamonds. She was a superb actress and could dress and talk like a patrician. She examined this stone and that and finally announced there was nothing suitable and rose to leave. Then the clerk noticed to his chagrin that seven expensive stones were missing, worth about fifty grand. She and the clerk were the only persons within touching distance. Was it possible she had dropped them into her handbag? The lady drew herself up in haughty indignation. The clerk called a store

detective . . . and she was escorted into a room and searched by a matron. Nary a stone was found on her, and she threw the place into an uproar, threatening damages for humiliation, false arrest, etc. . . . eventually, she exited, the management apologizing. As Sophie said, "the most sullen and baffled apology you can imagine. They were not stupid. They knew I had taken the stones but they were helpless." . . . The next day her husband strolled nonchalantly into Tiffany's, bought a diamond ring from the same clerk his wife had tricked, and paid cash. While the clerk was making out the receipt, Billie slipped the seven stolen gems from the gum under the counter where Sophie had stuck them and walked out a happier and wealthier man.

Another audacious trick managed to take in both Tiffany's and Harry Winston's within the space of a few minutes. A well-dressed and attractive woman walked into Tiffany's and asked to see a selection of marquise diamond rings. The assistant was impressed by the fact that the woman already wore an expensive diamond ring of this type. Taking off her own ring and placing it on the counter she tried on a number of those laid out before her.

After a time she announced that she needed time to think about it and walked out of the store—straight into Winston's, a block away. There she repeated the procedure and left, apparently without making a choice. It was only when both salesmen checked their stock at the end of the day that it became clear what had happened. The woman had entered Tiffany's wearing a 2.75 carat diamond ring worth $7,500 and switched it for a 3.69 carat one worth $19,800. She had then walked into Winston's wearing the Tiffany ring and walked out again with a Winston ring of 5.3 carats valued at $38,500. Harry Winston wryly commented that she was clearly not a professional thief but "just a woman who wanted a more expensive ring to wear."

In 1932 Tiffany's was the scene of another bizarre robbery. A wild-eyed, shock-haired character dressed in outlandish clothes was being observed warily by the security guards as he wandered aimlessly from counter to counter. Suddenly, the man made a dash for

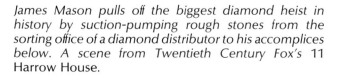

James Mason pulls off the biggest diamond heist in history by suction-pumping rough stones from the sorting office of a diamond distributor to his accomplices below. A scene from Twentieth Century Fox's 11 Harrow House.

the door with the two guards in hot pursuit. He did not get far. He was caught a few yards along Fifth Avenue and in the struggle, handfuls of sparkling diamonds spilled over the sidewalk. Handcuffed and with a burly guard firmly holding each arm, the prisoner was marched back to Tiffany's. Feeling a little bruised and shaken, the unkempt thief decided that things had gone far enough. He revealed that he was Harpo Marx and that he had pulled off the stunt as a bet. The diamonds were glass.

It is unfortunately true that no matter what precautions are taken, diamonds will continue to be one of the prime targets for the professional criminal; and diamond dealers have little choice but to accept the risks that go with their trade. For the private owner of expensive jewelry, however, there are options. Copies can be made of the best pieces and worn while the originals rest safely in a bank vault. Given the excellence of many simulants, this is an increasingly common practice, and an added incentive is provided by the prospect of a sharp reduction in the insurance premium which could otherwise be prohibitively high. Diamond lovers are not noted for their eagerness to maintain a low profile, but in 1975 the committee of New York's famous annual charity event, the Diamond Ball, were forced to consider changing the name of the ball and cutting down on lavish advance publicity after one woman, Mrs. Elizabeth Fondaras, was relieved by four gunmen of $300,000 worth of diamonds as she returned from the ball. There may have been a few rhinestones among the diamonds on display at the Diamond Ball in 1976 and 1977 but most of the guests continued to wear their best pieces. Diamonds have an air of danger and excitement about them which seems to be as attractive to the owners as it is to the potential thief!

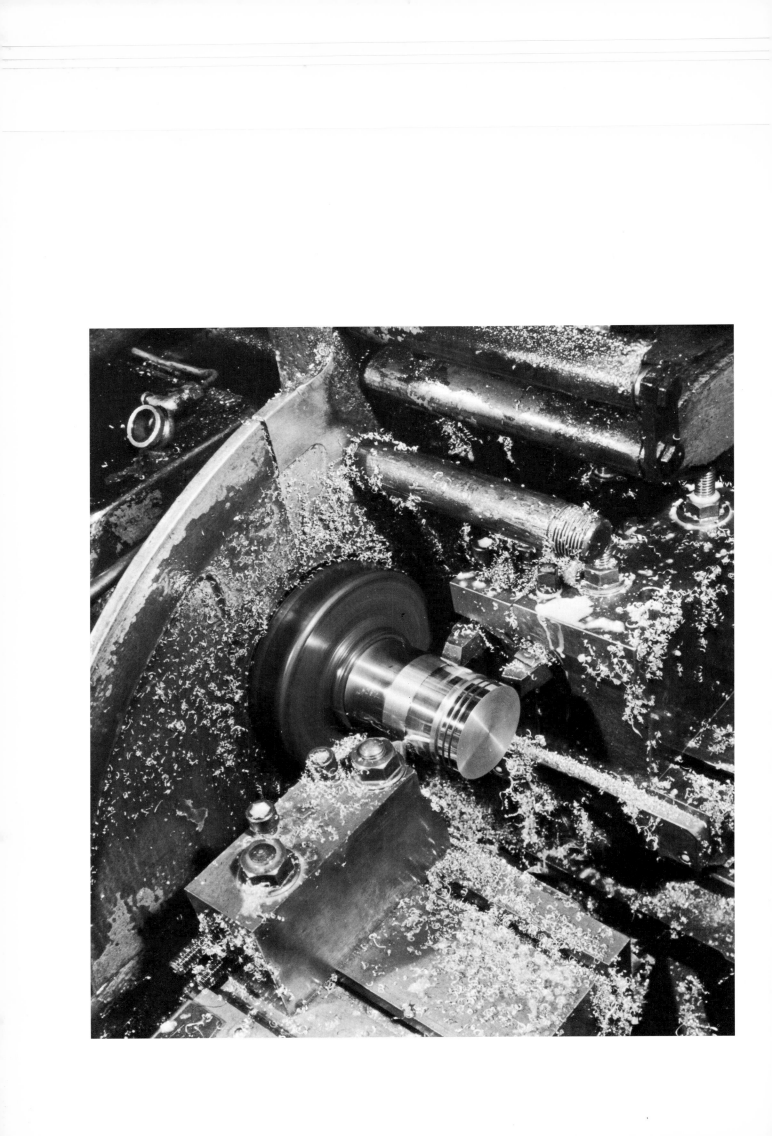

HARDER THAN STEEL

Very few people think of the diamond as anything but a gem and yet only about 20 percent of total natural diamond production is used in jewelry. The other 80 percent, together with as much again in synthetic production, goes to industry where it is used in an almost infinite number of applications. The widespread use of diamonds in industry is a relatively recent development, however. They had been used for centuries in simple cutting tools and in powder form within the diamond industry itself, but it was the rapid growth of industrial technology during and after World War II along with intensified research effort that revealed the true value of the diamond to industry. As a result, the world's annual industrial consumption of diamonds has grown from something like 5,000 carats in 1939 to a figure well in excess of 80 million carats today.

The research effort was very much the brainchild of Sir Ernest Oppenheimer. The growing demand for gem diamonds inevitably involved the mining of a proportionately greater number of non-gem quality stones, and it was clearly in the interests of the diamond producers to encourage the development of industrial uses for these diamonds. It was not long before the research and marketing activities of De Beers began

OPPOSITE *Diamond-turning operation on an aluminum-alloy automobile engine piston. Traditionally, a high-quality near-gem industrial diamond toolstone has been used for such machining applications on non-ferrous metals, but today synthesized diamond composite tool tips are also used.*

to make an impact on industry, and their efforts were given considerable impetus by two inventions. One was the discovery of how to incorporate crushed diamond into a resinoid bond and then to form it into the shape of grinding wheels. The other was the creation of an abrasive material by impregnating metal powder with crushed diamond, heating the compound to sintering point and pressing it. Diamond powder and grit rapidly became the standard materials used in the engineering industry for grinding, polishing and sawing of hard, abrasive workpieces and some 85 percent of industrial diamond consumption is accounted for in this way.

The principal uses for whole diamonds are in rock drilling, the turning and boring of nonferrous metals, the dressing of abrasive wheels, and wire drawing, tasks which before had been carried out mainly by carbide tools. The adoption of diamond tools in these roles took longer to achieve because of their initial high cost but it soon became recognized that the enormous gains both in precision and in tool life made them far more economical in the long run.

One example which is typical occurred in the machining of carbon molds used to seal electrical transistors. When carbide tools were employed, they needed sharpening after

OPPOSITE *An advertisement for diamond tools which appeared in US trade journals in 1880. Founded in 1841, Dessau & Co. is the oldest diamond tool manufacturer in America.*

The diamond wire-drawing die is one of the most important single tools in modern industry, for it is responsible for the production of the fine wires on which the world's electrical and electronics industries depend. Only natural industrial diamond crystals of the highest quality can withstand the stresses of drawing wire at speeds of up to 8,000 feet per minute (40 meters per second) while maintaining the close tolerances and high-quality finish required in continuous wire production.

every 100 operations. The diamond tool went on unaffected for 100,000 runs. The finest wires for the electrical and electronic industries are made by drawing the metal at speeds of up to 100 mph through tiny holes in diamond dies. The durability of these dies means that precision is guaranteed and that they do not have to be constantly replaced. Only a natural diamond crystal of good quality is strong enough to withstand the stresses involved in the operation, and even when the die begins to wear it can be repolished and used for larger diameter drawing. As many as seventeen resizings are possible with a single diamond die. Similarly, the introduction of a diamond-impregnated wheel in the manufacture of the stainless steel sleeves of the jet engine thrust reversers on

THE DIAMOND DIE

It follows from the extreme durability of diamond wire-drawing dies that it was no easy operation to pierce a hole, often less than one-thousandth of an inch in width, in the first place. Originally laborious and time-consuming techniques were used and a large stone could take days to make into a die. In 1937 electrolytic piercing was introduced which sped up production considerably, but the real breakthrough came in 1962 when the laser beam was used for the first time. Piercing can now be done in a matter of seconds, but the exact shaping of the hole is still carried out in the traditional manner with fine micron diamond powder.

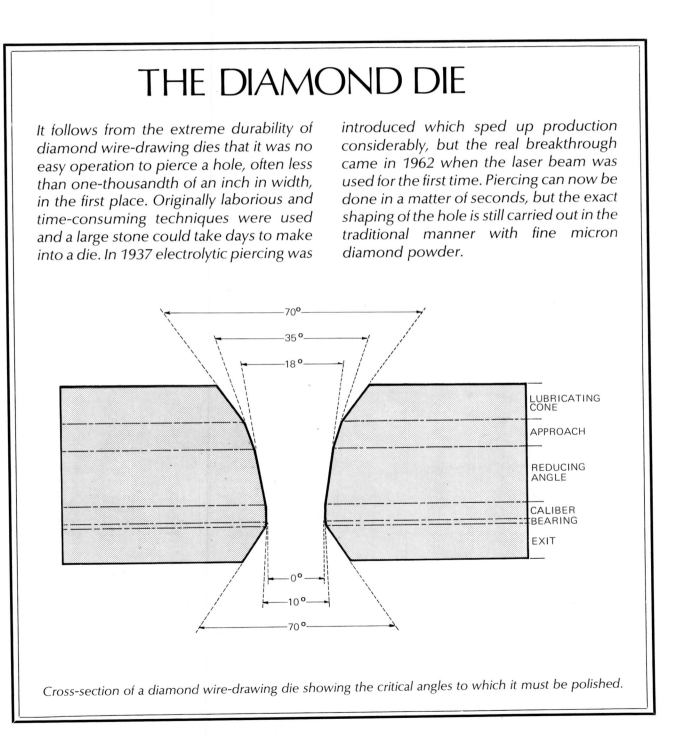

Cross-section of a diamond wire-drawing die showing the critical angles to which it must be polished.

In certain types of glass engraving—such as stippling—the vibrator tool, equipped with a diamond point, can work much faster than the more traditional diamond-tipped hand scriber. Glass designer Jane Webster, seen here at work on a presentation piece, employs the vibrator to supplement her regular use of the hand scriber in the engraving of fine detail.

the Lockheed C5A not only halved production time but also achieved a far better finish. The diamond wheels replaced aluminum oxide wheels which had required two operations to complete the job. But it is not only in metal working industries that the diamond is used. It has a great variety of applications in ceramics and in glass and plastics, where once again it does the work of alternative materials in much less time and with far greater precision. A good example is in the production of optical lenses. Diamond-impregnated milling and grinding tools are used in the shaping of lenses like the five-ton paraboloid mirror at the Greenwich Observatory in England, down to the smallest camera lens. For centuries artists have used diamond-tipped tools to engrave glassware and today they are widely employed along with diamond grinding wheels to provide delicate effects of line and tone. Applications range from the highest-quality domestic tableware to the windows of Coventry Cathedral.

Diamond-impregnated blades are used to cut grooves in highways and aircraft runways in order to prevent aquaplaning in wet weather and they do it with a degree of speed and precision far superior to that which could be attained by conventional abrasives. They are also used to cut expansion slots in walls of buildings, again with a high degree of speed and precision: in one day a diamond saw blade can cut eighteen expansion slots compared with the ten days needed to cut just one slot using a hardened metal blade.

Mining is another important application. Diamonds mounted in the heads of drills can cut through thousands of feet of the hardest rock. Because of the large diameter of many of the holes needed to be bored in rock, it is in this application that the sizes of diamonds used are the greatest. The head of a rock drill may be studded with brown and yellow diamonds of up to 5 carats each. The first recorded use of diamonds in rock drilling was in 1864 when the Mount Cenis Tunnel was driven through the Alps.

Many road and airport runway accidents which occur in bad weather are attributable to aquaplaning, a phenomenon which occurs when a tire mounts a film of water, losing all contact with the road or airport runway surface. Planing machines equipped with diamond cutting heads will grind a pattern of grooves into the surface with skid resistance characteristics equal to, or even better than, those of a newly laid surface.

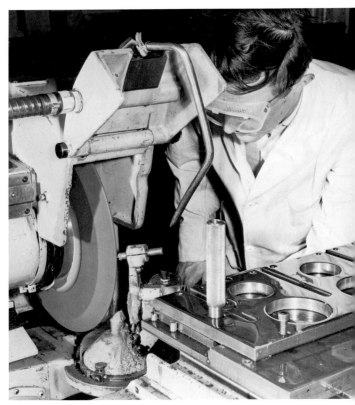

OPPOSITE: **ABOVE LEFT** *An 85 inch (2.2 meters) diameter circular saw blade, whose cutting teeth contain De Beers diamond grit, saws through a block of Welsh slate at high speed.* **ABOVE RIGHT** *Diamond crowns 12 inches (305 millimeters) in diameter or more, containing up to 900 carats of high-quality drill stones, are used in drilling through hard rock for oil wells. Smaller bits, such as the one illustrated here, are used for core sampling and mineral prospecting.* **BELOW LEFT** *Dice are diamond-finished to ensure "fair shakes."* **BELOW RIGHT** *Diamond dressing tools are widely used in the engineering industry to remove clogged or dulled surfaces on conventional abrasive grinding wheels.* **THIS PAGE: ABOVE** *A copper-coated photogravure printing cylinder weighing nearly a ton is diamond-turned to a mirror finish and a concentricity of 0.001 inches (0.03 millimeters).* **BELOW** *The heart of the Science Research Council's new £2 million infrared telescope, which is being installed on Hawaii's Mauna Kea mountain, is a glass ceramic disc 152 inches (3.8 meters) in diameter. In this picture the telescope mirror's 40-inch (1-meter) diameter center hole is being machined with a 45° edge bevel using a wheel containing De Beers natural diamond abrasive.*

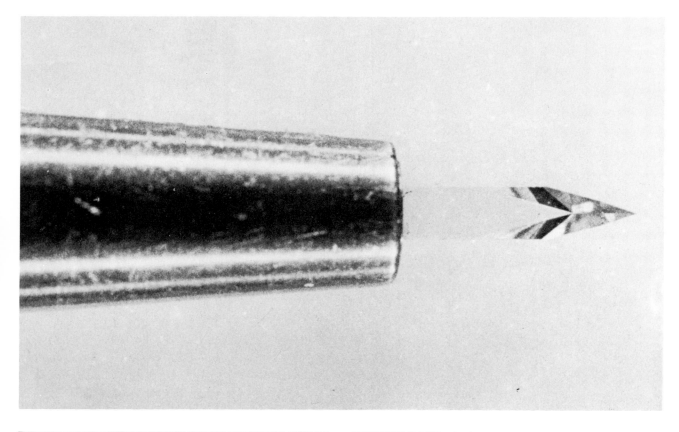

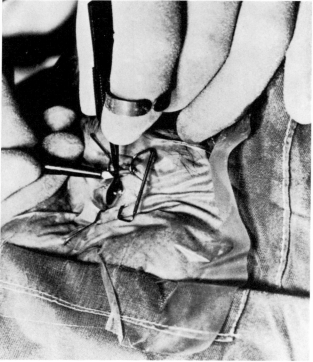

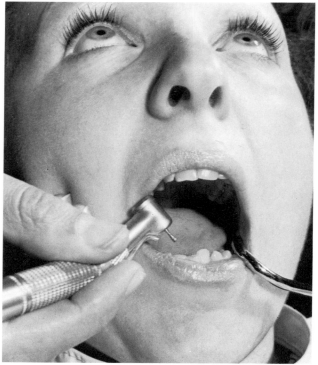

The general public knows the industrial diamond best in its noncutting uses, and without doubt the most familiar example is the record player stylus. Minute though they are, the styli are shaped with the utmost precision. Automatic equipment is used to ensure that a 78 rpm diamond tip is machined to a radius of 0.0035 inches, while that for a long-playing record fines down to 0.0007 inches. The highest-quality stereo reproduction requires a 0.0002-inch radius tip. Precision is also essential in research laboratories and diamond feeler styli are used on surface-measuring equipment which is able to check surface finishes to the extent of detecting scratches no wider than two-millionths of an inch.

One great spur to industrial diamond manufacturers has been the challenge provided by steel. Because of a tendency to overheat and fracture, diamonds had never

OPPOSITE: ABOVE *A diamond-edged surgical knife, or scalpel, has a cutting edge 1 ½ to 2 ½ millimeters long. It replaced the ophthalmic surgeon's traditional stainless steel knife. With a diamond, a sharper, more accurate type of instrument can be produced for new micro-surgical techniques.* **BELOW LEFT** *The diamond surgical knife in action.* **BELOW RIGHT** *Diamond-coated dental burrs, used in conjunction with ultrafast air-bearing drills, enable dentists to cut tooth enamel much more quickly and less painfully than with older tools and equipment. The diamond tools seen here are actually cheaper than steel or carbide.* **THIS PAGE** *The vast majority of diamond's industrial applications involve the removal of material, either by cutting or abrading. However, there is a small but important group of uses in which no material is removed. One of these—and one of the few forms in which the general public ever sees industrial diamonds—is as record player styli. The tiny diamond tip, greatly magnified, is highly polished and normally has a radius of about 0.0007 inches (17 microns).*

been considered suitable for the grinding of steel; only silicon carbide and aluminum oxide were used. Eager to obtain a share of the market for grinding the most common of metal alloys, De Beers' engineers embarked upon a series of experiments which eventually produced a synthetic diamond grit capable of doing the job. They called it the Ductile Materials Experimental Diamond Abrasive (DXDA) and then improved it by a revolutionary new process of metal-cladding devised by the Swedish company ASEA, partners of De Beers, who were pioneers in the manufacture of synthetics. Metal cladding involves the application of a fine metal coating to the diamond before it is bonded in resin. The result is a stronger bond which holds the diamond in place for much longer periods, prevents premature fracturing, and slows down the transfer of heat from the diamond points to the resin bond. DXDA-MC also works successfully on combinations of carbide and steel. There are also many varieties of micromesh natural and synthetic diamonds with an almost infinite variety of industrial uses which are dictated by the nature of their bond or cladding. Even the smallest diamond crystals have their distinctive shapes and are graded accordingly, and as far as synthetic diamond is concerned, great progress has been made toward actually tailoring the product for the job.

But if the diamond has a great advantage over other materials in certain industrial uses because of its extreme durability, there are new areas of technology being developed where there is no alternative to using diamond tools. In the field of space technology, for example, no other material is capable of achieving the degree of precision required. There is a story from the early days of the space program about a specification being issued to potential precision tool suppliers. A tool was required by the McDonnell Corpo-

OPPOSITE *Sharpening the tungsten carbide teeth of a woodworking saw with a resin-bond diamond grinding wheel. Some 50 percent of all industrial diamond grit is used in wheels of this type for grinding carbide-tipped tools.*

ration to machine the reentry configuration of the heat shield of the Gemini spacecraft which would have to operate at white heat without a coolant. The suppliers claimed that no such tool could be devised and that even a diamond one would rapidly burn up. In the event, McDonnell decided to make up a tool to their own specifications. They bonded a ¾-carat cut diamond to a copper stock and mounted it at the corner of a triangular steel block. With the copper acting as a heat sink, the 3,500°F cutting temperature was tolerated long enough for the diamond-tipped tool to complete three to four heat shields before renewal.

Ultrafine finishes are also vital in the manufacture of air bearings for space vehicle guidance and control devices. These, too, are almost impossible to obtain without the use of diamond compounds because the surfaces to be polished are made of hard-anodized aluminum and are themselves extremely hard. The diamond compounds were found to produce completely scratch-free surface finishes of 0.5 microinch as against the 2-microinch finishes which had been the best attainable by other methods.

The high thermal conductivity of the diamond, which is superior to that of the best metallic conductors (six times as effective as copper), makes the substance indispensable in many industrial operations in which extreme heat is generated. The diamond is capable of carrying heat away almost instantaneously from areas where high-speed, high-precision work is necessary, as in the example of the machining of the Gemini heat shield already mentioned. It can also act as a heat sink for the high-power transistor microwave radio transmitters used in guided missiles. These are very tiny devices and their efficiency depends entirely upon the ability of the whole system to carry away the heat that they generate.

PRIVATE COLLECTION

An unusual application for a diamond tool is the removal of the black masking ink which Japanese customs officials diligently apply to strategic parts of the female body displayed in imported girlie magazines. A flexible diamond micron impregnated eraser has been found to be totally effective in this task.

A marked difference in the physical properties of individual diamonds has prompted their classification into Type I and Type II. Broadly, Type I diamonds are those that contain slight traces of nitrogen (up to 0.3 percent), while those in Type II contain it only in the most negligible amounts. The former are much more common, but because Type II diamonds are three to five times more efficient as conductors, they are much sought after by industry.

Of Type II diamonds, those with exceptional optical and thermal properties are called Type IIa, and those with semiconducting properties, Type IIb. Both types of diamond are exceptionally pure and very rare in nature. The latter are much rarer and generally blue in color: the famous Hope diamond is of this type. A new use devised for Type IIa diamonds is as windows for infrared detecting sensors. These sensors "see" in the dark by focusing on areas or objects generating heat whether they be the human body, a gun barrel or the exhaust pipe of a vehicle. They then convert this infrared image into a visual one. Since Type IIa diamonds are highly transparent when exposed to infrared radiation, thin slabs of diamond make ideal windows for the devices. They are also used in the same way in the Golay cell, another heat-detecting system used in the laboratory for the measurement of infinitesimal amounts of heat, and in the windows of weather satellites circling the earth.

There is, of course, no such thing as perfection in any natural material but the purest diamond approaches it nearer than anything produced synthetically. As a result, the engineer and the scientist in a nuclear or space laboratory today regard the diamond with much the same respect as did their ancestors more than two thousand years ago. The diamond is as much a scientist's best friend as it is a girl's!

APPENDIX
POLISHED DIAMONDS OVER 100 CARATS

KEY

The first line of each entry contains the following coded information:

Name of diamond/Carat weight/Color/Shape/Country of origin. The second line denotes the diamond's last recorded owner.

ABBREVIATIONS

Color	Shape	Country of origin
W—White	♀ —Pear	SA—South Africa
P—Pink	▯ —Cushion	I—India
Y—Yellow	▽ —Table	SL—Sierra Leone
B—Black	⊙ —Brilliant	BR—Brazil
C—Canary	▢ —Square	?—Unknown
CH—Champagne	⌂ —Rose	
BL—Blue	⊖ —Double Rose	
BR—Brown	◊ —Oval	
?—Unknown	○ —Round	
± —More or less	▯ —Emerald	
	◇ —Octahedron	
	? —Unknown	

*indicates that information is an estimate or cannot be verified.
†indicates old carats.

Adapted from "Notable Diamonds of the World . . .," a publication by De Beers Consolidated Mines, Limited, and used with their permission.

CULLINAN I *530.20/W/♀/SA*
British crown jewels, Tower of London, 1971

This was the largest lump of gem diamond crystal ever discovered. In the rough, it weighed 3,106 carats, or about 1⅓ pounds. Since the rough had a cleavage face, many experts believe that the huge stone was only a piece of a much larger diamond which was broken up in the weathering process.

Found in the Premier Mine of South Africa by the mine superintendent, Frederick Wells, it was named after Sir Thomas Cullinan, who had discovered the mine in 1902 after persistent prospecting in the area.

The Transvaal government bought the rough for £150,000 and presented it to King Edward VII on his sixty-sixth birthday, November 9, 1907. Touched by the loyalty of his subjects, the king promised to keep the diamond among the crown jewels.

In 1908 King Edward sent the stone to Asscher's in Amsterdam for cutting. The yield was nine major gems, ninety-six small brilliants, and more than 9 carats of polished fragments. Only the two largest were retained for the crown jewels.

King Edward bought one for his consort, Queen Alexandra. The people of South Africa bought the other six major gems and presented them to Queen Mary in 1910. Thus, two of the Cullinans are among the crown jewels and the other seven belong to the royal family:

I—530.20-carat pear shape—is the largest cut diamond in the world. Also called the Great Star of Africa, it is set in the Imperial Scepter and is on permanent display in the Tower of London.

II—317.40-carat square-cut brilliant—is the second largest diamond in the world. Also called the Lesser Star of Africa, this diamond is in the Imperial State Crown in the Tower of London.

CULLINAN II *317.40/W/▯/SA*
British crown jewels, Tower of London, 1971
(See Cullinan I above)

GREAT MOGUL *†280.00/W/⌂/I*
Lost after sack of Delhi in 1739

This great diamond weighed 787.5 carats when it was found in the Gani Mine in India about 1650. It was presented to Shah Jehan, famed builder of the Taj Mahal.

Aurangzeb, the son of Shah Jehan, showed it to Tavernier, who reported that the diamond was "rose cut, round and very high on one side," much like "the form of an egg cut in half." At the time Tavernier saw it, the diamond weighed 280 carats. Aurangzeb had hired one Hortensio Borgio to cut the huge 787.5-carat rough. When Borgio cut away two-thirds of the stone to remove some flaws, the furious Aurangzeb refused to pay him and fined him 100,000 rupees for his cutting mistake.

When Nadir Shah looted Delhi in 1739, he probably took the Great Mogul back to Persia. If so, it was probably stolen with his other jewels after his death in 1747, and recut to escape detection.

The Orloff, Darya-i-Nur and Koh-i-Noor all have been identified with the Great Mogul, but most experts agree there is no relationship.

NIZAM †277.00/W/◖/I
Nizam of Hyderabad, 1934

According to hearsay, the Nizam was discovered in the productive Golconda mines as recently as 1835, and has been owned by the wealthy nizam of Hyderabad ever since.

The diamond apparently was cut with irregular facets to retain as much weight as possible. Most descriptions give its weight at 340 carats, but the diamond reportedly had been broken up during the Indian Mutiny of 1857, and its original weight has been estimated to be as much as 440 carats.

As far as is known, the Nizam has never left India. All information comes from visitors who had seen it there.

GREAT TABLE †250.00/*P/▽/I
Cut into Darya-i-Nur (185.00 carats) and the Nur-ul-Ain (60.00 carats), 1966

Tavernier saw this diamond in India and published a sketch of it in his book. It was flat and oblong in shape, with one corner chipped off. It was assumed to have been carried back to Persia by Nadir Shah after the sack of Delhi in 1739, but nothing was known of it in later years.

In 1966 Dr. V. B. Meen and Dr. A. D. Tushingham, in their study of the crown jewels of Iran, reached the conclusion that the Darya-i-Nur and the Nur-ul-Ain had been cut from the Great Table that Tavernier had described.

INDIEN †250.00/W/♀/*I
Unknown; listed by the duke of Brunswick in 1869

The duke of Brunswick listed this diamond in his 1869 catalog of precious jewels. It was described as a white pear-shape, valued at 12,500,000 francs, then in the hands of a prince in the "Grandes-Indes."

JUBILEE *245.35/W/◻/SA*
Paul-Louis Weiller, Paris, 1971

The Jubilee was found in the Jagersfontein Mine, South Africa, in 1895. Weighing 650.80 carats in the rough, it was named the Reitz diamond after F. W. Reitz, then president of the Orange Free State.

After being cut in 1897 to a 245.35-carat pure white cushion-shaped brilliant, it was renamed the Jubilee because that was the year of Queen Victoria's Diamond Jubilee. A 13.34-carat pear shape was cut from the same rough, but its whereabouts are unknown.

Many gemologists believe the Jubilee is the most perfectly cut of all large diamonds. Its facets are so exact that it can be balanced on the culet point which is less than two millimeters across.

The Jubilee was displayed at the Paris Exposition in 1900. Shortly afterward, it was sold to Sir Dorab Tata, the great Indian industrialist. After Tata's death, it was acquired by Paul-Louis Weiller, a well-known Paris manufacturer, who lent the stone to the Smithsonian Institution for an exhibit in 1961 and to the Diamond Pavilion in Johannesburg in 1966.

DE BEERS †234.50/Y/?/SA
Unknown, sold to an Indian prince about 1890

This diamond was cut from a 428.5-carat yellowish octahedron which was found in the De Beers Mine, South Africa, in 1888. It was reportedly sold to an Indian prince, but nothing further is known. Iain Balfour strongly suggests that this is the same diamond as the Victoria 1880.

VICTORIA 1880 †228.50/Y/◉/SA
Unknown; sold to an Indian prince about 1890

Little is known of this diamond, except that it was a yellowish rough of 428.5 carats found in the De Beers Mine, South Africa, in 1880, cut into a brilliant of 228.5 or 288.5 carats, and sold to an unnamed Indian prince. Iain Balfour suggests that this diamond is the same diamond as the De Beers.

RED CROSS †205.00/C/◻/SA
Unknown; sold in London in 1918

This large canary square-shaped brilliant was cut from a 375-carat rough found in the De Beers Mine, South Africa. A series of inclusions in the stone, arranged in the form of a Maltese cross, can be seen through the table. In 1918 it was presented to the British Red Cross Society and the Order of St. John in Jerusalem, then auctioned for $50,000. Its present ownership is unknown.

BLACK STAR OF AFRICA *202.00/*B/?/*SA*
Unknown; exhibited in Tokyo in 1971

Supposedly the largest colored diamond in the world, the Black Star of Africa was highlighted in a special exhibition of Belgian gems held in Tokyo in 1971. It was valued at $1.2 million.

ORLOFF *189.60/W/◠/I*
Russian Diamond Fund, Kremlin, 1968

Tales of the Orloff differ from account to account. Some believe it was the Great Mogul, seen by Tavernier in India, and stolen in 1739 by Nadir Shah. However, most authorities believe its history started about 1750 in a temple in Srirangam, near Trichinopoly, southern India, where it formed one of the bright eyes of the Hindu god Sri-Ranga.

According to this story, a French grenadier, fighting in the Carnatic Wars, deserted the army and stole the diamond eye which was "the shape of half an egg." He escaped to Madras, where he sold the gem to an English sea captain for £2,000. The captain, in turn, took it to London, where he sold it to a Persian merchant named Khojeh. Toward the end of 1775, Khojeh sold the diamond in Amsterdam to Prince Gregory Orloff for £90,000.

In an attempt to regain her favor, Orloff presented the diamond to Catherine the Great. She accepted the gift, but refused to reinstate Orloff to his powerful position in court.

Catherine never wore the Orloff, but had it mounted on top of the double eagle in the imperial scepter. It remains in the same setting today, housed in the Diamond Treasury of Soviet Russia in the Kremlin.

DARYA-I-NUR (IRAN) **185.00/P/▽/I*
Iranian crown jewels, Teheran, 1968

This great pink diamond, the "Sea of Light," is a rectangular step-cut table stone, set in a cap device, and is one of the prizes among the Iranian crown jewels. It cannot be weighed because of its mounting, but it is estimated to be between 175 and 195 carats.

It has an inscription in Persian, "The Sultan, Sahib Qiran, Fath Ali Shah, Qajar 1250." That date is 1834, the year of Fath Ali's death.

According to tradition, this is one of the diamonds carried off by Nadir Shah after the sack of Delhi in 1739. Harford Jones saw it in 1791, when it and the Taj-e-Mah were set in two armbands worn by Lutf Ali Khan Zand, the Persian ruler. He was struck by its resemblance to the Great Table diamond described by Tavernier, although the weights were different. Sir Malcolm Jones also saw the diamonds in the armbands in 1827.

The next recorded appearance of the diamond was in 1902, when Musaffer ud-Din wore it in his karakul hat, apparently in its present setting, on a trip to England.

In 1966 Dr. V. B. Meen, Dr. A. D. Tushingham and Mr. G. G. Waite of the Royal Ontario Museum in Toronto studied and authenticated the Iranian crown jewels on a grant from the Birks Family Foundation. They believe that the Darya-i-Nur seen by Hartford Jones was indeed Tavernier's Great Table, that it was damaged at some time before 1834, and that Fath Ali had it recut to remove the damaged area.

Another pink diamond among the crown jewels, the Nur-ul-Ain, the world's largest rose-pink diamond of brilliant cut (60 carats), is a crystallographic match with the Darya-i-Nur. To test their theory, they made a model of the Great Table and they proved that both present diamonds could have been cut from it.

The Darya-i-Nur was worn on a military cap by the present Shah of Iran at his coronation in 1967.

VICTORIA 1884 *†184.50/W/0/SA*
*Unknown; reported sold to the Nizam of Hyderabad, *1900*

Found in the Jagersfontein Mine, the 469-carat rough from which the gem was taken was shown in London in 1884, then cut in Amsterdam into an oval brilliant of 184.5 carats and a circular brilliant of 20 carats. The stone, also called the Imperial and the Great White, was sold to the nizam of Hyderabad for about $100,000.

MOON *183.00/±Y/O/SA*
Unknown; sold at Sotheby's in 1942

This brilliant-cut diamond with a tinge of yellow, probably of South African origin, was sold at auction at Sotheby's in 1942 for the low sum of $12,480. H. W. Thorne was the successful bidder, but the stone soon passed into the hands of a foreign potentate whose identity has never been disclosed.

IRANIAN 1 *152.16/±Y/0/SA*
Iranian crown jewels, Teheran, 1968

The name Iranian has been given to twenty-three diamonds among the crown jewels of Iran. When Dr. V. B. Meen and Dr. A. D. Tushingham made their study in 1966, they found literally buckets full of diamonds and other gems, but they had time to study only the largest.

Three of these stones (19, 22 and 23) are white, and one (20) is peach-colored. These are probably of Indian origin.

The other nineteen are all yellows of South African origin. Most of them were probably bought by Shah Nasir ud-Din during his trip to Europe in 1889.

The weights and shapes of the five largest are:

1—152.16 cushion
2—135.45 cushion
3—123.93 cushion
4—121.90 octahedron
5—114.28 cushion

DARYA-I-NUR (DACCA) †150.00/*W/*□/I
Unknown; offered for sale in Dacca in 1959

The East India Company showed this diamond at the Crystal Palace Exhibition of 1851. According to a contemporary steel engraving, which shows it with the Koh-i-Noor, it was almost square cut, and its weight is estimated from comparison with the Koh-i-Noor.

Afterward it was reported sold to the Nawab of Dacca (now in East Pakistan). It could well be the same diamond that the Nawab offered for sale in 1955 and again in 1959, but its present whereabouts are not known.

NAWANAGER 148.00/W/⊙/?
Rajmata Gulabkumberba of Nawanager, 1970

In 1970 Dr. E. Gubelin reported that the Maharanee Gulabkumberba of Nawanager owns an exceptionally fine brilliant-cut diamond of 148 carats.

Monnickendam reported that in 1930 Ranji Singh, Mahrajah of Nawanager, asked his advice about a fine diamond of about 130 carats, supposedly from Russia. He put a value of £250,000 on it and advised the maharajah to buy it. This could be the same diamond.

TURKEY I †147.00/*W/?/I
Unknown; reported in Turkish crown jewels 1882

This large diamond and its 84-carat namesake, Turkey II, were last reported in 1882 in the Turkish Regalia. Nothing has been heard about these stones since that time.

REGENT 140.50/W/□/I
Louvre Museum, Paris, 1971

One of the finest diamonds in the world, the Regent has had a long, adventurous history.

The rough stone, weighing 410 carats, was found in India. A slave stole it and escaped to the seacoast, hiding the diamond in the bandages of a self-inflicted leg wound. In return for passage, he offered a ship captain half the value of the stone, but the greedy captain murdered the slave and took the diamond. After selling it, the captain is said to have squandered the proceeds, and then hanged himself.

In 1702 Jaurchund, an Indian merchant, sold the stone to Thomas Pitt, governor of Madras, for about £20,000. Pitt sent it home to England where it was cut into a 140.50-carat cushion-shaped brilliant, a rectangular diamond a little more than an inch long and three-quarters of an inch deep. The cutting took two years and cost him almost £5,000 but the great gem became known as the Pitt diamond and its owner "Diamond Pitt."

In 1717 Pitt sold the gem to Philippe, duke of Orleans and regent of France during the minority of Louis XV, for more than £135,000. Renamed the Regent, it became part of the crown jewels and was worn in the crown of Louis XV at his coronation in 1722.

Removed from the crown, it was worn by Queen Marie Leczinska in her hair. Two generations later, Marie Antoinette frequently wore the Regent in a big black velvet hat.

The diamond was stolen along with the other crown jewels in the great robbery of 1792, but it was quickly recovered. The Directory gave it, with other state diamonds, as security for a loan from a Berlin banker in 1797, but the gem was redeemed five years later.

Napoleon Bonaparte had the great diamond set in the hilt of the sword he carried when crowned emperor of France in 1804. After Napoleon's exile, his second wife, Empress Marie Louise, carried the Regent with her to the Chateau of Blois. But her father, Emperor Francis I of Austria, later returned the gem to the French government.

Charles X wore the Regent at his coronation in 1825, and the gem remained in this crown until the time of Napoleon III. Then a place was made for it in the Greek diadem designed for Empress Eugénie.

In 1887 the French crown jewels were sold at auction, but the Regent was reserved from the sale and put on exhibition in the Louvre. Before the Germans captured Paris in 1940, the diamond was taken to the Chateau Chambord and hidden behind a stone panel. After World War II, it was returned to its place in the Louvre, where it rests today.

FLORENTINE 137.27/±Y/ϴ/I
Stolen from Austrian royal family about 1920

Legends of this great yellow diamond go back to 1477, when Charles the Bold, duke of Burgundy, supposedly was wearing it when he fell at the Battle of Nancy. A soldier found the diamond on the duke's body and, thinking it was glass, sold it to a priest for a florin. Afterward, it changed hands many times, one of its owners being Pope Julius II (1503–1513).

The first authentic reports of the Florentine date from

about 1657. In that year Tavernier, the famed French traveler and gem dealer, visited the Medici family in Florence, and was shown a clear yellow diamond by the duke of Tuscany. He described the stone as a double rose cut of 126 facets with an irregular nine-sided outline.

From the Medicis, the Florentine passed to the house of Austria through Francis of Lorraine who became grand duke of Tuscany in 1737, and his wife, Maria Theresa of Austria.

After the fall of the Austrian Empire in World War I, the crown jewels went into exile with the imperial family, and the Florentine was among them, mounted in a brooch.

There are various opinions about the later history of the stone. One of the most popular is that it was stolen by an adviser to the imperial family and taken to South America. In the 1920s it supposedly entered the United States, was recut and sold. As a matter of record, however, it must be listed as missing.

Although best known as the Florentine, this great yellow diamond has also been called Tuscan, the Grand Duke of Tuscany, the Austrian, and the Austrian Yellow.

QUEEN OF HOLLAND 136.25/B/0/?
Unknown; sold to Indian maharajah after 1925

Of mysterious origin, this intensely blue diamond was cut to its present cushion shape in 1904 by F. Friedman of Amsterdam. It was shown at the Paris Exhibition of Arts & Industry in 1925. Later, a Paris jeweler sold it to an Indian maharajah for a reported $1,000,000.

IRANIAN 2 135.45/±Y/0/SA
Iranian crown jewels, Teheran, 1968
(See Iranian 1 above)

MOUNTAIN OF SPLENDOR †135.00/W/?/I
Unknown; reported among Persian crown jewels, 1838

Streeter reported that this diamond was in the Persian Regalia in the nineteenth century. But it was not among the crown jewels of Iran in 1966.

LIGHT OF PEACE 130.27/W/0/*SL
Zale Corporation, Dallas, 1971

In January 1970 the Zale Corp., New York City, unveiled a 435-carat West African diamond, one of the largest roughs on record.

Measuring approximately two inches high, the stone was in the process of cutting for more than a year. The largest stone cut from it was this 130.27-carat pear-shape worth about $3,500,000.

The large diamond will not be sold. Funds derived from its exhibition will be donated to a cause for peace, which shall be decided by a commission headed by former UN Ambassador Arthur Goldberg.

GREAT BRAZILIAN 130.00/*W/?/?
Shown at Sears Roebuck stores, 1956

Once part of the crown jewels of Portugal, in 1956 this diamond was reported to be set in a $1,250,000 diamond necklace and shown at Sears Roebuck stores.

STAR OF THE SOUTH 128.80/W/0/B
Rustomjee Jamsetjee, Bombay, *1940

This stone was discovered in 1853 by a slave woman working at the Bagagem Mines in Brazil, and for reward she received her freedom and a pension for life. Weighing 261.88 carats, the rough was sold for about $15,000 and then changed hands several times before it was cut at the great Coster plant in Amsterdam. After cutting, the diamond was an oval brilliant of 128.80 carats, with a beautiful pinkish "inner glow" of refracted light.

Bought by a Paris syndicate and named the Star of the South, the diamond was shown at the London Exposition of 1862. Some five years later it was sold to Mulhar Rao, Gaekwar of Baroda, for $400,000. In 1934 his son told Robert W. Shipley, the American gemologist, that both the Star of the South and the English Dresden were mounted in a necklace among his family jewels. More recently, however, the Star of the South was reported to be owned by Rustomjee Jamsetjee of Bombay.

TIFFANY 128.51/Y/0/SA
Tiffany & Co., New York, 1971

The Tiffany, the largest golden diamond known today, was not worn as jewelry for almost eighty years after its discovery. But it has been seen by more than 25,000,000 people in almost seventy years of continuous display.

The rough diamond, weighing 287.42 carats, was believed to have been found in the Kimberley Mine in South Africa in 1878.

Whatever its origin, the diamond was bought by Tiffany & Co. in 1879, and cut in Paris to a cushion-shape brilliant of 128.51 carats. It was given 90 facets—32 more than the standard brilliant cut—and these extra facets give the great yellow diamond the effect of smoldering fire.

The Tiffany was shown at the Columbian Exposition in Chicago in 1893, at the Pan American in 1901, the Century of Progress in Chicago 1933–34 and the World's Fair in New

York 1939-40. The diamond has also been on almost continuous display through the years at Tiffany's, New York, where it is still exhibited today.

The first time the diamond was worn as an ornament was in 1957 at the Tiffany Ball in Newport. Mrs. Sheldon Whitehouse, the ball's chairlady, had the honor of wearing the Tiffany, mounted for the occasion in a necklace of white diamonds. The diamond is now valued at $5 million.

PORTUGUESE 127.02/W/▯/B
Smithsonian Institution, Washington, D.C., 1971

This emerald-cut diamond was fashioned from a 150-carat cushion-cut believed to be of Brazilian origin.

Once owned by the Portuguese royal family, it has since passed through several hands, including Harry Winston's. In 1963 it was acquired by the Smithsonian Institution, where it is now on display.

MOON OF THE MOUNTAINS †126.00/W/?/*I
Unknown; among Russian crown jewels in nineteenth century

Tradition has it that this diamond was part of the Mogul treasure taken by Nadir Shah in 1739. After Nadir's assassination in 1747, it supposedly came into the possession of an Afghan soldier. Later—after robbery, murder and fratricide—an Armenian merchant named Shaffrass acquired the stones and set himself up as a respectable gem merchant.

Many years later Catherine the Great bought the diamond from Shaffrass. It was known to be in the Russian crown jewels in the nineteenth century, but has since disappeared.

JONKER 125.65/W/▯/SA
Queen of Nepal, 1959

The story goes that Jacobus Jonker found a 726-carat diamond on his farm, about three miles from Premier Mine, after a heavy rain in January 1934. A few days later he sold it to the Diamond Corporation in Johannesburg for $315,000.

The Jonker rough was mailed to London (at a cost of 64 cents) and was met by Harry Winston, who had taken an option on it. After a month's study, he bought the stone for an undisclosed price and mailed it to New York. From the customs house it went directly to the American Museum of Natural History, where it was exhibited before being cut, in 1936.

IRANIAN 3 123.93/±Y/▢/SA
Iranian crown jewels, Teheran, 1968
(See Iranian 1 above)

JULIUS PAM †123.00/Y/?/SA
*Unknown, *1950*

This is the name given to a yellow diamond which was cut from a 246-carat rough found in the Jagersfontein Mine in 1889. No other information is available.

STEWART †123.00/±Y/◉/SA
Unknown; cut after 1882

For many years, this was the largest "river stone" found in the alluvial beds of South Africa. Weighing 296 carats in the rough, with a slightly yellowish cast, it was cut to a fine brilliant of 123 carats.

Antoine Williams was working his claim on the Vaal River in 1872 when his pick struck a rock so hard that it bounced. He uncovered the stone and took it to his partner, Robert Spaulding, after whom the diamond was first named. Williams later said he was so excited at the time that he could not eat for two days.

The partners sold their rough diamond to a Port Elizabeth merchant named Stewart for $30,000. Stewart later sold the diamond, still uncut, for $45,000, but the gem has kept his name. After being cut, the Stewart passed into private hands and its present location is unknown.

IRANIAN 4 121.90/±Y/◇/SA
Iranian crown jewels, Teheran, 1968
(See Iranian 1 above)

MEISTER 118.05/Y/▢/*SA
Walter Meister, Zurich 1970

This very vivid yellow cushion-cut was bought by Walter Meister, the Zurich jeweler, at the Sotheby auction in Zurich in April 1970. Meister says that the stone probably came from the early days of Kimberley, and that it had been in the possession of a single (unnamed) family "for a lifetime."

TAJ-E-MAH 115.06/W/◮/I
Iranian crown jewels, 1968

The Taj-e-Mah (Crown of the Moon) is a flawless white diamond, a mogul cut in an irregular oval. Although earlier gemologists had reported its weight at 146 carats, the Canadian gemologists studying the crown jewels of Iran weighed it at 115.06 carats.

By tradition, this diamond is considered the sister stone to the Darya-i-Nur, with which it was once set in armbands. Like the Darya-i-Nur, it was part of the treasure carried off by Nadir Shah in his sack of Delhi in 1739, and today is one of the finest gems among the crown jewels of Iran in Teheran.

UNNAMED *114.03/Y/0/?*
Unknown; sold at Christie's in 1962

CROSS OF ASIA *109.26/CH/▽/?*
Unknown; exhibited at Joske's, San Antonio, 1947

This champagne-colored diamond is said to be cut so that a Maltese cross is visible from above the table. It was last reported by an unnamed charitable institution which received it by will from a "prominent American." The diamond has been exhibited in stores, like Joske's of San Antonio (1947). A small admittance fee is charged, which is given to the institution.

Copeland says that efforts to establish the ownership of the Cross of Asia by the Gemological Institute of America have been unsuccessful.

EARTH STAR *111.59/±BR/♀/SA*
Baumgold Bros., New York, 1971

This pear-shaped, coffee-brown diamond was cut from a 248.90-carat rough found in the Jagersfontein Mine, South Africa, in 1967. Thought to be the largest brown diamond in the world, it is owned by Baumgold Bros. of New York.

KOH-I-NOOR *108.93/W/0/I*
British crown jewels, Tower of London, 1971

The Koh-i-Noor was first reported in 1304 as a diamond in the possession of the rajah of Malwa. Later it fell into the hands of Baber, and for the next two centuries, it was one of the precious jewels of the Mogul emperors.

In 1739, Nadir Shah of Persia invaded Delhi. His systematic pillage of the city failed to uncover the huge stone, but then he was told by one of the harem women that the conquered Mogul emperor had hidden it inside his turban. Taking advantage of an oriental custom, Nadir Shah invited his captive to a feast and suggested they exchange turbans. Retiring from the feast. Nadir Shah unrolled the turban and released the great gem. Seeing it, he is supposed to have cried, "Koh-i-Noor" (mountain of light). Tradition has it that this christened the diamond.

The gem went back to Persia with Nadir Shah. But he was assassinated in 1747, and the diamond was fought over by his successors. It was in the jewel chamber of Lahore, capital of Punjab, when that state was annexed to British India in 1849, and the East India Company took it as a partial indemnity for the Sikh Wars. The Koh-i-Noor was presented to Queen Victoria in 1850 to mark the 250th anniversary of the founding of the East India Company by Elizabeth I.

Valued at $700,000, the Koh-i-Noor was displayed at the Crystal Palace Exhibition in London in 1851. Since people were disappointed that the diamond did not show more fire, Victoria decided to have it recut. Mr. Voorsanger, the most able cutter of Coster's in Amsterdam, was brought to London for the job, which reduced the size of the diamond from 186 carats to 108.93 carats.

Acceding to the wishes of her Indian subjects, Victoria wore the great diamond as a personal ornament. From this probably came the superstition that only queens could wear the Koh-i-Noor safely. Victoria willed it to her daughter-in-law, Alexandra, who wore it at her coronation in 1902.

In 1911 a new crown was made for the coronation of Queen Mary with the Koh-i-Noor as the central stone. In 1937 it was transferred to the crown of Queen Elizabeth (now Queen Mother) for her coronation. On state occasions, the Queen Mother continues to wear the diamond in the circlet of her crown. At other times, the Koh-i-Noor is displayed with the crown jewels in the Tower of London.

ROJTMAN *107.46/Y/0/?*
Mrs. Marc Rojtman, New York, 1966

This yellow diamond is owned by Mrs. Marc Rojtman of New York and was exhibited at the De Beers Diamond Pavilion in Johannesburg in 1966. Nothing is known of the history of the stone before its acquisition by the late Mr. Rojtman, but it bears a resemblance to the 107.5-carat Star of Diamonds mentioned by Streeter in 1882.

IRANIAN 5 *114.28/±Y/0/SA*
Iranian crown jewels, 1968
(See Iranian 1 above)

STAR OF DIAMONDS *†107.50/?/?/SA*
Unknown; reported by Streeter in 1882

As its name indicates, this was one of the finest and largest diamonds discovered in the South African diamond fields. The nineteenth-century gem expert, Louis Dieulafait, said it was "a lovely stone, which attracted attention by revealing under the microscope a prospect of pointed mountain crests, lit up by broad sunlight in all the colors of the rainbow."

It is possible that this and the Rojtman are the same diamond.

STAR OF EGYPT *† 106.75/*W/0/*I*
Unknown; appeared in London after 1850

This diamond was said to have been cut from an oval stone

of 250 carats which was discovered in 1850 and immediately acquired by a viceroy of Egypt. In 1939 it appeared on the London market in its present weight, but its ownership today is unknown.

CENT SIX† *106.00/?/?/?*
Unknown; reported by Streeter in 1882

Mentioned by Streeter in 1882 as being a cut diamond. Its name obviously comes from its weight. No other details are given.

DEEPDENE *104.88/Y/O/?*
Unknown

For many years, this golden yellow, cushion-cut diamond was on loan to the Academy of Natural Science in Philadelphia through the courtesy of Cary Bok, whose family's estate was called Deepdene.

About 1954 it was acquired by Harry Winston, who sold it to an undisclosed American buyer.

Nothing further was heard about the stone for some time. Then a stone called Deepdene, of the same description and weight as the original, was put up for auction at Christie's in Geneva by its German owner. It went to the Paris jewelers, Van Cleef & Arpels, for a record bid of £190,000. However, when Van Cleef & Arpels had the stone examined by leading British and Swiss gemologists, they found that the stone had been falsely colored. The diamond was subsequently returned to its German owner.

The whereabouts of the real Deepdene are unknown, but it is still believed to be owned by the undisclosed buyer to whom Harry Winston sold it.

UNKNOWN (see above) *104.52/Y(treated)/O/?*
Auctioned in Geneva, May 1971

GREAT CHRYSANTHEMUM *104.15/±BR/Q/*SA*
Julius Cohen, New York, 1971

This pear-shaped diamond was cut from a 198.28-carat brown rough supposedly found in South Africa in 1963. Julius Cohen, a New York City dealer, bought the rough and had it cut to reveal the diamond's rich golden brown chrysanthemum-like color. The stone is valued at $540,000.

In 1971 the diamond was exhibited at the Kimberley Centenary Exhibition in South Africa. The diamond also was shown in the Diamonds-International Academy Collection at the Diamond Pavilion in Johannesburg in 1965.

RAULCONDA †*103.00/*W/?/I*
Unknown; seen by Tavernier

This cut stone was seen by Tavernier in the Raulconda Mine, India, where diamonds were cut as well as mined. Nothing more is known of it.

ASHBERG †*102.00/A/?/?*
Unknown; sold in Stockholm in 1959

This amber diamond is reputed to have been among the ancient czarist crown jewels brought to Sweden after the Bolshevik Revolution. It was exhibited by a Swedish collector named Ashberg at the Amsterdam Diamond Exhibition in 1949. Later it was sold to a private collector.

HASTINGS †*101.00/?/O/I*
Unknown, disappeared in eighteenth century

In 1786 Warren Hastings, governor general of India, presented this diamond to George III as a gift from the nizam of Deccan. Political scandal followed, and Hastings, who was later impeached, was accused of trying to bribe the king. Nothing is known of it since then.

JACOB †*100.00/W/?/*I*
Unknown: offered for sale in 1956

Long part of the collection of the nizam of Hyderabad, this diamond was held for sale by the Bank of India in 1956 at an asking price of $280,000. The present owner is not known.

BIBLIOGRAPHY

Berquen, Robert de. *Les Merveilles des Indes*. Paris, 1669.
Bruton, Eric. *Diamonds*. London, 1974.
Dickinson, Jean. *The Book of Diamonds*. New York, 1965.
Dieulafait, Louis. *Diamonds and Precious Stones*. London, 1874.
Emanuel, Harry. *Diamonds and Precious Stones*. London, 1867.
Hahn, Emily. *Diamond*. London, 1956.
Herbert, Ivor. *The Diamond Diggers*. London, 1971.
International Diamond Annual, 1971 and 1972.
Jackson, Stanley. *The Great Barnato*. London, 1970.
Lenzen, G. *History of Diamond Production*. London, 1970.
Purtell, Joseph. *The Tiffany Touch*. New York, 1972.
Roberts, Brian. *The Diamond Magnates*. London, 1972.
Streeter, Edwin W. *Precious Stones and Gems*. London, 1898.
Tavernier, Jean Baptiste. *Travels in the East*. London, 1679.
Walker, David E. *Adventure in Diamonds*. London, 1955.
Williams, Gardner F. *The Diamond Mines of South Africa*. New York, 1905.

GLOSSARY
GEOLOGICAL AND TECHNICAL TERMS

Blue ground Kimberlite as yet unweathered by exposure to the elements, which is found at a depth of between 60 to 80 feet (20 to 25 meters). In the early days of the South African mines, the blue ground used to be spread out over large areas and left to disintegrate. It is now crushed and processed mechanically. *See also* Kimberlite.

Boart Minutely crystallized or crypto-crystalline gray or black material which is usually only suitable for crushing to be used in grinding and polishing applications. On rare occasions a piece of boart can contain a perfectly formed diamond in its center, and it may even take such an exceptional form that it can be a gem itself, as in the case of the Amsterdam (see p. 69). The name derives from the Afrikaans word for bastard.

Carat The oldest weight measurement for diamonds and other gem stones, the carat was originally the seed of the carob tree, a small black bean which is remarkably uniform in weight. There were many regional differences until an international metric carat standard was established earlier this century with the carat set at 0.2 gram.

Carbonado The Brazilian word for boart. It is found in quantity in certain mining areas in Brazil.

Coated crystals Diamonds are often found covered with a layer of inferior-quality diamond containing many small inclusions of foreign material. The coating is usually gray, green, brown or black, and while in some cases it may conceal a diamond of the highest quality, in other cases the diamond underneath may turn out to be of even lower quality than the coating. Purchasing a coated crystal which has not been "opened" by cutting two facets opposite each other is a very speculative venture.

Comparison stones These are stones of known color which are used as a standard for comparison by graders. They are usually limited to the first four or five grades of whiteness.

Dop Originally a cup on the end of a thick copper stalk in which the diamond is set in solder ready for cutting, it now usually refers to a clamp in which the diamond is held. Only that part of the diamond which is to be cut is exposed. The word comes from the Dutch word for cup.

Doublet Usually devised with the intent to deceive, a doublet consists of a diamond top cemented to a base made of some simulant. It can be that two diamonds will be joined together in order to give the impression of one large diamond.

Fluorescence This is the term applied to the glow produced by a diamond when exposed to ultraviolet light. Many diamonds fluoresce blue and since ordinary daylight contains ultraviolet, the slight blue fluorescence produced can often mask the presence of a less desirable color, e.g., yellow.

Foiling The practice of backing the diamond with reflective foil to improve its appearance has been going on for the past five centuries. In the early days it was almost as important an art as cutting is today, since only by foiling could a diamond begin to show its hidden brilliance.

Grain A diamond, like a piece of wood, has a grain. It is related to the crystal structure and axes, and sometimes appears as fine parallel lines when the diamond is looked at through a lens.

Inclusions Often erroneously called carbon spots, the dark spots which can be seen inside most diamonds are in fact inclusions of other minerals which were present in the original magma in which the diamond was formed. The most common are olivine and garnet.

Indicator materials Diamonds are almost always found in association with certain other minerals, notably garnets, ilmenites, zircons and chrome diopsides, and because they are much more common than diamonds, prospectors tend to concentrate initially on the search for these red, green and yellow "indicator minerals." The famous Siberian Zarnitza pipe was discovered in 1953 after a geologist had spotted red pyrope garnets.

Kimberlite The composition of the diamond-bearing rock called Kimberlite (after the town of Kimberley) is by no means uniform, varying from a conglomerate that is finely granular and compact to one containing huge boulders of different types of rock. The variation is consistent with the theory that the original magma in which the diamond was formed at depths of around 120 miles (200 kilometers) picked up many other rocks and minerals on its way to the surface. Kimberlite is not volcanic lava.

Lapidaries A feature of medieval literature, these are accounts of the attributes of gems with a special emphasis on their magical and medicinal properties. They demonstrate the great importance which was attached to precious stones in medieval times.

Mêlée A broad categorization of diamonds made during initial sorting. The word covers all crystals under a certain weight (usually around the one-carat mark).

Parure A matching set of jewels consisting of from three to seven pieces. A diadem, necklace and earrings were a popular combination.

Pavé A type of setting in which many small cut diamonds are placed close together rather like paving stones. Indentations are made in the metal setting and small ridges are raised to hold the stones.

Phosphorescence This is the glow which the diamond continues to emit after removal from the ultraviolet light source.

Rivière A style of necklace consisting of a string of individually set stones to form literally "a river of diamonds."

Solitaire A single diamond set in a fine ring.

Stomacher A large corsage brooch covering the front of the dress across the midriff. Usually V-shaped to accentuate the slimness of the waist.

Strass High-density lead glass developed by Joseph Strasser in the eighteenth century. Apart from being very much softer and thus liable to show signs of wear very quickly, strass is an excellent diamond simulant. It is often known as "paste."

Tang The fixed tool holder in use in the diamond cutting industry from the earliest days. It takes the form of an arm resting on the wheel.

Trigons A characteristic feature of the diamond, these triangular markings can often be seen with the naked eye on the octahedral face. They are shallow pits shaped like an equilateral triangle. Apart from those clearly visible, many more appear under high magnification.

Vesteller This is the name given to the man who mounts the diamond in the solder in the dop. With the advent of the mechanical dop using clamps instead of solder, this trade has practically disappeared.

Yellow ground Weathered kimberlite which continues to roughly 60 feet (18 meters) below the surface in a diamond pipe. Relatively soft, it is easily mined.

INDEX

Page numbers given in *italics* indicate black-and-white illustrations. Page numbers given in **bold** indicate the pages between which the color plates can be found.

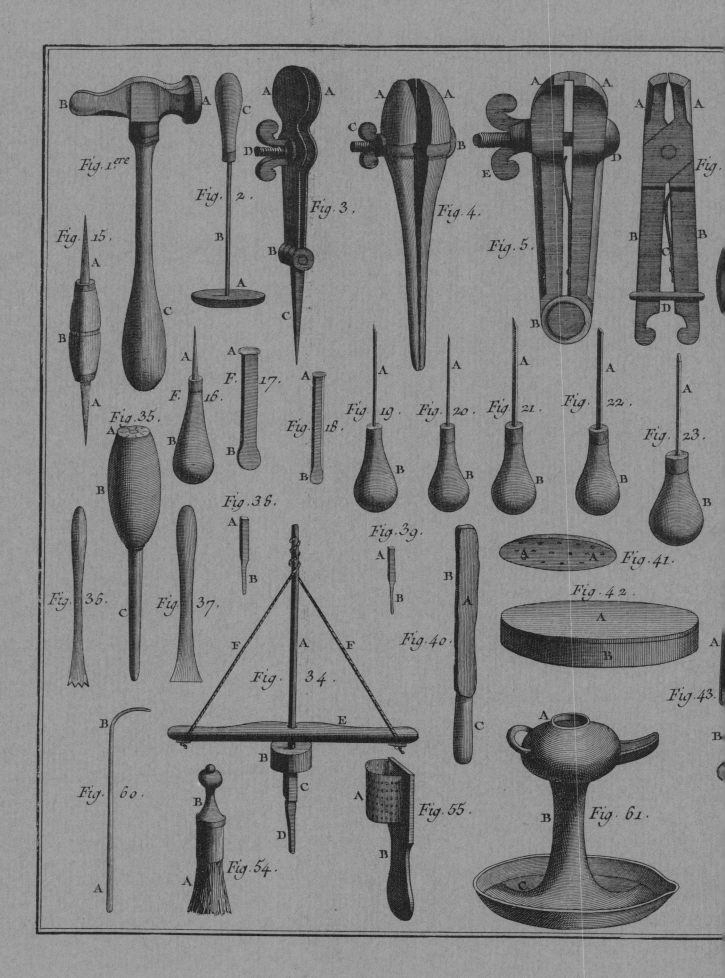

Fig. 1.ere

Fig. 2.

Fig. 3.

Fig. 4.

Fig. 5.

Fig.

Fig. 15.

Fig. 35.

F. 16.

F. 17.

Fig. 18.

Fig. 19.

Fig. 20.

Fig. 21.

Fig. 22.

Fig. 23.

Fig. 36.

Fig. 37.

Fig. 38.

Fig. 34.

Fig. 39.

Fig. 40.

Fig. 41.

Fig. 42.

Fig. 43.

Fig. 60.

Fig. 54.

Fig. 55.

Fig. 61.